Domestic Violence in Asia

This book explores the changing patterns of domestic violence in Asia. Based on extensive original research in the Maldives, it argues that forces of globalization, consumerism, Islamism and democratization are changing the nature of domestic relations, with shifting ideas surrounding gender and Islam being particularly significant. The book points out that domestic violence has been relatively low in the Maldives in comparison with other Asian countries, as a result of, the book argues, a history of relatively equal gender relations, an ideology of masculinity that is associated with calmness and rationality where violence is not considered an acceptable means of dealing with problems, and flexible marriage and divorce practices. The book shows how these factors are being undermined by new ideas which emphasise the need for wifely obedience, increasing gender inequality and the right of husbands to be coercive.

Emma Fulu completed her doctorate at the University of Melbourne, Australia.

Asian Studies Association of Australia Women in Asia Series
Editor: Lenore Lyons (The University of Sydney)
Editorial Board:
Susan Blackburn (Monash University)
Hyaeweol Choi (The Australian National University)
Michele Ford (The University of Sydney)
Louise Edwards (University of Hong Kong)
Trude Jacobsen (Northern Illinois University)
Vera Mackie (University of Wollongong)
Anne McLaren (The University of Melbourne)
Mina Roces (University of New South Wales)
Dina Siddiqi (The City University of New York)
Andrea Whittaker (The University of Queensland)

Mukkuvar Women
Gender, Hegemony and Capitalist Transformation in a South Indian Fishing Community
Kalpana Ram 1991

A World of Difference
Islam and Gender Hierarchy in Turkey
Julie Marcus 1992

Purity and Communal Boundaries
Women and Social Change in a Bangladeshi Village
Santi Rozario 1992

Madonnas and Martyrs
Militarism and Violence in the Philippines
Anne-Marie Hilsdon 1995

Masters and Managers
A Study of Gender Relations in Urban Java
Norma Sullivan 1995

Matriliny and Modernity
Sexual Politics and Social Change in Rural Malaysia
Maila Stivens 1995

Intimate Knowledge
Women and their Health in North-East Thailand
Andrea Whittaker 2000

Women in Asia
Tradition, Modernity and Globalisation
Louise Edwards and
Mina Roces (eds) 2000

Violence Against Women in Asian Societies
Gender Inequality and Technologies of Violence
Lenore Manderson and
Linda Rae Bennett (eds) 2003

Women's Employment in Japan
The Experience of Part-time Workers
Kaye Broadbent 2003

Chinese Women Living and Working
Anne McLaren (ed.) 2004

Abortion, Sin and the State in Thailand
Andrea Whittaker 2004

Sexual Violence and the Law in Japan
Catherine Burns 2004

Women, Islam and Modernity
Single Women, Sexuality and Reproductive Health in Contemporary Indonesia
Linda Rae Bennett 2005

The Women's Movement in Post-Colonial Indonesia
Elizabeth Martyn 2005

Women and Work in Indonesia
Michele Ford and *Lyn Parker* (eds) 2008

Women and Union Activism in Asia
Kaye Broadbent and *Michele Ford* (eds) 2008

Gender, Islam, and Democracy in Indonesia
Kathryn Robinson 2008

Sex, Love and Feminism in the Asia Pacific
A Cross-Cultural Study of Young People's Attitudes
Chilla Bulbeck 2008

Gender, State and Social Power
Divorce in Contemporary Indonesia
Kate O'Shaughnessy 2008

Gender, Household, and State in Post-Revolutionary Vietnam
Jayne Werner 2008

Young Women in Japan
Transitions to Adulthood
Kaori Okano 2009

Women, Islam and Everyday Life
Renegotiating Polygamy in Indonesia
Nina Nurmila 2009

Feminist Movements in Contemporary Japan
Laura Dales 2009

Gender and Labour in Korea and Japan
Sexing Class
Ruth Barraclough and *Elyssa Faison* (eds) 2009

Gender Diversity in Indonesia
Sexuality, Islam and Queer Selves
Sharyn Graham Davies 2010

New Women in Colonial Korea
A Sourcebook
Hyaeweol Choi 2012

Women Writers in Postsocialist China
Kay Schaffer and *Xianlin Song* 2013

Domestic Violence in Asia
Globalization, Gender and Islam in the Maldives
Emma Fulu 2014

Domestic Violence in Asia
Globalization, Gender and
Islam in the Maldives

Emma Fulu

LONDON AND NEW YORK

First published 2014
by Routledge
2 Park Square, Milton Park, Abingdon, Oxfordshire OX14 4RN

Simultaneously published in the USA and Canada
by Routledge
711 Third Avenue, New York, NY 10017

First issued in paperback 2016

Routledge is an imprint of the Taylor & Francis Group, an informa business

© 2014 Emma Fulu

The right of Emma Fulu to be identified as author of this work has been asserted by her in accordance with the Copyright, Designs and Patent Act 1988.

All rights reserved. No part of this book may be reprinted or reproduced or utilised in any form or by any electronic, mechanical, or other means, now known or hereafter invented, including photocopying and recording, or in any information storage or retrieval system, without permission in writing from the publishers.

Trademark notice: Product or corporate names may be trademarks or registered trademarks, and are used only for identification and explanation without intent to infringe.

British Library Cataloguing in Publication Data
A catalogue record for this book is available from the British Library

Library of Congress Cataloguing in Publication data
Fulu, Emma, author.
   Domestic violence in Asia : globalization, gender and Islam in the Maldives / Emma Fulu.
     pages cm. – (Asian Studies Association of Australia women in Asia series)
   Includes bibliographical references and index.
   Summary: "Explores changing patterns of domestic violence in Asia. Based on extensive original research in the Maldives, it argues that forces of globalisation, consumerism, Islamism and democratisation are changing the nature of domestic relations, with shifting ideas surrounding gender and Islam being particularly significant" – Provided by publisher.
   1. Family violence – Maldives. 2. Intimate partner violence – Maldives. 3. Family violence – Religious aspects – Islam. 4. Globalization – Social aspects – Maldives. 5. Women in Islam – Maldives. I. Title.
   HV6626.23.M42F85 2013
   362.82'92095495–dc23
   2013005939

ISBN 13: 978-1-138-65231-6 (pbk)
ISBN 13: 978-0-415-67397-6 (hbk)

Typeset in Times New Roman
by Out of House Publishing

For my son Felix

Contents

List of illustrations — x
Series editor's foreword — xii
Preface: insider/outsider — xiii
Acknowledgements — xvi

Introduction: domestic violence in Asia and globalization from below — 1

1. Coercive control: patterns of intimate partner violence in the Maldives — 19

2. The protective factors: lessons for violence prevention — 39

3. 'A good wife obeys her husband': the changing nature of the family — 65

4. 'For the love of women': increasing gender inequality — 90

5. A social crisis in the Maldives — 111

Conclusion: creating peace cultures – the way forward — 125

Appendices — 133
Glossary of foreign terms — 145
Bibliography — 146
Index — 168

Illustrations

Figure

I.1	The globalized ecological model	14

Tables

A1	Prevalence of physical and/or sexual violence by an intimate partner among ever-partnered women, according to when the violence took place	133
A2	Severity of physical partner violence reported by ever-partnered women	134
A3a	Frequency of intimate partner violence, by type	134
A3b	Association between frequency and severity of physical partner violence, among ever-partnered women aged 15–49	134
A4a	Percentage of ever-partnered women reporting various controlling behaviours by their intimate partners	134
A4b	Percentage of ever-partnered women reporting controlling behaviour by partner according to their experience of physical and/or sexual partner violence	135
A4c	Mean number of acts of controlling behaviour reported by ever-partnered women according to their experiences of intimate partner violence	135
A5a	Percentage of women who experienced controlling behaviour, by severity of physical partner violence	135
A5b	Percentage of women who experienced controlling behaviour, by frequency of partner violence	135
A5c	Logistic regression model for association between controlling behaviour and experiences of physical partner violence	136
A6a	Percentage of women aged 15–49 who have ever experienced financially controlling behaviour from their current husband, by women's experiences of IPV	136

A6b	Logistic regression models for association between financially controlling behaviour and experiences of intimate partner violence	136
A7a	Percentage of women, who have ever been in a relationship, reporting selected symptoms of ill health, according to their experience of physical and/or sexual partner violence	137
A7b	Logistic regression models for the associations between selected health conditions and experiences of intimate partner violence among ever-partnered women	137
A8a	Percentage of ever-pregnant women reporting having had a miscarriage, abortion, stillbirth or child who died, according to their experience of partner violence	137
A8b	Logistic regression models for the association between selected reproductive health outcomes and experiences of intimate partner violence, among ever-pregnant women	138
A9a	Physical and/or sexual partner abuse and circumstances of last pregnancy, among women who gave birth in last five years	138
A9b	Logistic regression models for the association between unplanned pregnancies and experiences of intimate partner violence, among ever-pregnant women	139
A10a	Comparison of suicidal ideation and behaviour for ever-partnered women according to their experiences of physical partner violence	139
A10b	Logistic regression models for associations between suicidal thoughts and experiences of intimate partner violence	140
A11a	Percentage of ever-partnered women aged 15–49 who experienced partner violence in past 12 months, by background characteristics	140
A11b	Percentage of ever-partnered women aged 15–49 who experienced partner violence in past 12 months, by husband's characteristics	141
A11c	Correlates of ever-partnered woman's likelihood of having ever experienced partner violence in the past 12 months	142

Series editor's foreword

The contributions of women to the social, political and economic transformations occurring in the Asian region are legion. Women have served as leaders of nations, communities, workplaces, activist groups and families. Asian women have joined with others to participate in fomenting change at micro and macro levels. They have been both agents and targets of national and international interventions in social policy. In the performance of these myriad roles women have forged new and modern gendered identities that are recognisably global and local. Their experiences are rich, diverse and instructive. The books in this series testify to the central role women play in creating the new Asia and re-creating Asian womanhood. Moreover, these books reveal the resilience and inventiveness of women around the Asian region in the face of entrenched and evolving patriarchal social norms.

Scholars publishing in this series demonstrate a commitment to promoting the productive conversation between Gender Studies and Asian Studies. The need to understand the diversity of experiences of femininity and womanhood around the world increases inexorably as globalisation proceeds apace. Lessons from the experiences of Asian women present us with fresh opportunities for building new possibilities for women's progress the world over.

The Asian Studies Association of Australia (ASAA) sponsors this publication series as part of its on-going commitment to promoting knowledge about women in Asia. In particular, the ASAA Women's Forum provides the intellectual vigour and enthusiasm that maintains the Women in Asia Series (WIAS). The aim of the series, since its inception in 1990, is to promote knowledge about women in Asia to both academic and general audiences. To this end, WIAS books draw on a wide range of disciplines including anthropology, sociology, political science, cultural studies, media studies, literature and history. The series prides itself on being an outlet for cutting edge research conducted by recent PhD graduates and postdoctoral fellows from throughout the region.

The series could not function without the generous professional advice provided by many anonymous readers. Moreover, the wise counsel provided by Peter Sowden at Routledge is invaluable. WIAS, its authors and the ASAA are very grateful to these people for their expert work.

Lenore Lyons (The University of Sydney)
Series Editor

Preface
Insider/outsider

I write this book from the perspective of an insider/outsider in the Maldives. I am not totally foreign, not totally local; both and neither at the same time. My mother is Australian and my father is Maldivian. I am a dual citizen. I was born and raised in Australia and, while I visited the Maldives a number of times on family trips as a child, it was not until 2004 that I actually lived and worked in the Maldives as an adult. I came to the Maldives to work for the Ministry of Gender and Family (then called the Ministry of Gender, Family and Social Security) in 2004 after finishing my honours degree in Gender and Development Studies in Australia. I hoped that I could reconnect with my heritage, learn Dhivehi (the Maldivian language), get to know my extended family better and be employed in an area that I was passionate about. At the Ministry of Gender and Family I began working on the issue of violence against women. The strong interest I developed for this subject area led to this book on domestic violence in Asia.

Having grown up in Australia, I generally feel culturally Australian rather than Maldivian, but in Australia my colouring has often led to the classification of me being from somewhere else. I am constantly asked where I am from, even though I am from Melbourne. I am often told that my English is good when it is my first language. I am asked if I am an international student when I was born in Australia. It is at such moments that I am reminded, as was Fatimah Rony when watching *King Kong*, and W.E.B. Dubois when glanced at by a young white girl, that I am sometimes marked as 'other' (Rony 1996: 3–4). In Australia and throughout the western world whiteness usually remains 'unexamined – unqualified, essential, homogeneous, seemingly self-fashioned, and apparently unmarked by history or practice' (Frankenberg 1997: 1). When whiteness is paraded as the norm, I become a deviation that must be scrutinized. This constant questioning of my Australian identity had made me acutely aware of my Maldivian characteristics.

In the Maldives my indigenous status is also questionable – this time because of the light colour of my skin, my poor Dhivehi and my 'western' mannerisms, movements and ideas. Nevertheless, in recent years I have undergone some sort of secondary socialization (or resocialization), which does not supply me with the same authority as a native, but perhaps identifies me as a 'halfie' as Kirin Narayan (1993) and Lila Abu-Lughod (1991) have termed it. That is, someone with a mixed cultural identity, or someone who negotiates transnational identities. I am on the fringe of Maldivian society but also paradoxically privileged because I was educated in Australia and can return to my comfortable Australian life any time I wish.

In the Maldives, nationality has until very recently been passed through the father's line.[1] I have a Maldivian passport and am subject to Maldivian laws when I am in the country. Having this passport and identity enabled me to work for the Ministry of Gender and Family, which in turn allowed me to gain access to Maldivian women and their stories from around the country. The Maldivian government has historically been restrictive of whom they allow into the country to conduct research. Given the sensitive nature of my research, this work was only made possible by the access I gained to women through family contacts and the Ministry of Gender and Family. Working as both a practitioner and researcher has had its tensions. However, in the end my various roles have complemented each other and this insider status was vital to my research.

Being part of a Maldivian family enabled me to participate in everyday Maldivian life and also to be a part of important religious and cultural events such as weddings, circumcision parties, funerals, Eid celebrations and Ramazan (fasting). My insider status enabled me to learn about gendered roles first hand, which was invaluable to my understanding of Maldivian society. My aunt, with whom I initially lived, took responsibility for me and cared for me like a daughter. Over time I became more sensitive to certain cultural expectations about dress and mobility. I also became acutely aware that I reflected my family's reputation and was more conscious of femininity and modesty, being instructed about appropriate clothing, curfews and chaperoning. I became very conscious of the public places that were barred to me as a Maldivian woman. While expatriate friends of mine entered teashops to buy take-away fish snacks, I always waited outside, feeling very uncomfortable to be seen near, let alone inside, a male-dominated establishment. This internalized modesty became clearly apparent when my Australian mother came to visit me in Malé. She was welcomed as a member of the family and I felt that therefore she too reflected the reputation of both my family and myself. As such I was very insistent that she dress modestly despite the heat and she jokingly awarded me the nickname of the 'clothes police'.

But even as my skin darkened, my Dhivehi improved and my western-ness was moderated by Maldivian sensibilities, I was still not fully an insider in the Maldives. I still walked that tightrope between insider and outsider. I always will. While this position is challenging socially, I think it proved useful for my research. Regardless of where we are from, we often suffer from 'blindness' to aspects of our own culture. For example, white Americans or

Australians often fail to recognize whiteness as a racially inherited condition, or their accents as 'accents', or their culture as 'culture'. Those things are associated with the 'other'. Therefore, it is useful to be able to sit within society enough to gain access to people and places but also to be able to examine a culture from without. In viewing Maldivian society from two vantage points, as both insider and outsider, I hope I have been able to expose the intimate lives of women and men as well as how they are negotiating outside forces that are contributing to shifting social norms and structures, religious practices and gendered regimes of power.

7 October 2012, Bangkok, Thailand

Notes

1 In 2008 the law was changed to allow children who have a Maldivian mother and foreign father to still obtain Maldivian citizenship.

Acknowledgements

The amazing and often challenging journey of writing this book, which began as a doctoral thesis, would not have been possible without the help of many people. First, I would like to acknowledge my supervisory panel. Thanks to Jacqueline Siapno who was my co-supervisor in the earlier stages of my thesis and shared not only her rigorous intellectual insights but a deep friendship and even her home in East Timor. I am grateful to Abdullah Saeed, who kindly took on the role of co-supervisor towards the end of the process; having a Maldivian academic on my panel who could truly understand the context I was writing about was extremely helpful. I would particularly like to thank Kalissa Alexeyeff who was my primary supervisor throughout my candidature and provided unwavering personal and academic support, even continuing to supervise me during her maternity leave.

I am thankful for the advice and encouragement from my thesis examiners, Linda Rae Bennett and Dorothy Counts, and the comments of anonymous readers engaged by Routledge. In particular, I would like to sincerely thank the Women in Asia Series editor Lenore Lyons, whose insightful comments on numerous versions of this manuscript have been invaluable in shaping this book. I would also like to acknowledge Shaarif Ali and Xian Warner who worked as research assistants during different periods of my research.

I am extremely grateful to my Maldivian family who sheltered and supported me throughout much of my fieldwork, taught me about Maldivian life and shared many of the stories that are interwoven throughout this book. I would especially like to thank my father for being my connection to this beautiful country, reading this book and sharing his wisdom. I would never have done this had I not been his daughter.

I would also like to thank my Australian family who has equally influenced this book. To my mother, in particular, who has been a continual support to me, reading drafts and encouraging and nurturing me when I needed it most – thank you.

My deepest gratitude goes to my husband, Chris, who has continuously supported and encouraged me throughout this extremely long process.

For loving me from a distance during our extensive periods apart for this research, I will be forever grateful.

I owe a great debt to all the wonderful people I worked with at the Ministry of Gender and Family and UNFPA in the Maldives, particularly Shadiya Ibrahim, Dheena Moosa, Aishath Mohamed Didi, Maana Rafiu, Aishath Shehenaz and Athifa Ibrahim.

Most significantly, I would like to acknowledge all the women and men who participated in this research: thank you for so openly and bravely sharing your often-painful stories. I only hope I did justice to the richness of your lives and your resilience.

Introduction
Domestic violence in Asia and globalization from below

On 7 February 2012, the first democratically elected president of the Maldives, Mohamed Nasheed, resigned under duress. This followed weeks of protests by opposition party supporters in response to President Nasheed's ordering the arrest of the criminal court chief judge, whom he accused of incompetence and corruption. The protests escalated and Nasheed claims that police officers and army personnel mutinied and forced him to resign. In an opinion piece published in the *New York Times* the day after his resignation, Nasheed wrote, 'I believe this to be a coup d'état and suspect that my Vice President, who has since been sworn into office, helped to plan it' (Nasheed 2012).

At the same time that Nasheed was resigning, a handful of men stormed the National Museum and destroyed its display of priceless artefacts and Buddhist statues from the nation's pre-Islamic era. Echoing the 2001 destruction of the Bamiyan Buddha statues in Afghanistan by the Taliban, this is testament to the rise of Islamic extremism in what has generally been considered a very liberal Islamic state. Former President Nasheed, former Foreign Minister Ahmed Naseem, the international media and some commentators suggested that Maldivian Islamic extremists played an instrumental role in forcing Nasheed to resign (see Davis 2012; Jayasinghe 2012).

The ultra-conservative Islamic party, the Adhaalath Party, has now pledged its support for the new president, Dr Mohamed Waheed, and is part of a new coalition government that includes parties that have strong links to the 30-year dictatorship that preceded Nasheed's election. Waheed appointed four un-elected Adhaalath Party members to his cabinet, raising fears among many people that progress towards democracy is slipping away. At the time of writing in 2012, the Maldives remained in a state of political turmoil; Nasheed's party, the Maldives Democratic Party (MDP), was calling for new elections, and clashes between anti-government protesters and police continued to escalate.

These events are reflective of an unprecedented period of social transformation in the Maldives. The rise in Islamic extremism must be understood in the broader context of democratization, globalization and social change. The Maldives, a previously economically and politically insular country, has opened up to the world and global flows of ideas, discourses, media, capital and people are having an impact on all levels of society. This book argues that the implications of such social change are most profound for women and those on the margins of society, exposing them to greater discrimination and oppression. As Shadiya Ibrahim, member of the newly formed Gender Advocacy Working Group and a long-time campaigner for women's rights, said in the wake of the 2012 coup, 'being a woman is harder now' (quoted in Doherty 2012). Perhaps in recognition of this, women of the Maldives have been leading the protests calling for new democratic elections. Hundreds of women marched across the capital on 24 February 2012, then on 6 March a group of women marched to the President's Office to deliver a set of letters requesting Waheed's resignation, while others sat outside the office holding boards with slogans such as 'Where is my vote?' and 'Justice now'. Even more women came out in protest on International Women's Day.

As with the Arab Spring, global technologies such as Twitter, Facebook and YouTube are being used to mobilize people, call for democratic elections and share on-the-ground reports, footage and photos of events in Maldives, and women are also at the forefront of these movements. Many of the images being shared through social media sites are of violence and brutality by the police against protesters, often women. The police have used water cannon, tear gas and physical force to try to disperse protesters and Amnesty International has specifically condemned attacks on a group of women demonstrators in Addu Atoll by the Defence Force (Lubna 2012; Robinson 2012).

A more common but less visible form of violence against women is domestic violence. Violence by a male intimate partner is in fact the most common form of violence faced by women in the Maldives and around the world (Fulu 2007a; Garcia-Moreno *et al.* 2005). It is both a consequence of women's subordination and oppression and a tool used to maintain patriarchy. It is a serious human rights, development, health and social issue and it provides an indicator or gauge of the status of women in a society. I believe that the forms of violence taking place in the Maldives in 2012 – political oppression, destruction of Buddhist artefacts and domestic violence – are interconnected.

In her book *The Algebra of Infinite Justice*, Arundhati Roy (2002: xxiii) writes that it is important to 'never simplify what is complicated or complicate what is simple'. This is a useful idea when trying to understand the issue of domestic violence in Asia. In many ways international work on violence against women has simplified what is extraordinarily complicated. It tries to create slogans and replicable programmes that can be applied by development agencies around the region and indeed around the world. The fact that the prevalence of violence against women has not decreased in any significant way in the region, and may perhaps be increasing in some contexts, despite decades of work and millions of dollars spent, indicates that we still fail to understand this complex phenomenon. Other scholars have understandably rallied against such universalism and stressed the unique experiences of women across different socio-cultural settings, suggesting that cross-border analysis can be problematic (Frankenberg 1997; Grewal and Kaplan 1994; Mohanty 1991). While it is vital to address the specificities of different situations, it is important to maintain a sense of solidarity rather than disconnection in the political project of ending violence against women. Although the diversity of experiences of violence across the Asian region is significant, having lived, worked and conducted research on violence against women in a number of countries in the Asia-Pacific, I am often struck by the common threads and common stories from different places.

Chimamanda Ngozi Adichie (2011), a Nigerian novelist, speaks eloquently of the dangers of using a single story; single stories create stereotypes and 'make one story become the only story'. The other problem with a single story, she notes, is that 'it makes our recognition of our equal humanity difficult'. This book examines women's lived experiences of intimate partner violence in the Maldives through the lens of domestic violence in Asia, particularly through a process of comparison with the countries of South Asia and Muslim nations in Southeast Asia. I weave multiple stories together – stories from women who have experienced violence, stories from my family, stories of love, stories from politicians and stories by documentary film makers, among many others. However, this is not simply a book about violence in the Maldives. It provides a model for better understanding and responding to the complexities of domestic violence in Asia as a whole. I believe that the multiple stories from the Maldives and Asia in this book show not just how we are different but, importantly, how we are similar. Through this case study we can recognize complexity at the same time as commonality.

On the surface it may seem that, as a small and historically isolated island nation in the middle of the Indian Ocean, the Maldives offers little that is relevant to other countries in the region. However, the Maldives is on the border between South and Southeast Asia, with elements of similarity to both regions. In addition, the prevalence rate of intimate partner violence in the Maldives is lower than almost any other country in Asia, offering insights into violence prevention from the experiences of a relatively non-violent society. Importantly, rapid social transformation in the Maldives, which is similar to many other countries in the region, highlights that the prevalence, causes and consequences of domestic violence can no longer be understood outside the realities of globalization and social change. In fact, the elements that have historically kept intimate partner violence low in the Maldives are the very elements that are now being challenged by dramatic changes to the Maldivian social fabric. In this book I argue that domestic violence in the Maldives is increasing and will continue to do so if the current patterns of social change persist. By looking at the experiences of democratization, globalization and Islamism, this book offers a study of the causes of change in domestic violence that are particularly relevant in Asia.

This book is based on qualitative research and participatory observation carried out during various trips to the Maldives from 2004 to 2008, as well as data from the Maldives Survey on Domestic Violence and Women's Health, which I coordinated in 2006. Over this period I conducted informal and semi-structured interviews about gender and violence with key informants such as government ministry staff, police officers, magistrates, health-care workers, activists and UN workers. I also conducted in-depth semi-structured interviews with women who had experienced intimate partner violence. Focus group discussions were also conducted to explore general community attitudes and beliefs about violence against women.[1]

The Maldives in flux

The Maldives is undergoing a period of rapid social transformation stemming from an increase in global cultural flows. The impacts of economic development, increasing consumerism and western influences, internal migration and urbanization, Islamism and democratization have been particularly evident in shifting ideas and discourses surrounding gender and Islam. Such changes have been emerging over the past 30 years; however, this book focuses particularly on the period from 2004 to 2012, a period characterized by rapid and dramatic change in the Maldives.

The Maldives remained relatively isolated from the rest of the world until the 1980s when tourism started to take off. A number of older people I spoke to said that until the 1970s, change came at a very slow pace. In many ways, life in the mid twentieth century was, for most islanders, similar to how it had always been, with life's necessities harvested from the sea and coconut trees and the surplus bartered for cloth and rice. Writing in 1976, anthropologist Clarence Maloney (1976: 654) argued that the Maldives was among the least known of all independent countries in Asia. He went on to state that 'the impact of the modern world has hit the Maldives late, and in a hundred island villages even now it is scarcely noticeable' (Maloney 1976: 671). Webb (1988: 11) suggested that in the late 1980s the populations inhabiting the remote islands of the Maldives were perhaps some of the few people left in the world who were surviving totally on their immediate environment.

The Maldives is a chain of approximately 1,200 small coral islands in the Indian Ocean spread over a distance of 900 kilometres on the equator. Of the 1,200 islands, 198 are inhabited (Republic of Maldives 2008a). *Dhivehi Raaje* is the name Maldivians use for their country and Maldivians refer to themselves as *Dhivehin*. The islands of the Maldives are grouped into 20 administrative atolls and the population of 360,000 is widely dispersed. More than one-third of the inhabited islands have a population of fewer than 500 people and 70 per cent of the inhabited islands have a population of fewer than 1,000 people (Republic of Maldives 2008a).

The Maldives is a Sunni Islamic state but has a Buddhist history and Hindu influences (Bell 1940; Heyerdahl 1986). The Maldivian language, first scripts, architecture, customs and manners all point to a time when the Maldives was a Buddhist kingdom. However, there is reluctance, even opposition, to studying early history because of what many regard as the contemptible past before Islam (Mittra and Kumar 2004: 2). Maldivian Buddhist history is either omitted or just briefly mentioned in most local history books. Maldivian law explicitly prohibits the importation of any objects that are revered or used for worship in religions other than Islam. According to official Maldivian records, Islam was universally adopted in 1153 CE. Maldivians follow the Shafi'i school of law, founded by Iman al-Shafi'i. The Maldives has often been described as moderate or liberal in its practice of Islam (discussed more in Chapter 3).

Outsiders are often shocked at the tiny size and isolated nature of these islands floating in the middle of the vast Indian Ocean. Of the 198 inhabited islands only 28 have a land area greater than one square kilometre (Republic of Maldives 2008a). Maldivians tend to identify with their home island even if they have lived on Malé, the capital, for most of their lives and often travel between islands to visit family and friends. Despite the fact that the population is spread across hundreds of islands and separated by vast tracts of ocean, all Maldivians speak the same language, Dhivehi, although there are a number of dialects mostly in the Southern atolls.

Traditionally, the Maldives was a seafaring nation and fishing is still the second biggest industry in the country, after tourism. The Maldives expanded economically in the 1970s with the arrival of tourism, mechanized boats and freezer vessels that enabled greater fish catches and export. The first tourist resort was opened in 1972; there are now nearly 100 resorts and the number of annual tourist arrivals has risen to nearly 800,000 – double the Maldivian population (Republic of Maldives 2006a, 2011b). The burgeoning tourism industry along with multilateral and bilateral aid has promoted economic growth rates of 7 to 9 per cent in the past ten years. In 2011, the Maldives had the highest GDP per capita in South Asia at US$2,900 (Republic of Maldives 2008c).

Economic growth has led to major improvements in a range of social indicators. In 2010 the Maldives had a Human Development Index of 0.602, ranking 107 out of 169 countries (UNDP 2010). Life expectancy has increased from 60 years for females and 62 years for males in 1985 to 76 years for males and 79 years for females in 2010 (Republic of Maldives 2005a, 2008a). The Maldives has achieved five out of eight Millennium Development Goals ahead of the 2015 deadline, making it South Asia's only 'MDG+' country (Republic of Maldives 2011a). The Millennium Development Goal indicators show that a net primary school enrolment rate of 95 per cent has been achieved for both girls and boys and the literacy rate for 15–24-year-olds was over 98 per cent in 2007 (Republic of Maldives 2008c). The infant mortality rate has been reduced from 62 per 1,000 live births in 1997 to 11 per 1,000 in 2010 (Republic of Maldives 2006a: xxi, 2011b). The under-five mortality rate has also decreased from 48 per 1,000 live births in 1990 to just 12 per 1,000 live births in 2009 (Republic of Maldives 2005a).

Most inhabited islands have at least one school and one health-care facility, although the level of service provision varies from island to island. Some islands have only primary-level education and basic health posts. Other larger islands have secondary and upper secondary schools and well-equipped health clinics and hospitals. Five regional hospitals and five atoll hospitals are located across the country. The proportion of the atoll population living on islands with schooling available up to grade ten increased from one-quarter to two-thirds between 1997 and 2004 (Republic of Maldives 2006a), and in 2009 all except five inhabited islands were providing education at least up to grade seven (Republic of Maldives 2011a). Services such as electricity, sanitation, medical services and potable water have also increased significantly over the last ten years. For example, in 1997, 28 per cent of the atoll population received less than six hours of electricity per day. By 2004 this figure had dropped to 2 per cent of the atoll population (Republic of Maldives 1998, 2006a).

However, the process of economic development has been accompanied by increasing urbanization and income disparity and this has impacted on domestic violence in the Maldives, as discussed later in the book. Malé, the capital island, is less than two square kilometres; however, it is home to more than 100,000 people, making it the most densely populated city in the world. Malé brings together people from all over the Maldives and, as such, it is a microcosm of the country: revealing the multiple realities of the Maldives and providing a visible sense of the past and future.

Less than 30 years ago Malé used to have wide, white sandy streets and bicycles were the only wheeled form of transport. Absurdly, there are now thousands of cars and motorbikes on the island – even imported sports cars for those who can afford it – competing for space in the maze of narrow streets. Modern, high-rise buildings and apartments have become commonplace since the turn of the century. Cranes take up the whole width of a street, diverting traffic. Iron rods stand out of slabs of concrete like pick-up sticks and migrant construction workers use them to balance as they manoeuvre around the work site in sandals or bare feet. The constant construction gives a hint of the rapidly expanding Malé population; growing primarily through migration from the atolls (for work and education) rather than a particularly high fertility rate.[2] Malé is the centre of almost all business and government activity: the home of parliament, government offices, banks, key public and private organizations as well as the international offices of the United Nations and World Health Organization; it thus offers the most employment opportunities.

Malé is not a planned city and it continues to grow in a chaotic or organic fashion. With the ocean as a barrier to outward expansion, the city of Malé seems to grow in and up; tighter and denser. Malé locals could never have imagined that the population would double as it has in only the last ten years. They often complain about the current incarnation of the city, a far cry from the spacious island they recall from their childhood. One friend explained, 'You can tell things are moving too quickly when people in their twenties and thirties are nostalgic about what life was like on this island when they were young'.

Space has become so scarce that the rent on a typical two-bedroom apartment is approximately four times the average per capita income, forcing many people to share rooms and even sleep in shifts (Republic of Maldives 2008a). Recently, in an attempt to reduce some of the congestion in Malé, the government built an island between the airport and Malé called Hulhumalé. Unfortunately, this has not alleviated the crowding in the capital. Mahjoob Shujau, the man in charge of the Hulhumalé development, is reported as saying, 'We built it, but the people are not coming' (Rosenberg 2008: 26).[3]

With increasing urbanization and overcrowding, symptoms of social disorganization are becoming visible. In 2004 I saw for the first time beggars on the street and young men and women who were suffering from drug addiction. Violent crime is also on the increase. In 2004 I was comfortable walking around the streets at night on my own; however, by 2006 I was being warned repeatedly by family and friends that this was no longer safe. Everyone was talking about bag-snatching, men carrying knives and houses being burgled.

Politically things have also changed dramatically since the early 2000s. The Maldives used to be a sultanate and became a republic in 1968 with Ibrahim Nasir the first president. In 1979 Maumoon Abdul Gayoom succeeded him and remained in power until 2008, making him the longest-serving leader in Asia. During the 30 years of Gayoom's rule, political parties were banned and elections were not free or fair and the media was state-run and -controlled. Until recently the president was nominated to a five-year term by a secret ballot of the *Majlis* (Parliament), which was then confirmed by a national referendum. The public could only vote 'yes' or 'no' for the president, with no alternative candidates. The president was considered to hold supreme authority – he was the Commander-in-Chief of the armed forces, Protector of Islam and also appointed cabinet ministers who need not necessarily be Members of Parliament. For many years, Amnesty International criticized the Maldives government for various human rights abuses including arbitrary detention of political prisoners, torture and inhumane treatment (Amnesty International 2003). In practice, the Maldives under Gayoom denied freedom of religion, freedom of the press, freedom of expression and the right to free association and assembly. The Freedom in the World Index, which is a measure of political rights and civil liberties published by Freedom House, judged the Maldives as 'not free' in 2007 and 2008.

During my fieldwork between 2004 and 2006, political tensions were increasing. Public assembly was deemed illegal and protests and demonstrations of any kind were virtually unheard of. However, in September 2003 a young prisoner was beaten to death by wardens. Other prisoners revolted and the government gave the order to shoot. Five more prisoners were killed, sparking massive protests in Malé. This was the catalyst for the establishment of the MDP, the first opposition party set up in exile in Sri Lanka as political parties were illegal in the Maldives at the time. After this event in September 2003 there were unprecedented civil protests in Malé demanding improvements in the political and human rights situation. Government crackdowns also became more visible, with the government riot squad out in force. I vividly remember getting caught in a protest in 2006 by accident and being surrounded by police in riot gear. At another time in 2006 the government called a state of emergency, instituting a curfew to try to prevent any more political demonstrations. One of the most bizarre scenes I witnessed was a full-scale armoured tank rolling down the tiny streets of Malé in the middle of the day. It seems totally incongruous with the Maldives I knew before.

The Maldivian political situation largely remained under the international radar for a number of reasons, including geographical isolation, political insularity and a high level of self-sufficiency. However, when the Indian Ocean Tsunami struck on 26 December 2004 the country was suddenly thrown into the international spotlight. The tsunami was the worst natural disaster in Maldivian history – more than 1,300 people suffered injuries and 108 people died (World Bank *et al.* 2005). Despite the relatively small death toll, the Maldives experienced a disaster of national proportions with only eight of the 198 inhabited islands left unaffected. Some 56 islands sustained major physical damage and 14 were completely destroyed and had to be evacuated, some rendered permanently uninhabitable (World Bank *et al.* 2005).[4]

The country was inundated by international agencies and funding. Previously there had been internal pressure for the government to democratize, particularly from the MDP. Now there was also considerable international pressure to establish democratic institutions, promote a multi-party system and allow free and fair elections. As such, the democratic reform process was sped up and parliament voted unanimously for the creation of a multi-party system on 2 June 2005. The government formed the Dhivehi Rayyithunge Party (Maldivian People's Party; DRP), and the MDP returned to the Maldives from exile in Sri Lanka to become the major opposition party. Other new parties such as the Islamic Democratic Party and the Adhaalath Party were also established. In October 2008 the first democratic elections were held in the Maldives. Mohamed Nasheed, leader of the MDP, who had been a political prisoner in the past, became the president. The MDP did not win an outright majority and had to form a coalition government that included the Adhaalath Party, among others. The vast ideological differences between members of the coalition resulted in frequent clashes over various issues – such as selling alcohol on inhabited islands, which had previously been illegal under Islamic law, making Islam an optional rather than a compulsory subject in secondary school and the introduction of religious unity regulations, as discussed in Chapter 3. In September 2011

Adhaalath withdrew its support for Nasheed and the government, citing his lack of cooperation with its efforts to strengthen Islam in the Maldives.

Nasheed's government struggled with a declining economy and a parliament dominated by opposition parties, leading to constitutional gridlock. Further tension arose when the then government attempted to reform a judiciary that was largely staffed by loyalists to the previous Gayoom government and that many regarded as corrupt (Aljazeera 2012; Bajaj 2012). In January 2012, Mr Nasheed ordered the army to arrest the chief judge of the criminal court, Abdulla Mohamed, whom he accused of corruption and incompetence. The arrest was widely condemned as an unconstitutional overreach of authority and prompted the nightly protests in Malé that led to Nasheed's resignation on 7 February 2012. He was replaced by Vice President Dr Mohammed Waheed, who is currently serving as president although he has not been elected by the people.

Domestic violence in the Maldives and Asia

The story of violence against women in the Maldives is complex. In early 2006 as part of my research for this book, I coordinated the first ever nationally representative survey on violence against women in the Maldives, using the World Health Organization (WHO) Multi-Country Study on Women's Health and Domestic Violence methodology (Garcia-Moreno *et al.* 2005). The *Maldives Survey on Violence against Women* (hereafter the Maldives Survey) found that 20 per cent of Maldivian women aged 15–49 who had ever been in a relationship reported that they had experienced physical or sexual violence, or both, by an intimate partner (Fulu 2007a). Some 6 per cent reported that they had experienced physical and/or sexual violence by an intimate partner in the previous 12 months (Fulu 2007a).[5]

Prior to this study there was a strong public perception that violence against women in the Maldives was rare or non-existent and many people were shocked at the findings. Ali Rasheed, a documentary filmmaker who was employed by the Ministry of Gender and Family in 2004 to make a documentary on violence against women in the Maldives in an attempt to bring the reality of women's experiences to light, recounted his experiences:

> I remember seeking advice from someone who had years of experience in community development across the country. 'What's your film about?' he asked us. When we told him, he replied, 'Forget it. There's no violence against women in the Maldives, at least not enough to warrant real concern.'
>
> (Rasheed 2006b: 29)

There has been a high level of denial and silence surrounding the issue of domestic violence in the Maldives. On International Women's Day in 2002, the then Minister of Women's Affairs and Social Security, Ms Raashida

Yoosuf, attempted to address this denial and encourage more open discussion of violence against women. She said,

> Violence is an issue we are hesitant to talk about. We have to keep in mind that victims keeping silent about their suffering encourages perpetrators to continue with their actions. If we want to make our environment safe, free and conducive for all individuals, we have to start openly talking about the actions of perpetrators of violence.
> (Quoted in Fulu 2004: 4)

The failure to openly discuss violence against women is not unique to the Maldives. Domestic violence remains hidden in many countries because it is often considered a private, family issue and is frequently associated with shame. Scholars writing about South Asia have suggested that many communities are preoccupied with maintaining cultural integrity and cohesion, as well as projecting a positive image to the outside world, which results in a certain level of denial of unpleasant issues (see Bhattacharjee 1992; Dasgupta 2000a; Kallivayalil 2007; Venkataramani-Kothari 2007).

Given this context, many people were hesitant to accept the findings of the Maldives Survey. They felt that the prevalence rate was too *high* to be accurate. My own response was somewhat different. I was aware that the prevalence rates of partner violence in other countries were much higher. In other countries such as Samoa, Ethiopia, Peru and New Zealand, where the WHO Multi-Country Study had been conducted, the prevalence rates of partner violence were much higher, as high as 71 per cent in Ethiopia (Garcia-Moreno *et al.* 2005: 28). I was left with the question: What makes the rate of violence in the Maldives so *low*?

The prevalence of partner violence in the Maldives is also particularly low compared with other countries in the South Asian region. A survey of almost 10,000 women in seven Indian cities found that 70 per cent of women had experienced at least two forms of physical partner abuse (Duvvury 2000). In a more recent study in Bengal and Jharkhand, 52 per cent of women reported experiencing psychological partner violence, 16 per cent physical violence and 25 per cent sexual violence (Babu and Kar 2010). In Sri Lanka, it is estimated that around 60 per cent of women are subjected to domestic violence (Republic of Sri Lanka 2004). Based on data from the 2009 study on domestic violence in Nepal, 58 per cent of women had experienced some form of sexual coercion by their husbands (Adhikari and Tamang 2010). The WHO Multi-Country Study on Women's Health and Domestic Violence conducted in one urban and one rural site in Bangladesh in 2005 found that 53 per cent of women in the urban site and 62 per cent in the rural site reported experiencing physical and/or sexual intimate partner violence (Garcia-Moreno *et al.* 2005). This high prevalence was confirmed by a 2011 study on men's perpetration of violence against women in the same sites in Bangladesh that revealed that

55 to 57 per cent of men reported using physical and/or sexual violence against a partner (Naved *et al.* 2011).

In Southeast Asia rates of violence against women tend to be lower than in South Asia; however, they are still higher than in the Maldives. In Thailand, the prevalence of physical and or sexual partner violence was determined to be 41 per cent in one urban site and 47 per cent in one rural site (Garcia-Moreno *et al.* 2005). A 2010 national study on domestic violence against women in Vietnam using the same WHO methodology reported that 34 per cent of ever-married women aged 18–60 had experienced physical and/or sexual partner violence (Government of Viet Nam 2010). In East Timor, 25 per cent of women reported having experienced physical partner violence in the previous 12 months (Hynes *et al.* 2003).

Even compared to many industrialized countries such as Australia, the United Kingdom and the United States of America, where the status of women is assumed to be higher and policies and programmes to address violence against women have been in place for decades, the prevalence of intimate partner violence in the Maldives is low. In Australia, research suggests that over one-third of women who had a current or former intimate partner have experienced at least one form of partner violence in their lifetime (Mouzos and Makkai 2004). In the United States and United Kingdom, the prevalence rates are 30 per cent (Wilt and Olson 1996) and 26 per cent (Walby and Allen 2004), respectively.[6]

Research on violence against women using the same WHO methodology conducted in 2009 in Kiribati, another small atoll nation that is geographically very similar to the Maldives, revealed one of the highest rates of intimate partner violence among all the countries where this research had been undertaken. In Kiribati, among women aged 15–49 who had ever been in an intimate relationship, 68 per cent reported being physically or sexually abused by an intimate partner (Secretariat of the Pacific Community 2010). Unlike Maldivians, who were shocked at what they considered to be an unrealistically high prevalence of violence at 20 per cent, people in Kiribati were not particularly surprised to hear that more than two-thirds of women reported experiencing intimate partner violence, because they saw violence to be a relatively normal part of family life.

These results reinforced my belief that the results of the Maldives Survey were particularly interesting and had the potential to offer powerful lessons to guide policy and programmes to address this issue around the world. If we could shed light on some of the socio-cultural elements that have served to protect women from high rates of intimate partner violence in the Maldives, then perhaps this could inform approaches aimed at addressing violence against women in societies where it is more prevalent. Research on violence against women to date has tended to focus on the risk factors for violence or the 'root causes of violence' (see Abramsky *et al.* 2011; Heise 2011). However, if we accept the premise that human systems move in the direction of what they continuously study, analyse and discuss, then this calls us to study the 'root causes of success', rather than the 'root causes of failure' (Whitney et al. 2010: 27). Therefore, I felt that it was important to ask: What can we learn about the 'root causes of peace' from a relatively non-violent society?[7]

Violence against women is not a static phenomenon – it must be understood in the context of social change. The quantitative, qualitative and ethnographic data in this book is reflective of the impact of social changes on women's experiences of violence. I argue that in fact domestic violence is on the rise in the Maldives because the 'root causes of peace' are being eroded. Given that there is no baseline data prior to 2006, it is difficult to determine whether the 20 per cent prevalence of intimate partner violence is an increase from the past. However, my research indicates that there are already signs of an increase in violence against women and that it will continue to increase beyond the 2006 levels if the underlying issues are not addressed.

The globalized ecological model: an integrated understanding of intimate partner violence

This book focuses on male partner violence against women because it is the most common form of gender-based violence in the Maldives, and indeed around the world (Fulu 2007c; Garcia-Moreno et al. 2005; UN General Assembly 2006; WHO 2002). Intimate partner violence is defined as 'behaviour within an intimate relationship that causes physical, sexual or psychological harm, including acts of physical aggression, sexual coercion, psychological abuse and controlling behaviours' (Heise and Garcia-Moreno 2002). For the purposes of this book, the prevalence rate of intimate partner violence includes physical and/or sexual violence by a current or former intimate male partner. In this book I also explore emotional abuse in more qualitative terms.[8]

It is evident that women also perpetrate violence against men and there are even a number of scholars who suggest that partner violence is gender-symmetric (Fergusson et al. 2005; Finkelhor et al. 1983; Gelles and Straus 1979; Hammel 2009). However, the data from the Maldives and other countries in the region indicate that women rarely initiate partner violence. Although I did not interview men directly about their experiences of violence by a female partner, in the Maldives Survey we asked female respondents if they had ever hit or physically mistreated their partner when he was not hitting or physically mistreating them. This does not generate data specifically on the victimization of men, but it does address the question of whether women frequently initiate violence against a male partner (Garcia-Moreno et al. 2005: 38). Only 4 per cent of women reported that they had initiated violence when their partner was not hitting them. Similarly in almost all other developing country settings where this research was carried out, woman-initiated violence was extremely rare (Garcia-Moreno et al. 2005: 38). These rates may be underestimations because the data is obtained from women, however, other studies that ask men directly about their experiences of violence by their wives also tend to suggest that female-initiated violence is less common than male-initiated violence (Kishor and Johnson 2004a, 2004b; Nelson and Zimmerman 1996).[9]

This book adopts an interdisciplinary perspective on domestic violence because violence against women is an interdisciplinary issue: it is a health issue, a legal issue, a human rights issue, a gender issue, a development issue and a social issue. As Bell and Naugle (2008: 1101) argue, new theories on intimate partner violence should be more comprehensive in nature, 'integrating views from multiple academic disciplines'. Similarly, Arias (1998) suggests that scholars in the United States have tended to examine family violence from within the confines of their relative disciplines, and as such the complexity and interconnectedness of the determinants of violence have been lost and this has hampered the impact of interventions. In a conscious attempt to avoid this, I draw on literature from a wide range of disciplines including public health, development, sociology, gender studies and anthropology. I incorporate epidemiological analysis of the Maldives Survey, feminist epistemology in the approach to interviewing women, as well as ethnography in the use of participant observation. However, my research comes primarily from a gender studies or feminist social science perspective in that my foremost assumption is that intimate partner violence is a gendered phenomenon that fundamentally stems from gender inequality within society. Asymmetric gender relations contribute to violence against women, and violence also serves to preserve asymmetric gender systems of power (Bennett and Manderson 2003; O'Toole et al. 2007).

As an analytical framework, I draw on and expand upon the ecological model that was first introduced in the late 1970s by Garbarino and Crouter (1978), and has been used by several authors since to conceptualize gender-based violence (Heise 1998; Kocacik et al. 2007). It attempts to explain the multi-faceted nature of violence and explores the relationship between individual and contextual factors. This model examines the characteristics of the individual including psychological factors (such as having a childhood history of domestic violence) and demographic factors (such as educational attainment). It also considers the intimate relationship where the abuse takes place, including the distribution of power within the relationship, as well as the community and societal context that refers to the dominant cultural views and attitudes within the society, laws, social and economic policies and social norms (Heise 1998, 2011; WHO 2002). Importantly, it also acknowledges the links between these factors.

I have developed the Globalized Ecological Model (Figure I.1) based on Heise (1998, 2011) to understand what contributes to partner violence in the Maldives and how these factors are changing over time. However, the model has applicability for other countries in the Asia-Pacific region and beyond. It identifies five dimensions to domestic violence – individual/relationships, family, community, society and global. The categories in this model are

14 Introduction

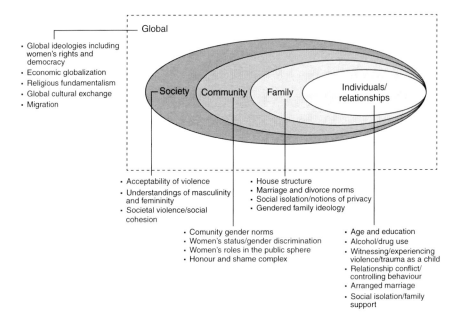

Figure I.1 The globalized ecological model: factors related to intimate partner violence in the Maldives at the different levels of the social ecology

used for the sake of conceptual organization and the levels are interconnected and overlapping, as shown by the concentric circles. In addition, all the layers of the model are in a state of flux, and this book explores the 'moments of change' of these 'overlapping scales' (see Jimenez 2005: 158). It includes factors specifically related to the Maldivian context rather than a comprehensive list of all possible risk and protective factors (for such a list, see Heise 2011).[10]

The individual/relationship level refers to the socio-demographic characteristics of the woman and her partner such as age, education, use of drugs and alcohol and childhood experiences of violence. It also considers elements of the relationship such as whether the marriage was arranged and if a woman can count on members of her own family for support. These elements are useful in understanding what individual- and relationship-level factors put some women at increased risk of violence compared to other women within the same society.

The outer three levels of the ecological model – family, community and society – help to understand what broader contextual factors contribute to women's experiences of violence, and specifically what elements at these different levels can be used to explain why partner violence is low in the Maldives. The family level looks at the nature of family life, including the structure of the family home, notions of the domestic sphere as private, and marriage and divorce practices. The community level looks at gender roles within the community, including the status of women, women's roles in the public sphere and also how notions of honour and shame are played out. The society level refers to the broader socio-historical context. It examines how violence is culturally understood, whether it is acceptable and whether it is used as a form of discipline in society. In this section I also consider the level of crime in society and how masculinity and femininity are defined.

Expanding further on Heise's ecological model, I include an overarching global framework of analysis, examining how global processes impact upon the other levels of the ecological model. I look at the influence of democratization, globalization and Islamism on women's experiences of violence in the Maldives, offering a study of the causes of change in domestic violence that are particularly relevant in Asia.

While definitions and conceptualizations of globalization remain contested, there exists a broad consensus that the increasing interdependence of communities across the globe has created a new kind of world (Doyal 2002; Giddens 1990, 2003; Rege 2003; Sandbrook and Romano 2004). Globalization is not merely an economic phenomenon of greater economic integration but, for the purposes of this book, refers to increased flows of commodities, flows of people, flows of migration and flows of transnational discourse (Appadurai 1991).

Lindberg (2009) argues that many, both within and outside Asia, have problematically interpreted globalization as a uni-directional, neo-colonial imposition of western culture. This Eurocentric perspective fails to recognize, for example, the proliferation of Vietnamese restaurants in cities throughout Asia and the world, the frequent use of Indian textile designs in European clothing labels and the immense global popularity of Korean and Cantonese pop bands. As Lindberg (2009: 107) explains, 'at its core, globalization implies reciprocity between different areas'. These multidirectional flows, varyingly resisted and accepted, are clearly evident in Asia, particularly among young Muslims in Indonesia, Malaysia and elsewhere who view their Islamic faith as a way of being modern and globally engaged without being western (Lindberg 2009; Rinaldo 2008; Robinson 2009; Sharify-Funk 2008).

Padilla *et al.* (2007: xii) suggest that there is a gap in the literature in terms of scholars who have examined the linkages between macro-structural trends of globalization and the subjective experiences and local meanings of actors in specific cultural settings (for exceptions to this, see Abaza 2001; Featherstone 1998; Robertson 1990; Robertson and Khondker 1998). As Mendieta (2007: 18) explains: 'The planet is globalized, indeed, but not all in the planet are globalized in the same way. Some are more globalized than others, some are affected more than others, and some are globalized adversely while others beneficially.' Beasley (2008: 99) argues that there is a need for 'more rigorous and culturally specific evaluation of globalization as an uneven process entailing complex forms of accommodation and resistance'. Recognizing the need to address this gap in the effects of globalization on the human experience, this book explores how Maldivians are negotiating changes to gender and Islam, among other things. In particular, I examine the uniquely localized way in which the lived experiences of violence in the Maldives are being affected by the 'shifting terrain of globalizing processes' (Padilla *et al.* 2007: xii).

This book therefore offers a gendered understanding of globalization. This is important because, as Ferguson *et al.* (2008: 2) argue,

> Gender is not exterior to globalization, nor is it simply one more vector or circuit: rather, the complexities of globalization are always already gendered, already doing their contradictory work on sexed, raced, and laboring bodies: gendered family relations; and masculinized and feminized institutions, ideologies and identities.

While extensive feminist literature exists on globalization's impact on women, there have been calls for further analysis on how violence against women, as it is conceptualized within a broader spectrum of violence, is impacted by cultural and social factors related to globalization (Krug *et al.* 2002: 1088). Some scholars have addressed globalization in relation to specific empirical circumstances of violence against women (Merry 2001; Radford and Tsutsumi 2004); however, as Pinnewala (2009) notes, there are very few studies on partner violence in Asia, and almost none on women's perspectives on ending violence. In addition, there has not been a concentrated effort to incorporate globalization into theoretical frameworks of violence against women.

This book offers a space for both positive and negative readings of globalization 'on the ground', providing a theoretical and empirical basis for understanding the intersection between the global and the local. The Globalized Ecological Model presents a new framework for understanding domestic violence in Asia. It demonstrates that violence must be understood holistically, examining social, cultural, religious and political contexts. It also makes clear that domestic violence is not static and must be recognized as a dynamic phenomenon, affected not only by local factors but also by global forces. Although global cultural flows are making violence against women more prevalent in the Maldives, the fact that experiences of violence are changeable offers hope for a reduction in the rates of violence in Asia. Furthermore, the factors that have historically kept intimate partner violence low in the Maldives suggest a way forward in this endeavour of reducing violence against women.

Chapter outlines

Chapter 1 examines the nature, patterns and consequences of intimate partner violence in the Maldives. I analyse the characteristics of individuals to see what makes some women more vulnerable to violence than others and show how these accounts confirm or challenge previous research findings from other settings, particularly from Asia.

In Chapter 2 I explore why the prevalence of intimate partner violence in the Maldives is lower than in other countries in the Asian region. I first present a statistical analysis of the risk and protective factors associated with partner violence from the Maldives Survey. Based on this I argue that there are three interconnected reasons for the relatively low rate of violence: the flexible nature of marriage and divorce; relatively equal gender relations with a moderate honour/shame complex; and a culture where crime has been rare and violence has not been considered an acceptable means of dealing with problems.

Chapters 3, 4 and 5 explore how those elements that have historically kept intimate partner violence low in the Maldives are being challenged by the dramatic changes to Maldivian social fabric stemming from globalization. By looking through the lens of globalization we see that domestic violence is not static, and that the prevalence of violence has the potential to increase, not just in the Maldives but also in other parts of Asia that are also negotiating the conflicting and contradictory effects of globalization. Specifically, Chapter 3 investigates the impact of global flows of people and ideas on the shifting ideologies of love, romance, marriage and divorce and how these changes impact on women's experiences of partner violence. Chapter 4 examines the impact of globalization on women's roles in the public sphere. Chapter 5 examines how some elements of globalization have contributed to the fragmentation of communities, a state of social disorganization and what many are referring to as a 'social crisis' in the Maldives.

In the final chapter I present the way forward as I see it. I explore the global implications of this research and how it highlights the need for a paradigm shift in the work on violence against women. I advocate for an understanding of violence against women that acknowledges the dynamic intersections of the global and the local. We must anticipate the new challenges that we see arising with globalization and social transformation, to ensure that the benefits of global spaces are shared with all. I suggest that to respond effectively to violence against women we need to have an integrated approach that moves beyond a deficit model towards a more creative and holistic promotion of peace.

Notes

1 The statistics presented in this book come from the Survey on Domestic Violence and Women's Health, and the analysis was conducted directly by the author. All original direct quotations come from in-depth interviews, key informant interviews and focus group discussions conducted by the author and her research assistants. The survey and all focus group discussion and in-depth interviews were conducted in Dhivehi and the key informant interviews were conducted in English. All interviews and focus group discussions were transcribed in

18 *Introduction*

    the original language and translated from Dhivehi into English by a research assistant.
2 The total fertility rate fell from 6.4 in 1990 to 5.4 in 1995 and 2.8 in 2000 (Republic of Maldives 2005c).
3 Hulhumalé has attracted only about 5,000 people since 2003 but the planners say 150,000 could fit into the 188-hectare island. Some people explained to me that Hulhumalé is more expensive than the government promised and in fact only the wealthy can afford to purchase land there. The wealthy are therefore keeping their homes in Malé and buying in Hulhumalé as an investment. Those living in the most crowded conditions in Malé cannot afford to move. Furthermore, the apartment blocks built by the government in Hulhumalé are small and unappealing, and many young people say that there is nothing to do in Hulhumalé. They would rather be close to the 'action' in Malé. And for Maldivians who are unused to commuting, the 20-minute boat trip from Hulhumalé to Malé seems like a long journey to make every day to come to work.
4 For more discussion on the impact of the tsunami, particularly on women and gender relations, see Fulu 2007b.
5 The survey asked a range of behaviour-specific questions related to each type of violence, see Appendix 1.
6 These rates were calculated using national surveys and not the WHO Multi-Country Study model; however, their methodologies and questionnaires were relatively similar. General comparison of prevalence rates is therefore possible.
7 Little research has been conducted on societies where family violence is rare. Levinson (1989) examined family violence from a cross-cultural perspective, and Howell and Willis (1989) have discussed approaches to the control and prevention of family violence by looking at societies in which family violence is rare. This research has looked only at small-scale societies rather than countries as a whole.
8 Defining and measuring emotional abuse is very challenging because the acts that are perceived as abusive are likely to vary between countries and even between groups within countries (Garcia-Moreno *et al.* 2005). Because of the complexity of defining and measuring emotional abuse, and the difficulty of comparing across countries, emotional abuse is not included in the comparable prevalence rates of domestic violence in this book.
9 Violence against men is an area that requires greater research, although it is outside the scope of this book. Intimate partner violence does not only occur in heterosexual relationships. A recent body of literature indicates that violence within same-sex couples is also relatively common (Burke and Follingstad 1999; Elliot 1996; Island and Letellier 1991; Letellier 1994; Mak *et al.* 2010; Renzetti and Miley 1996).
10 This is modelled for the Maldivian context but could be configured in different ways in different contexts. For example, Heise's (2011) ecological model separates the relationship from the individual and considers gender equity and legislation as part of the macro-social level.

1 Coercive control

Patterns of intimate partner violence in the Maldives

Aishath is a 45-year-old woman who lives in Malé and works at a government ministry.[1] She has two children, although she has been pregnant five times. Her other children died during pregnancy or childbirth. Aishath has been married twice but is now single. She experienced intimate partner violence by her first husband whom she married when she was 17 years old. He was ten years older than her and she recalls that he was a very quiet and respected person. She met him through mutual friends when she was in high school. At the time he was an officer on a boat and they kept in contact through letters and cards, and after a year they got married. She said,

> For the first 18 years with him I didn't even know that there was such a thing as domestic violence and that people go through such things because we didn't have any problems between us. For us it was always like we were on our honeymoon.

According to Aishath, the violence began after her husband started having an affair with another woman. 'After that I started experiencing violence in many ways from him', she explained. 'The whole person changed, the way he talked changed; he was louder.' He also started smoking and would burn cigarettes on her body, Aishath recalled. He abused her sexually and emotionally as well, humiliating her in front of her friends and keeping her isolated in the home. While she was pregnant he pushed her onto the ground and she hurt her back badly.

> Even just two days before the delivery when I was asleep he stepped on my throat and when I moved he would let go. He did that three times and when I woke up and looked at him he asked me if I was still alive.

Aishath stayed with her husband for 20 years but finally left because she said the abuse was getting 'worse and worse by the day'.

Hawwa is a 27-year-old woman with two children. She filed for divorce from her abusive husband a month prior to our meeting. Hawwa married her husband when she was 18 after knowing him for only a week.

> It all started as a bet I made with some of my friends. I saw him on the road one day, and my friends made a bet and asked me to marry him within one week. I wasn't so serious about it and took it all for fun and got married with him right after I turned 18, and that was within one week after I met him. He was 24 years old then. I didn't even check his background or any other details about him. In short, I didn't know him at all when I married him. And since then I have been living with him.

She said that at the time 'my thinking was immature and I didn't get any support from my family. My mother never explained these things to me, about what marriage is'. The violence started from the beginning of the relationship and included physical, sexual and emotional abuse.

Hawwa recalled: 'He would tell me to stay at home and don't go out. So I would obey him and stay home, so I didn't know what was happening outside.' Hawwa said that her husband was unable to maintain a permanent job and was not very reliable. 'He was lazy and bad tempered and had no positive qualities at all', she said. Hawwa kept the violence a secret for nearly ten years but finally, after realizing that his behaviour was never going to change, she applied for a divorce.

> I had no confidence at all then, I was very lonely and frustrated. But now I have a lot of confidence. I know that I can face this and I can speak up for myself, but earlier I didn't have the courage to say anything at all.

Patterns of intimate partner violence

Maldivian women experience various types of violence including emotional, physical and sexual abuse. As in most countries around the world, women in the Maldives are significantly more likely to experience violence by an intimate partner than by other men or women (Garcia-Moreno et al. 2005: 47; Heise et al. 1999; Johnson 1996; Tjaden and Thoennes 2000). In the Maldives Survey, 20 per cent of women who had ever been in a relationship (ever-partnered) reported experiencing at least one act of physical or sexual violence, or both, by an intimate partner at some point in their lives.[2] Among the ever-partnered women interviewed, 6 per cent reported that they had experienced physical or sexual violence within the 12 months prior to the interview. Physical violence was more common than sexual violence: 18 per cent of ever-partnered women aged 15–49 reported physical violence by an intimate partner and 7 per cent reported sexual violence. The most common acts of physical violence that women reported were being slapped or having something thrown at them, pushed or shoved, or hit with a fist.

However, many women reported that they had experienced more than one type of physically violent act, including more severe forms such as being kicked or choked. In terms of sexual abuse, the most common act reported was being physically forced to have sex when she did not want to, which was reported by 5 per cent of women. Five per cent also reported that they had sex when they did not want to because they were afraid of what their partner might do.

Multiple technologies of violence

As indicated above, 20 per cent of women reported physical or sexual violence by a partner, although this reflects a variety of different lived experiences. Some women had been hit only once while others experienced frequent and overlapping physical, emotional and sexual abuse. The majority of women who reported intimate partner violence, 76 per cent, had been hit once or a few times (fewer than five times). Violence for some women may be relatively infrequent but can still be severe and often involves multiple technologies of violence. In fact, Maldivian women are more likely to experience 'severe' physical violence, such as punching, kicking, choking or burning (11 per cent), rather than only 'moderate' forms of violence (7 per cent).[3] Of the women who reported physical violence, 39 per cent reported that they had experienced 'moderate' forms of violence while 61 per cent reported 'severe' forms of violence. However, there is a strong association ($p < 0.001$, see Appendix, Table A3b) between high frequency of violence and severity. That is, women who had experienced severe forms of violence were more likely to have experienced violence many times compared to women who reported moderate forms of violence. Similarly, women who reported experiencing a violent act only once were much more likely to have reported a 'moderate' act than a 'severe' one.

In reality, violence of all forms is a disturbing and complex experience. Such experiences are extremely difficult to define in neat linear categories. We cannot assume that a woman who has been hit only three times does not experience it as controlling, or that a woman who has been kicked has suffered more than a woman who has been slapped. Therefore, while acknowledging that there are many different lived experiences of violence, it is difficult to label them or differentiate them into distinct categories without oversimplifying the experiences. Rather than defining distinct categories of violence (Holtzworth-Munroe 2000), I describe a continuum of violent experiences that range in frequency and severity but still fit into the category of 'domestic violence' in that there are often multiple technologies of violence used and violence usually involves coercive control and has severe impacts on the victim's physical, mental and reproductive health (see Fulu 2007a).

There are some common patterns that emerge from both the statistical analysis of the Maldives Survey and women's own descriptions from in-depth interviews. As we saw in Aishath's and Hawwa's stories above, partner violence in the Maldives usually involves a complex range of overlapping violent acts that may include physical, sexual and economic maltreatment as well as degradation, humiliation, isolation, blaming, intimidation or threats. Prevalence rates of different forms of violence (i.e. physical, sexual and emotional) are useful for cross-cultural comparisons but in reality they are rarely separate events (Ellsberg 2000; Heise and Garcia-Moreno 2002; Jones *et al.* 1999). Of ever-partnered women aged 15–49, 30 per cent reported experiencing emotional abuse by a partner including being insulted or made to feel bad about herself, belittled or humiliated in front of other people, scared or intimidated on purpose, or threatened with violence (herself or someone she cared about).[4] Emotional abuse sometimes occurs without physical or sexual violence; however, physical and sexual violence very rarely occur on their own as isolated forms of abuse. Less than 1 per cent of women in the Maldives reported sexual abuse alone, and less than 4 per cent reported physical violence alone. This supports findings in many other studies indicating that women most often experience physical violence or a combination of physical and sexual violence. A number of women (19 per cent) in the Maldives who reported physical partner abuse also revealed that they were sometimes forced to have sex during or after a violent incident.

In Maldivian society, it is culturally accepted that a husband has some control over his wife's sexuality. For example, a woman must have her husband's permission to obtain contraception. Marital rape is not defined as a crime under Maldivian law, although a proposal to amend the Penal Code to include a provision that criminalizes marital rape was put before parliament in 2010. Under the Penal Code, rape is defined as 'forced *zina*' (literally meaning forced sex outside marriage). Therefore sex within marriage, even if forced, is not considered rape in the Maldives. Furthermore, under Maldivian law, rape is particularly difficult to prove. A man can only be convicted of rape if there are two male witnesses or four female witnesses willing to testify or if the accused confesses in court. Rasheed (2006b: 27) reports that no rapist has ever been convicted in Maldivian legal history. In other parts of South Asia, rape within marriage has been an alien concept (Dasgupta 2000b; Mazumdar 1998) because 'women's sexual consent within marriage is assumed with their consent to marry' (Bennett and Manderson 2003: 10). However, recently passed domestic violence legislation in Bangladesh,[5] Nepal,[6] Pakistan[7] and Sri Lanka[8] is starting to challenge this, with marital rape now defined as a crime in those countries.

Some 58 per cent of women in the Maldives Survey reported that it was a wife's obligation to have sex with her husband even if she does not want to. Most Maldivians, both men and women, who make this argument do so with reference to Islam. In the Maldives, the understanding that it is a wife's obligation to have sex with her husband stems in part from an interpretation of Islam, and in part from the belief that men have a much higher sex drive than women and it is women's responsibility to fulfil their husbands' needs.

This belief seemed to be held particularly by older women. Meena, an older woman in the focus group discussions, told us,

> We need to increase women's awareness about the needs of men. They should know that men's sexual needs grow as they get older. Most Maldivian women think that it is shameful to have sex after they reach 50. So the men are deprived from having sex and therefore find other means. This causes child abuse, prostitution and other social problems.

Other women aged 35 years and over in the focus group discussion argued that a woman should understand the sexual needs of her husband and that the mismatch of sexual needs within a relationship is one of the major reasons for divorce in the Maldives. One woman who spoke about her experiences of intimate partner violence in the documentary *Untold Stories* told how refusing to have sex with her husband incited his violence:

> I was having my period but he [husband] wanted to have sex. I told him and he hit me so hard in the mouth that six of my teeth became loose, I started to bleed, and my lips were badly cut. He abused me the next night, and the night after that.
> (Ministry of Gender Family Development and Social Security 2004)

While the majority of women in the survey thought a wife was obliged to have sex with her husband, only 5 per cent felt that a wife could not refuse sex with her husband under any circumstances. Furthermore, almost all of the participants in the focus group discussions, both men and women, agreed that a husband forcing his wife to have sex was rape. The younger women in particular asserted that women should not accept this type of behaviour. Here we see a distinction being made between force and submission. Many people felt it was a woman's responsibility to keep her husband sexually satisfied but that it was unacceptable for her husband to physically force her. Perhaps this is because they recognize that rape has little to do with sexual desire and more to do with violence and control.

Aishath's husband refused to have sex with her as a form of punishment for refusing to agree to him taking a second wife. He also forced her to have sex against her will:

> As a form of revenge he stopped having sexual relations with me and told me that I would have to live like this for the rest of my life and that he would never divorce me and just keep me like that. After six months without any sexual relationship between us one day he came from his boat. I had heard earlier that he was coming home but I didn't care and wasn't excited to see him like I used to be. He came home while I was taking a shower and he knocked loudly on the bathroom door. I didn't open the door as I was a little reluctant for him to see me since it had

been nearly six months since he had seen me naked. So I quickly dried myself and put on my clothes and opened the door. At once he grabbed my hand and threw me onto the bed, ripped off my dress and by force tried to have sex with me when I wasn't physically or emotionally ready. I didn't have any desire for it then and I bled a little because he had forcefully had sex with me. It was not pleasurable for me but it was for him. I felt like he was using me because as soon as he finished, after buttoning up his pants, he left without saying anything at all.

Aishath does not use the word rape to describe her experience because there is no word for rape in Dhivehi and, furthermore, as explained above it is difficult to conceptualize rape within marriage in the Maldives. It is interesting to note that although forced sex and withdrawal of sex seem to be opposite extremes, they can both be used by a violent partner, particularly as a means of controlling and punishing the woman. Watts *et al.* (1998b: 62), writing about violence against women in Zimbabwe, also found that the withdrawal of sex was often associated with changes in relationships, such as a partner getting a girlfriend or taking another wife. They argue that it appears to be used to force wives to accept the new situation. In Aishath's case, withholding of sex was used to try to force her to accept her husband taking a second wife, and when she refused, forced sex was used as a form of punishment. As Watts *et al.* (1998b: 62) argue, men are able to manipulate the situation in this way because of the substantial power inequalities that exist within relationships, and because of women's economic and emotional dependence on them.

Emotional abuse also constitutes a significant part of the combination of experiences that make up partner violence in the Maldives. This illustrates that the enactment of male power and control in violent relationships does not rely on violent acts alone (Wilcox 2006: 13). Mariyam, a 35-year-old woman with three boys and three girls, described how extreme control, fear and intimidation were used by her husband: 'He sometimes kept me starving for days, other times he would keep me awake for the whole night, disturbing me and scaring me verbally so I could not sleep.' Emotional abuse may also often involve threats of further violence, which in and of itself may be sufficient to maintain control, as Sharin, a survey respondent, described: 'He threatened me as well, saying he would hurt me in my private place to such an extent that it cannot be used.'

In the Maldives, physical partner violence is often combined with behaviour that aims to humiliate the victim, as Hawwa described:

He hits me, or slaps me on my face, and even takes off my clothes and pushes me out of the house onto the street, into the public. After I started wearing my headscarf, he even grabbed my scarf off my head when we were on the street or ripped my clothes off in public. He tears and destroys the things I wear and hits me as well.

Traditionally most Maldivian women have long hair. It is associated with beauty and femininity and for women who choose to cover their hair with a headscarf it becomes an intimate part of the body that only their husbands or close family members can see. As such, women described having their headscarf removed in public as a serious violation. Removing the headscarf or other clothing in public brings shame on a woman and denigrates her character, particularly in a culture where modesty is a highly valued quality. Some may suggest that this would also bring shame on the husband; however, in these examples the purpose is clearly to humiliate and shame the woman and it does not seem to reflect on the perpetrator's character.

Aishath also explained how her partner would humiliate her in public:

> He would humiliate me around my friends by saying that he is going to leave me because I am not woman enough for him and I can't satisfy him sexually and that I don't do all the things he wants me to do. I was very embarrassed.

According to Aishath, her husband's public comments about her inability to satisfy him were particularly humiliating because the public discussion of sexual relations is considered immodest in Maldivian society. Aishath's husband would also attack other parts of her character:

> At parties and around people he would say such embarrassing things such as I am very lazy. Once when a friend of mine asked me why I don't go out much and when I wasn't able to say anything my husband said, 'Where can she go? She is always in bed like a mattress, all lazy.'

Many women explained that even though acts of humiliation, degradation and isolation did not involve direct physical violence, they were often more painful because the injury lasted long after the incident and affected their sense of self and character. Garcia-Moreno *et al.* (2005: 35) support this finding, arguing that 'qualitative research routinely reveals that women frequently consider emotionally abusive acts to be more devastating than acts of physical violence'. Similarly, Kirkwood (1993:44) found that women experience emotional abuse as a 'deeper and more central form of abuse'. For some women emotional abuse was the most difficult to talk about because of its humiliating nature. For example, while Aishath could describe how her husband raped her, she could not bring herself to repeat in our interview the verbally abusive and offensive language that her husband used against her.

It is important to acknowledge that women are not merely passive victims. Of women who reported partner violence, more than half (53 per cent) indicated that they had physically fought back to defend themselves during the times that they were hit and 20 per cent reported fighting back many times. This is supported by other demographic health surveys in developing countries, which suggest that violence in self-defence is relatively common while woman-initiated aggression is relatively rare (Garcia-Moreno et al. 2005: 39). For those women who had experienced severe physical partner violence, an even higher proportion (63 per cent) reported fighting back. The fact that women fight back more when they experience severe violence indicates that perhaps when women feel that their lives are threatened they will do what they can to try to protect themselves. Hawwa told us: 'Lately at times I can't take it any more and get so mad that I even hit him back.' The majority (58 per cent) of women who had fought back reported that the result of fighting back was that the violence lessened or stopped.[9] Perhaps fighting back challenges the perpetrator's dominance and control within the relationship, reasserting some sense of equality.

While Aishath never physically hit her partner, she described a time when the situation became so desperate that she contemplated using violence against her husband as well as self-harm. When she started going into labour and told her husband that she had to go to the hospital, Aishath told us,

> He said why should he hurry and take me to the hospital as he wanted the baby dead. He said he would not take me soon … From that day onwards I lost all faith, trust and love I had for him and for the first time in my life I felt like killing him and stabbing him with a knife and then I would kill myself too. I never ever had this thought before but that day I did. But luckily I didn't do those things that I was thinking.

Shaikh (2007: 89), writing about marital violence in a South African Muslim community, also reported that women fought back and 'broke out of the traditional model of femininity by physical defending her bodily integrity'. Women may also resist in other, less physical ways. Idrus and Bennett (2003: 57) found that Bugis women in Indonesia chose to resist through silence, avoidance and withdrawal from their husbands; however, they also gave examples of women who verbally resisted their husbands' attacks.

Violence and coercive control

The Maldives Survey also measured the extent to which women experienced controlling behaviours. The respondents were asked whether they had experienced any of the following: tries to keep you from seeing your friends; tries to restrict your contact with your family of birth; insists on knowing where you are at all times; ignores you or treats you indifferently; is often suspicious that you are unfaithful; gets angry if you speak with another man; expects you to ask permission before seeking health care for yourself.

The use of physical and sexual violence in relationships is intimately linked to the perpetrator's use of a range of controlling behaviours including economic control, emotional abuse, isolation, intimidation and threats. Male use of controlling behaviour has been found to be common in violent intimate partner relationships in many settings, and many scholars now view domestic violence globally as a pattern of intimidation, coercive control and oppression (see, for example, Brewster 2003; Coan *et al.* 1998; Holtzworth-Munroe 2000; Pence and Paymar 1993; Shepard and Pence 1999; Stark 2007; Strauchler *et al.* 2004; Warrington 2001; Yllo 1993).

In the Maldives, there was a strong association between women's experiences of physical and/or sexual violence by an intimate partner and experiencing controlling behaviour by a partner ($p < 0.001$). Among women who had experienced intimate partner violence, 72 per cent reported that their partner displayed at least one act of controlling behaviour, whereas only 40 per cent of women who had not experienced intimate partner violence reported that their partner exhibited controlling behaviour. In addition, the average number of controlling acts reported was much higher for women who had experienced partner violence (see Appendix, Tables A4a–c).

Controlling behaviour is also associated with the frequency and severity of violence. That is, women who experienced 'severe' violence were even more likely to experience controlling behaviour than women who experienced 'moderate' violence (see Appendix, Table A5c). Controlling behaviour is also more strongly associated with women who reported experiencing violence either a few or many times, rather than only once. Women who experienced physical violence 'a few times' were 4.1 times more likely to experience controlling behaviour than non-abused women, and women who experienced violence 'many times' were 5.7 times more likely to have experienced controlling behaviour. But even women who had experienced only one act of physical violence were 1.7 times more likely to experience controlling behaviour than those who have never experienced violence. Although the frequency and severity of violence differs between individual women, all levels of partner violence in the Maldives are significantly associated with controlling behaviour (see Appendix, Tables A5a–c).

Controlling behaviour can also take the form of financial abuse (Hanmer 2000). For example, the reason why Aishath did not go out much was because her husband would not allow her to work and refused to give her money to buy clothes for herself and her children. 'He only gives money to cover the basic needs', she said. 'He stopped buying me clothes', she added, and during her pregnancy she grew out of her normal clothes. She recalled that

> I had to stay home, unable to go to the hospital or other places because the other clothes I had I couldn't wear because it was tight on my tummy ... Everyone kept asking me why I don't go out but I didn't tell anyone that it's because I didn't have any dress to wear but lied and told them that I don't feel like going out and that the doctor recommended that I take bed rest.

Where a husband exercises financial abuse, women are more likely to experience violence. There was a significant association between women who had ever given up or refused a job for money because their husband did not want them to work and experiences of partner violence. Furthermore, women who reported having had their earnings or savings taken from them by their partner against their will had more than twice the odds of experiencing violence as those who had never had their earnings or savings taken by their partner. Women were also asked if their partner ever refused to give them money for household expenses, even when he had money for other things. The odds of a woman whose husband refused to give her money experiencing violence were six times the odds of a woman whose husband had not refused to give her money experiencing partner violence (see Appendix, Tables A6a and A6b on financial control).

Fathimath, a survivor of intimate partner violence, also experienced extensive financial control. Fathimath is a 30-year-old woman, married with three boys and three girls. She has married, divorced and remarried the same man three times (which is relatively common practice in the Maldives, as will be discussed in the following chapter). The first time was when she was 13 years old, in an arranged marriage. He was 33 years old at the time. Fathimath's husband started physically abusing her when she was pregnant with their first child. During the pregnancy he pushed and slapped her and shoved her into the wall. She left him but returned to the marriage 'for the sake of her unborn child', she said. According to Fathimath, she did not have enough money to support the children so she did housework for neighbours, but her husband stole the money she earned and when she complained he beat her. She said that she was severely hurt but he would not give her any money to go and see a doctor. Fathimath reported,

> I was suffering from seizures and getting weaker by the day. I went to the island hospital and they advised me to have several tests but still he refused to pay. Finally when my eldest daughter begged him to let me go to Malé for medical treatment he agreed to let me go.[10]

Another common method of control is enforced isolation, which is used by perpetrators to prevent disclosure, instil dependence, express exclusive possession, monopolize their partner's skills and resources and keep them from getting help or support (Stark 2007: 262). Some participants in the focus group discussions suggested that women suffering domestic violence do not talk to people about their problem because their husbands isolate them. Zeena said, 'sometimes he may prevent them from meeting friends and family or even talking to a neighbour. He will provide just enough for her to survive daily so sometimes she's left with no option'. Mizna, another woman in the discussion, recounted that 'there are situations where nobody can come into the house where the woman lives. She is made to live in a small room, taking care of the kids, cleaning and cooking'. This was the case with Aishath, who explained,

> Even if I stand near the door of my house or if I talk to my friends he would get mad and slap my face ... he doesn't want me to socialize or talk with anyone and I don't know why.

Sexual coercion and extreme jealousy appear to be associated with violence in the Maldives, as is reported elsewhere (Stark 2007: 248). Many women living with violence reported that their partner was extremely jealous, possessive and did not want them to talk with other men in particular. Yumna said of her husband, 'he gets very angry if I talk to other men. He accuses me of seeing other men and would start beating me'. In fact, in the Maldives Survey a number of women who had experienced physical partner violence reported that one of the most common situations that tended to lead to their partner's violent behaviour was 'when he was jealous'.

The combination of humiliation, degradation and financial and physical control often further isolates victims of abuse. Stark (2007: 259) argues that perpetrators of partner violence 'use degradation as an isolation tactic, embarrassing their partners in public or among friends, family or workmates'. As we saw earlier, this is reflected in Aishath's case where her husband's abuse isolated her from sources of support such as friends and family because she stopped going out for fear of being humiliated. She explained: 'When he says these kinds of things I feel so humiliated and sad and can't manage to explain the real reason. Because of this I stopped going to parties or crowded places.' The ongoing attacks on Aishath's sense of self and her confidence led to an inability to recognize her own isolation, tell anyone or try to leave. She said poignantly that 'I was so isolated and didn't know that I was in a cage'.

The impact of intimate partner violence

The seriousness of the violence that many women face is reflected in the grave impact that it has on women's physical, mental and reproductive health. The Maldives Survey data shows strong and consistent associations between intimate partner violence in the Maldives and a wide range of physical, mental and reproductive health problems. Intimate partner violence also impacts on women's sense of self, their ability to care for their children and their ability to participate in society.

Injuries and physical health consequences

Injury from a violent incident is the first obvious impact on victims of abuse. Among women who had ever experienced physical or sexual partner violence, 36 per cent reported being injured at least once. The majority of women reported being injured once or twice, although a third of the women reported being injured many times. It is noteworthy that out of the women who reported injuries, half had experienced severe injuries such as gashes, fractures, broken bones or internal injuries.[11] Hawwa recalled: 'Once he poured hot water on me and my left thigh was burnt and has scars. Also all over my body there are cigarette burns. The violence became crueller and one night he threw hot milk in my face.'

Violence is not only a significant health problem because of direct injuries, but also because it indirectly impacts on a number of health outcomes (Garcia-Moreno et al. 2005). Women who had experienced violence by an intimate partner were significantly more likely than women who had not experienced violence to report poor or very poor health, general pain, problems carrying out daily activities, problems with memory and dizziness.[12] This is consistent with the experiences of other countries that undertook the WHO Multi-Country Study, as well as other studies from around the world showing that women who are physically abused often have many less-defined somatic complaints, including chronic headaches, abdominal and pelvic pains and muscle aches (Garcia-Moreno et al. 2005; Watts et al. 1998b). It is particularly noteworthy that the survey found an association between recent experiences of ill-health (within the last four weeks) and experiences of partner violence that occurred more than 12 months ago. This suggests that the impact of violence may last long after the actual violence has ended.

As in other countries (Heise et al. 1994), in spite of the isolation many Maldivian women living with violence experience, they visit health services more frequently than non-abused women. In addition, women who had experienced partner violence were more likely to have spent a night in hospital or have had an operation (apart from a caesarean) in the past 12 months compared with women who had never experienced intimate partner violence.[13] However, the controlling behaviour of abusive husbands combined with a health system that is not well equipped to deal with such cases means that many cases of domestic violence go unnoticed.

The treatment of violence against women as a health issue is new to the Maldives and there is not yet a well-developed system in place to deal with cases of intimate partner violence when they present at the hospital. Service providers sometimes still stigmatize and blame victims. For example, Shaylini described how a doctor blamed her for the violence when she sought help:

> Once, when I had gone to the doctor while bruises from the physical abuse were showing the doctor asked if somebody hit me ... Since I did not want to tell anybody about my husband, I did not tell the doctor. I said something fell and hit my hand. There was another blue mark on me and the doctor asked if it was a mark from being hit. When he saw it I could not deny it any more so I said yes, he does hit me. The doctor asked if I behaved in a way that I deserved to be hit. I said no but he does anyway. By then I had started crying.

In the Maldives, health-care professionals' lack of training on violence against women often means that when victims of violence do seek health care many feel unable to report the true nature and cause of their injuries. More than half of the women who had received health care for their violence-related injuries did not tell the health worker the real cause of their injuries. One doctor from Indira Gandhi Memorial Hospital (IGMH), the tertiary public hospital in the Maldives, supported this finding, saying that when women come in with a suspicious injury, 'We try to probe a bit but most of the time they won't say. Unless they say, we can't report it or refer it to anyone'.

A nurse who participated in a focus group discussion with health-care professionals recalled the following incident:

> A husband and wife came in the middle of the night and the husband said the patient was having difficulty breathing, and then we found a wound here [pointing to her arm] that was dressed in a very ordinary way. We asked what had happened and the husband said that it had been done by the patient. The husband was very drowsy and we sent him out to get a drink for her and she revealed that he was doing all these things. Once the husband came back she just stopped talking and the husband continued saying that she has been doing these things to herself.

As this example illustrates, women in the Maldives rarely seek medical attention on their own and are usually accompanied by family and often their husband/partner. Furthermore, when a woman is examined by a doctor or a nurse her husband is usually present because it is culturally inappropriate for the doctor to ask the husband to leave the room, especially if the examining doctor is male. It is very unlikely that a woman would feel safe enough to report that she had been abused in front of her abuser when she knows she must return home with him after her injuries are treated.

Reproductive health consequences

Women also suffer serious reproductive health consequences of violence. According to the Maldives Survey 6 per cent of women who had ever been pregnant reported being physically abused during at least one pregnancy. Among the women who reported violence during pregnancy, 39 per cent had been punched or kicked in the abdomen. Women who had experienced partner violence, particularly during pregnancy, were significantly more likely to report miscarriages, abortions, stillbirths and having a child who had died (see Appendix, Table A8a).[14] In an in-depth interview, Aminath shared the following story:

> My husband was away fishing and one of my sister's friends [male] came to speak to me and asked me whether I was living in this island. Someone saw this and told my husband, who got angry and tied me up face down on a bed with rope. I was eight months pregnant then. We lived alone at the house. When I started crying, neighbours gathered at my place, but my husband wouldn't let any of them in and so no one could help me. I had to stay there for four hours. When he untied me, my hands and

feet were swollen and cut. My tummy hurt real badly and because I was tied face down, the knots on the rope were pressed against my tummy and it was bruised. I cried. I had a stillbirth and the midwife told me that it's probably due to the violence I had suffered from my husband.

Similarly, studies in the United States indicate that women beaten during pregnancy run twice the risk of miscarriage and have four times the risk of having a low-birth-weight baby than women who are not beaten (Watts *et al.* 1998a). In a number of other countries, physical abuse has also been found to be associated with higher rates of abortion, miscarriages, stillbirths and delayed entry into prenatal care (Evins and Chescheir 1996; Kishor and Johnson 2004a; Velzeboer *et al.* 2003).

Abortions are illegal in the Maldives, except for explicit medical reasons.[15] However, they do take place, illegally, within the Maldives, overseas or through self-induced attempts at home. Maldivian women are therefore likely to under-report abortions for fear of legal repercussions and because of the social stigma associated with them. Despite this, some women reported having had an abortion and there was a statistically significant association found between abortions and partner violence. A woman in an abusive relationship may be more likely to abort because she does not want to bring a child into an abusive relationship or because her husband forces her to get an abortion. Aishath's husband tried to force her to have an abortion:

> After I knew I was pregnant I came home ready to give the happy news to my husband, but when I told him he told me to abort the baby if I wanted to stay as his wife ... He also threatened to take me to India to abort my baby and once he even sent a person to my house with an injection that would abort my child but I didn't let him inject me.

This research also supports findings in other countries that abused women face a greater risk of unintended pregnancies (Ellsberg 2000).[16] Women who had experienced intimate partner violence were significantly more likely to have not wanted to become pregnant when they did, compared with women who had not experienced partner violence. Furthermore, it was more likely that the respondent's partner did not want the pregnancy if she had been a victim of partner violence than if she had not, as in Aishath's case.[17] It is likely that this is because 'abused women living in an environment of fear and male dominance lacked the ability to control their fertility' (quoted in Garcia-Moreno *et al.* 2005: 69).

Mental health consequences

In the Maldives, a statistically significant association was found between domestic violence and levels of emotional distress.[18] The levels of emotional distress were found to be higher among women who had experienced sexual violence than for those who had experienced physical violence and was highest among women who had experienced both physical and sexual intimate partner violence. Hawwa told us,

> I had sleeping and eating difficulties, didn't feel like eating at all, didn't feel like talking to my friends or family ... I couldn't give time for anything or do anything as my mind was occupied by the violence I was going through.

As many scholars argue, the abuser's techniques of power and control lead to a systematic breakdown of the survivor's identity, rooted in her body (Wesely *et al.* 2000: 216). As Hawwa lost her sense of self-worth, nothing seemed worth doing, all desire and activity became empty and in vain, and she sank into apathy. Research shows that recurrent abuse can place women at risk of psychological problems such as fear, anxiety, fatigue, sleeping and eating disturbances, depression and post-traumatic stress disorder (Watts *et al.* 1998a). Loue (2001: 16) argues that initial psychological responses to intimate partner violence include shock, denial, withdrawal, confusion, numbness, fear and depression. Links have also been found in other countries between physical abuse and higher rates of psychiatric treatment, attempted suicide and alcohol dependence (Plitcha 1992).

Maldivian women who had experienced partner violence were also more likely to report having thoughts of suicide and attempted suicide than women who had never experienced partner violence.[19] This has been found to be a common pattern around the world (Garcia-Moreno *et al.* 2005; Plitcha 1992). Suicide is a taboo topic in Maldivian society because it is prohibited under the Maldivian interpretation of Islam. In fact, during the preparation of the questionnaire, many Maldivians expressed concern that we were even asking women about suicidal tendencies and thought this section should be removed from the questionnaire entirely. It was considered even more sensitive than asking about alcohol, drugs or sex. While a number of women reported suicidal thoughts, less than 1 per cent of women reported suicide attempts. Suicide is rare in the Maldives because it is so socially unacceptable. However, there could also be under-reporting because women may feel reluctant to admit to suicide attempts because of the associated stigma. Aishath recalls how the ongoing abuse led to thoughts of suicide:

> I spent most of the time crying and sometimes wished that it would be better if I didn't wake up the next day, that it would be better if I were dead ... I felt like it would be better if we both [her and her unborn baby] died because even if my baby was alive, he or she would be an unwanted baby, because the baby's father doesn't want it.

According to medical personnel, anxiety and depression cases are extremely common in the Maldives, particularly among women. In focus group discussions, foreign doctors working at a private hospital in Malé (ADK Hospital) suggested that anxiety issues are more common in the Maldives than in other countries where they have worked. The doctors at both IGMH and ADK Hospital reported that women are often brought in by family members in a state of unconsciousness. Other physical symptoms identified by health professionals were: fainting, headaches, blackouts, chest pain and breathlessness. One nurse from IGMH explained:

> Often women will come in with difficult breathing or with headaches and sometimes we find that the patient has been crying for a long time because of swollen eyelids. Or sometimes we see scratch marks, and we keep on asking questions but mostly they won't answer.

According to one IGMH doctor, 'a lot of them come without having food for the whole day; they are very weak, and they need IV [intravenous] fluid'. Another doctor added: 'All day they spend without eating, without talking to anybody, isolated and then they collapse.' The doctors at IGMH reported that that they get approximately eight to ten such cases per shift, especially during the night shift. According to both doctors and nurses the most common causes of this anxiety were family problems and relationship or marital problems.

Some nurses and doctors at IGMH described these cases as 'attention seeking behaviour', and indicated that they did not consider them to be serious medical problems. The medical community in the Maldives has only started to acknowledge mental illness as a health issue since the first mental health plan developed by the Ministry of Health was introduced in 2006. In 2012 there was still only one trained psychiatrist in the country and a handful of trained counsellors, although a counselling diploma course was established in 2007 to try to address the serious shortage of mental health professionals. Doctors in the focus group discussions pointed out that in the Maldives everything must have a physical diagnosis and that health is limited to the physical aspects rather than a broader understanding that incorporates mental health.

I believe that rather than this behaviour being simply attention seeking, it demonstrates the serious impact of violence and perhaps reflects help-seeking behaviour by women. It represents a culturally coded way of dealing with difficult situations. It makes sense that women would seek help at health facilities, given that there are virtually no other support services available to victims of domestic violence in the Maldives, and especially given the proven impact of violence on physical, reproductive and mental health. The results of the Maldives Survey show that health facilities are the second most common place where women seek help for intimate partner violence, second only to the courts where women seek divorces and child custody. In the crowded spaces of the Maldives, self-isolation and withdrawal offer a way (consciously or unconsciously) for women to demonstrate that something is wrong when, for various reasons such as the culture of secrecy, fear, social pressure and shame, they are unable to talk openly about the problem. Actions such as not eating, drinking or sleeping also manifest physical symptoms, which are taken more seriously by society than 'emotional' problems.

Intimate partner violence also often impacts the victim's children. According to the Maldives Survey, there are significant associations between women's experience of intimate partner violence and her children (aged 5–12 years) undergoing emotional and behavioural problems such as having nightmares, being aggressive and wetting the bed (Fulu 2007c). Hawwa explained the detrimental impact of her partner's violence on her children:

> He [her husband] acts badly in front of the children too, even coming up from behind me and grabbing my private parts in front of them and saying all sorts of filth. And my older child would say, 'Dad is very bad.' This wasn't good for the older child and he would be shocked. It also affected his studies. Before my child would bring home good results but later his performance became very poor. He also started getting angrier.

Hawwa finally decided that the impact on her children was too great and that it would be better to get divorced. There is a large body of empirical research providing evidence that children who witness domestic violence may suffer significant negative social, emotional, behavioural and academic repercussions (Fantuzzo *et al.* 1991; Geffner *et al.* 2003; Jaffe *et al.* 1990; Robertson and Busch 1994). Impacts may include development and learning problems, poor concentration, limited social skills, aggressive and non-compliant behaviour, low self-esteem, depression and anxiety (Fantuzzo *et al.* 1991; Fantuzzo and Linquist 1989; Geffner *et al.* 2003; Graham-Bermann 1998).

We see that intimate partner violence in the Maldives generally constitutes a form of abuse involving multiple technologies of violence designed to exert coercive control. The impact of such violence on women is serious and long lasting. In order to begin to address this problem we must establish what characteristics or factors make some women vulnerable to violence when the majority of women in the Maldives do not face such abuse. Furthermore, understanding the risk factors for violence should shed some light on why the prevalence of violence in the Maldives is lower than in other countries in the region.

Conclusion

Intimate partner violence against women occurs around the world and international research suggests that there are many commonalities among women's experiences that cut across class, religion, ethnicity and age.

At the same time, there is also a great deal of variation in the patterns, manifestations, contributing factors, consequences and responses to partner violence across cultures (Ellsberg 2000; Garcia-Moreno *et al.* 2005; Walker 1999; Watts *et al.* 1998a). As such, lived experiences of partner violence must be understood from the perspective of the couple's social and cultural environment, contextualized in time, space, history and language (Eisikovits and Buchbinder 2000: 5).

Maldivian women's stories, including those of Aishath and Hawwa, help us to understand the patterns of partner violence in the Maldives, but they also share similarities with other Asian women's experiences shedding light on the phenomenon of violence against women more broadly. While the frequency and severity of violence varies on a case-by-case basis, partner violence usually involves a complex range of overlapping violent behaviours that serve to assert and maintain control. Physical partner violence is more common than sexual partner violence; however, they rarely occur on their own as isolated forms of abuse. Non-physical acts such as humiliation, isolation and jealousy also constitute a significant part of the technologies of violence used by perpetrators of intimate partner violence. The use of physical and sexual violence in relationships is intimately linked to the perpetrator's use of a range of controlling behaviours including economic control, emotional abuse, isolation, intimidation and threats. While women rarely initiate violence in the Maldives, a number of women reported fighting back, especially when they experienced severe violence.

This chapter has examined women's lived experiences of violence in detail. However, it is equally important to understand why the majority of women in the Maldives do not experience domestic violence. In the following chapter, I analyse the various factors that increase or decrease women's risk of experiencing violence in the Maldivian context.

Notes

1 This name and all other names used in this book of women who have experienced violence are pseudonyms to protect the anonymity of the respondents.
2 The definition of 'ever-partnered women' is central to the survey because it defines the population that could potentially be at risk of partner violence, and hence becomes the denominator for prevalence figures. In the Maldives Survey, it was decided that we needed a broad definition of partnership, since any woman who had been in a relationship with an intimate partner, whether married or not, could have been exposed to the risk of violence. Unlike other South Asian countries, dating relationships are common and acceptable in the Maldives, even though men and women do not cohabit until they are married. Qualitative research and reports on violence against women showed that a number of young women experience violence by boyfriends and it was important to capture this. As such, the definition of 'ever-partnered women' included women who had ever been or were currently married or in a dating relationship (not living together).
3 For the purposes of analysis, the questions on physical violence were divided into those considered 'moderate' violence and those considered 'severe' violence,

where the distinction between moderate and severe violence is based on the likelihood of physical injury. 'Moderate' violence includes being slapped, shoved, pushed or having something thrown at them that could hurt them. 'Severe' violence includes being hit with a fist or with something else that could hurt her; being kicked, dragged or beaten up; threatening to use or actually using a gun, knife or other weapon against her.

4 These were the specific acts of emotional abuse that were included in the questionnaire. However, there is a relative scarcity of research on emotional abuse and developing a list of acts that are recognized as emotionally abusive across cultures was difficult.

5 The Prevention of Oppression against Women and Children Act (2000) and Suppression of Violence against Women and Children (Amendment) Act (2003).

6 The Nepal Civil Code for Gender Balance was amended in 2006 to criminalize marital rape. Also see the Domestic Violence (Crime and Punishment) Act (2008).

7 Domestic Violence (Prevention and Protection) Act (2009).

8 Prevention of Domestic Violence Act No. 34 (2005).

9 22 per cent reported no change in the violence and 20 per cent reported that the violence got worse.

10 Malé has the only tertiary hospital in the country and certain tests are only available in Malé.

11 For the purposes of categorization, mild injuries were defined as including cuts, punctures, bites, scratches, abrasions and bruises. Moderate injuries were defined as including sprains, dislocations and burns. Severe injuries included penetrating injuries, deep cuts, gashes, broken eardrum, eye injuries, fractures, broken bones, broken teeth and internal injuries.

12 All women, regardless of their partnership status, were asked whether they considered their general health to be excellent, good, fair, poor or very poor. They were then asked whether they had experienced a number of symptoms during the four weeks prior to the interview, such as problems walking, pain, memory loss, dizziness and vaginal discharge. Although in a cross-sectional survey it is not possible to demonstrate causality between violence and health problems, the findings give an indication of the forms of association. There were consistent differences at the bivariate level between women who reported experiences of violence by an intimate partner and those who did not report violence, for most symptoms of ill health that were asked about. See Appendix, Tables A7a and A7b for more details.

13 The Maldives Study showed that 46 per cent of women who had experienced violence had visited a health-care professional in the past four weeks compared with only 33 per cent of women who had not experienced violence. In addition, 16 per cent of women who had never experienced physical or sexual partner violence had spent a night in hospital in the past 12 months, compared to 28 per cent of women who had experienced some form of physical or sexual intimate partner violence. Some 7.7 per cent of women without a history of partner violence reported having an operation in the past 12 months compared with 9 per cent of women who had experienced physical and/or sexual partner violence.

14 The associations between all these reproductive health outcomes and experiences of intimate partner violence were found to be statistically significant. The crude and adjusted odds ratios for each reproductive health problem are presented in Appendix, Table A8b.

15 The prohibition of abortion is supposedly based on Islamic law; however, it is important to note that Islamic law is based on precedent and not all interpretations of Shariʻa prohibit abortion.

16 Women who reported having had a live birth in the past five years were asked whether, at the time they became pregnant (the last pregnancy), they had wanted to become pregnant then, wanted to wait until later, did not want (more) children or did not mind either way. The respondent was asked the same questions about her partner: did he want her to become pregnant then, wait until later, did not want (more) children or did not mind either way. Appendix, Table A9a shows the results of these questions according to the respondent's experience of physical and/or sexual partner violence.

17 26 per cent of women who had been physically or sexually abused by an intimate partner reported that, at the time of her last pregnancy, her partner did not want (more) children or wanted to wait until later. In comparison, 18 per cent of women who had not been abused by an intimate partner reported that their partner wanted to wait or did not want (more) children.

18 Mental health was assessed using a self-reporting questionnaire of 20 questions (SRQ-20), developed by WHO as a screening tool for emotional distress, that has been validated in a wide range of settings. It asks respondents whether, within the four weeks prior to the interview, they had experienced a series of symptoms that are associated with emotional distress, such as crying, tiredness and thoughts of ending life. The number of items that women respond 'yes' to are added up for a possible maximum score of 20, where 0 represents the lowest level of emotional distress and 20 represents the highest. Spearman's Rho coefficient = 0.229 ($p < 0.01$).

19 Multivariate logistic regression on the association between suicidal thoughts and experiences of violence by an intimate partner, adjusting for age, education and marital status, confirmed that women who had experienced physical and/or sexual violence were very significantly ($p < 0.001$) more likely to have thought of ending their lives. The odds of women who have experienced partner violence having suicidal thoughts is four times the odds that women who have not experienced partner violence have thought about ending their lives. See Appendix, Table A10b.

2 The protective factors
Lessons for violence prevention

The prevalence rate of physical and sexual partner violence in the Maldives, while significant at 20 per cent of women aged 15–49 who have ever been in a relationship, is less than in many other countries in the Asian region. This chapter examines the reasons for the relatively low prevalence of partner violence in the Maldives by examining different layers within the Globalized Ecological Model – individual, family, community and society (see Figure I.1). While these elements are all interconnected it is useful to examine them separately for the purposes of analysis. The influence of global processes on these levels will be explored in Chapters 3 to 5.

The individual level: risk and protective factors

The everyday violence that women experience simultaneously reflects overlapping social hierarchies that are based not only on gender, but also on their age, marital status, class, religion and ethnicity. 'Violence against women routinely functions to sustain multiple inequalities, reinforcing women's subordination within complex hierarchies of oppression' (Bennett and Manderson 2003: 1). While partner violence cuts across age, education, socio-economic status, religion and ethnicity there are some factors that make some women more likely to experience partner violence than others.

Using data from the Maldives Survey I undertook logistic regression techniques to explore the individual-level and relationship-level factors associated with women's experiences of physical/sexual partner violence experienced in the 12 months prior to the interview.[1] This is useful for understanding what contributes to partner violence in the Maldivian cultural context but also helps us understand why the overall prevalence of violence in the Maldives is relatively low. The list of risk factors included in the analysis was developed drawing upon existing conceptual models and other published analyses on risk and protective factors (Heise 2011; Hotaling and Sugarman 1986; Jewkes *et al.* 2002; Kishor and Johnson 2004b; Kyriacou *et al.* 1999; Lee 2007; Schafer *et al.* 2004; Straus *et al.* 1990).

According to this analysis, partner violence was not strongly associated with most socio-economic and demographic indicators such as age, education, employment and marital status. Patterns of current violence (12 months prior to the interview) by age group showed that women aged 25–29 were at the highest risk of intimate partner violence: 10 per cent reported current partner violence compared with 4 per cent of women aged 30–34. A pattern of increased risk of violence among younger women was also documented in other countries that undertook the WHO Multi-Country Study (Garcia-Moreno *et al.* 2005: 32–3) as well as in Canada (Johnson 1996) and the United States (Tjaden and Thoennes 2000). It therefore seems that violence may start early in a marriage, which then may break up over time. Qualitative interviews with survivors of violence revealed that often violence started very soon after marriage: for example, within the first year or after a woman's first pregnancy. It is also possible that older women in abusive relationships develop strategies that decrease the frequency of violence, or that they are less likely to report violence. However, the association in the Maldives is not statistically significant, highlighting that women of all ages are vulnerable to violence.

Women with lower levels of education were more likely to report experiences of intimate partner violence in the Maldives (see Appendix, Tables A11a and A11b), but again this association was not found to be statistically significant. Among women with no education, 10 per cent reported experiencing violence compared to 7 per cent of women who had achieved secondary-level education. More highly educated women may have greater choices in partners and more freedom to choose when to marry, and are able to negotiate greater autonomy and control of resources. On the other hand, it is possible that more educated women may be less likely to disclose violence because of social stigma. Other studies in Asia have found education to be a significant factor associated with violence. For example, in Nepal literate women were found to have 28 per cent less chance of experiencing sexual coercion by husbands than illiterate women (Adhikari and Tamang 2010), and a large-scale national survey in Pakistan found that women were more likely to have experienced violence if she or her husband had no formal education (Andersson *et al.* 2009). In Eastern India, higher levels of male and female education were associated with lower levels of domestic violence (Babu and Kar 2010).

Although age and education were not found to be key factors explaining women's experiences of violence in the Maldivian context, a number of other factors were found to be significantly associated with intimate partner violence (see Appendix, Table A11c). Women who had experienced sexual abuse under the age of 15 were more likely to experience partner violence. Women who had experienced childhood sexual abuse were nearly three times more likely to have experienced intimate partner violence within the last 12 months than women who had not been abused as children. Highlighting the inter-generational cycle of violence, this finding contributes to our understanding of the causes of violence in the Maldives as well as broader implications for violence prevention elsewhere. Studies from various different country contexts have illustrated that childhood exposure to violence greatly increases a person's likelihood to either perpetrate or suffer from intimate partner violence as an adult (Andersson *et al.* 2009; Ellsberg *et al.* 1999; Fehringer and Hindin 2009; Jewkes and Abrahams 2002; Martin *et al.* 2002; Wekerle and Wolfe 1999; Whitfield *et al.* 2003). A number of other studies have also found similar associations between partner violence and childhood sexual abuse (Coid *et al.* 2001; DeLillo *et al.* 2001; Jehu 1988).

In the Maldives, women whose marriages were arranged were more likely to report intimate partner violence than women who chose their husbands themselves. Women who had an arranged marriage were 2.7 times more likely to experience partner violence than women whose marriage was not arranged. This supports local beliefs about the deleterious effects of arranged marriages. One woman told us: 'You must choose the man you are going to marry, not your parents. If you listen to your parents and marry the man they choose you will get pain and suffering.' Unlike many other countries in South Asia, arranged marriages are very rare in the Maldives. Only 7 per cent of women who participated in the survey reported that their parents had chosen their husbands for them and less than 1 per cent of women interviewed reported that their husbands' parents had arranged the marriage. Many people consider marriage to always be intimately connected to love and affection (see Chapter 3). My father recalled that until he travelled overseas and read stories like Jane Austen's *Pride and Prejudice* about marriage and status, he had no idea that marriage could be based on anything other than love. The majority of women who reported having an arranged marriage in the Maldives Survey were aged between 30 and 49 and would have been getting married during the period of Islamic revivalism in the 1970s and 1980s (discussed in Chapter 4). However, the practice never really took hold and those who experienced it appear not to have promoted it in the next generation. One woman from the survey whose parents had forced her to marry someone they had selected reported: 'I got married against my will. I will not let that happen to my children.' In the context of the Maldives, arranged marriage puts women at greater risk of violence. This is perhaps because when arranged marriages do take place they reflect a more conservative family ideology than the norm. There appears to be a higher risk of marital violence within unions that are the result of arranged marriages elsewhere in the world (see Hilsdon (2003); Hoelter *et al.* (2004); Idrus and Bennett (2003). A large-scale study in Pakistan also found that women who were married without their consent, were in polygamous marriages or had bride price were more likely to experience intimate partner violence (Andersson *et al.* 2009). The Maldives Survey also asked questions about polygamy. While there was some indication that women who were in polygamous marriages were at increased risk of violence, the overall number of women who reported polygamy was too small to come to any statistically significant conclusions.

Women who reported being able to count on their family for support in times of trouble were less likely to experience violence than those who could not count on their family. Social isolation has been shown to be a risk factor for partner violence in other studies (Hanmer 2000; Nielsen *et al.* 1992; Warrington 2001). As demonstrated above, social isolation, particularly from family and friends, is a common pattern among abusive relationships. Stark (2007: 263–6) says that controllers make women's relationships with their family and friends a primary target of isolation because they represent possible support networks.

Hawwa explained that not having family support was extremely challenging. She said, 'I just coped on my own. I was always lonely and never got family support so I managed on my own and I don't know how I managed everything myself'. Results from the Maldives Survey showed that when women do seek help, they most often seek support from their friends and family, rather than formal services such as the police. Talking to friends and family is one of the most important coping strategies for women living with violence. After nine years Hawwa told her friends about her experiences of violence and she explains how their support was instrumental in her regaining self-confidence and finally deciding to apply for a divorce:

> I felt like no other person would accept me, I was totally hopeless and felt that I would never get a man or a job. And even if I do get a job, I won't be able to go because I have my children and I can't go and leave them. I had no confidence at all. But when I started going out, I began to get more aware, and my friends gave me good advice. I started exercising with them and going swimming and I started to get fit. So finally I decided that divorce is the only option I have, and from my friend's help I gained confidence in myself ... Finally I realized that I can live without him, that I don't need him, that I can get someone else, even if I have two kids.

A number of scholars have noted the importance of supportive relationships for abused women because they create a sense of connection that gives women strength (Davis 2002; Landenburger 1989; Ulrich 1998). In fact, it has been found that in the United States, the development of social supports has the most influence on women's ability to cope in a positive way (Lu and Chen 1996).

Most of the characteristics found to be significantly associated with violence relate to the woman's partner. There is a significant association between the respondent's partner being involved in physical fights with other men and partner violence. In fact, women who reported that their partners had ever been involved in a physical fight with other men were nearly eight times more likely to have experienced partner violence in the last 12 months compared with women whose husbands had not been involved in physical fights. This may indicate that if a man sees interpersonal violence as a strategy for resolving disputes, then it is more likely that he will employ violence when conflicts arise in intimate relationships. Torres and Han (2003: 672–3) refer to this characteristic as 'the generality of violence', that is, whether the offender was violent outside the family. They found this to be significantly associated with the level of physical abuse. Gondolf (1988) and Saunders (1992) also found that generalized violence is associated with the most frequent use of severe partner violence. Levinson (1989: 45) argues that

> we can expect to find more wife beating in communities where men brawl with one another when drunk, where women fight with other women, where men fight with other men ... the severity of wife beating incidents is consistently related to the presence of violence in a society.

The logistic regression analysis also indicates that having a partner who had an affair is a high-risk factor for intimate partner violence. Women whose husbands had had affairs were four times more likely to experience current violence than women whose husbands had not been unfaithful. Perhaps this is because having affairs highlights a belief in the sexual availability of women and reflects an unequal dynamic within the relationship.

As discussed in the previous chapter, there is a strong positive association between women experiencing controlling behaviour and violence. Women whose partner exhibited at least one form of controlling behaviour had six times the odds of experiencing partner violence than women whose partner did not exhibit controlling behaviour. Similarly, in Nepal women who experienced higher levels of patriarchal control from husbands were more likely to be sexually coerced (Adhikari and Tamang 2010).

In the Maldives Survey women were asked whether their partner ever used intoxicating substances, including alcohol or drugs. In the Maldives alcohol is a prohibited substance and was therefore considered in the same category as drugs. Alcohol is difficult to come by and its consumption is relatively rare. Drug use has historically been relatively uncommon; however, as I discuss in Chapter 5, its use is on the rise. The use of intoxicating substances was found to be very strongly associated with intimate partner violence in the Maldives. Women whose partner used alcohol or drugs were more than ten times more likely to experience intimate partner violence than women whose partner did not use intoxicating substances. This is an extremely significant risk factor for violence in the Maldives.

Men's drinking patterns have been found to be associated with marital violence across various ethnic groups and classes in several developed and developing country settings (Cocker *et al.* 2000; Jewkes and Abrahams 2002; Koenig *et al.* 2003; Moraes and Reichenheim 2002; Rao 1997; Scott *et al.* 1999; White and Chen 2002). Data from a 2009 study on domestic violence in Nepal found that women whose husbands consumed alcohol were more likely to report sexual coercion (Adhikari and Tamang 2010), and a quantitative study in Eastern India also found men's alcohol consumption to be a risk factor for all types of domestic violence (Babu and Kar 2010). Studies have also found that abusers' alcohol use was related to a greater likelihood of physical injury (Brecklin 2002).

The influence of alcohol or drugs on intimate partner violence is complex. Historically, feminists have been hesitant to accept this association because it fails to deal with what they consider the root cause of violence against women: patriarchy and gender inequality in society. They have argued that many men who drink or take drugs are not violent and many violent men do not drink or take drugs, therefore we cannot say that alcohol or drugs cause violence. Abrahams *et al.* (quoted in Jewkes *et al.* 2002: 1613) have argued that some South African men drink in order to give women the beating they feel is socially expected of them. Lee (2007) has suggested that alcohol may be used as an excuse for violence occurring in intimate relationships, which allows the victim to forgive the abuser. Others suggest that conflict when inebriated may be more likely to result in violence because of the disinhibiting effect of alcohol. However, social anthropologists have argued that the connections between violence and drunkenness are socially learnt (quoted in Jewkes *et al.* 2002: 1613).

The association between alcohol and drug use and partner violence is likely due to a combination of these factors; it contributes to violence through enhancing the likelihood of conflict, reducing inhibitions and providing a social space for punishment. It is important to remember that the use of alcohol or drugs does not explain the underlying imbalance of power within relationships where one partner exercises coercive control. Therefore, while decreasing the use of alcohol or drugs may reduce the risk of partner violence, it will not eliminate it.

Factors found to be significant risks for women's experiences of partner violence include not being able to count on family for support and experiences of childhood sexual abuse. For male partners key characteristics included exhibiting controlling behaviour, use of intoxicating substances, infidelity and fights with other men. At the relationship level, arranged marriage is a risk factor in the Maldivian context. Interestingly, these characteristics and practices are relatively uncommon in Maldivian society, which help to explain why the overall prevalence of violence is low. That is, 'love' marriages and supportive family relationships, which are the norm in the Maldives, are in fact protective. Furthermore, violent fights between men and alcohol use are rare. Factors at the family, community and societal levels are explored below to understand the Maldives' low prevalence of violence and prevention implications.

The family level: flexible marriage and divorce practices

Flexible marriage and divorce practices in the Maldives have been instrumental in keeping rates of partner violence low compared to many other countries in the Asian region, particularly compared to South Asia.

Romantic love is and has been an important element of Maldivian culture and social life for centuries. It is not a recent cultural invention related to westernization, modernization or development as suggested in much academic literature about love outside the west. Contradicting the Eurocentric assumption that romantic love is limited to or is a product of western culture, recent ethnographic work shows that love in various forms plays a strong role in South Asian culture (Marsden 2007; Orsini 2006; Osella and Osella 2000; Trawick 1990). Although the expression of love is often culturally specific, Jankowiak and Fischer (1992) in their cross-cultural study on love document the occurrence of romantic love in 89 per cent of the cultures they considered.

Orsini (2006: 1) argues that culture and language play a crucial role in defining love at every stage: from sexual arousal to codified sentiment, from norms of comportment to 'significant stories' such as fables and myths. The 'significant stories' that Orsini (2006) refers to are particularly important in analysing love and marriage in the Maldivian context because academic and ethnographic material on the subject is virtually non-existent. Traditional fables and stories, songs and poetry provide useful insights into love, women's position in society and the practice of marriage.

The Maldivian word for love is *loabi*. It means romantic love as well as all other types of love. It is often used to describe babies and translates as 'cute' in English. Maldivians do not often say 'I love you', although the phrase is used in the written form in poetry and in letters. Sometimes Maldivians use the Arabic word *ishq* for romantic feeling.

Dhivehi has Sanskritic and Pali origins and, according to Orsini (2006: 5), Sanskrit and Perso-Arabic poetry includes many ideas and stories about sexual love and passion. For example, an Urdu *masnavi* was a 'ballad-like' linear narrative about two ordinary individuals focusing on the emotional state of the lovers expressed in a distinctively lyrical style. According to Orsini (2006), *masnavi* claim to be real stories with characters, locale and time explicitly mentioned, which culminate invariably in the tragic death of one or both protagonists. *Raivaru*, a traditional style of Maldivian love poetry and song that has a unique form of rhyme and rhythm, could be considered the Maldivian equivalent of this. While usually sung, *raivaru* also refers to written love poems. My father recalls that when he was a young boy on the islands he would see men engraving *raivaru* onto coconut leaves with sharp knives. The engravings would turn brown and be easily legible. They would roll up the palm frond, tie it with twine and slip it into the hands of their lover or girlfriend or perhaps get a friend to pass it on to the object of their affection.

Dhon Hiyala and Ali Fulhu, a popular *raivaru* from the Maldivian oral story-telling tradition is set from about 1450 to 1550 CE and has been described as 'arguably the most important epic work in Maldive literature' (Romero-Frias 2003: 39). It is based on the *Raivaru of the Princess of Buruni* but was transformed into prose in 1976 by Abdullah Sadiq, considered by many to be the foremost authority on Maldivian literature. Sadiq (1976: 6) recalls:

> I heard this same *raivaru* being sung by the famous Kara Kuda Thakkaan in a house in Galolhu ward, Malé. As I listened, my heart went through inexplicable feelings. This was no longer just a *raivaru*; it was a fascinatingly beautiful romantic story told in the special *raivaru* form of rhyme and rhythm. I had never heard anything like this in *Dhivehi* prose. It contained no hint of influence, simile, or metaphor from foreign literature. The story relied solely on the *Dhivehi* language and customs for inspiration. In short, it was a linguistic picture of atoll life from a much earlier time.

After listening to this, Sadiq decided to write the story in prose and travelled around the country listening to different versions of this *raivaru*, which became the inspiration for *Dhon Hiyala and Ali Fulhu*. He has used plain language to retain the originality of the *raivaru* form. Now the story is studied by school children as part of their Dhivehi lessons, although apparently there was opposition among Maldivian Wahhabi scholars to the inclusion of the story in the education syllabus because of the *fanditha* (magic) and the story's strong female characters (O'Shea 2004: 97). Many of the images and idioms from *Dhon Hiyala* have now become part of everyday language in the Maldives. For example, the word *Hiyala*, meaning beautiful girl, was used for the title of the Ministry of Gender and Family's annual magazine on women's issues, referencing this famous tale. My grandmother also recalls this tale in detail and remembers hearing it sung on her home island of Thinadhoo when she was young.

Dhon Hiyala and Ali Fulhu tells the story of a Maldivian *raaveri* family; a family of toddy collectors who were traditionally of low status.[2] It is a story that attests to the significance of magic, astrology, religion and fishing in Maldivian life; however, ultimately it is a tragic love story of Dhon Hiyala, a beautiful girl from a *raaveri* family on the island of Buruni, and Ali Fulhu. The story begins with Dhon Hiyala's grandfather (Raaveri Ali) and describes his first and second marriages and is useful in understanding marital practices more than 500 years ago. Marriage is a common theme throughout the story and clearly an important part of Maldivian life. When Raaveri Ali was 20 his mother told him it was time for him to get married.

> At the southern end of the island he [Raaveri Ali] met Sakeena, an orphan with no one looking after her. Ali spoke softly and Sakeena agreed to marry him. On the seventh night of the month of Rajan, the wedding date was set for Friday the fourteenth, and only then did Ali tell his mother about his plans. On Thursday night, two witnesses were sent to Sakeena to get her official consent and dowry price for accepting Ali. She had no parents, so at midnight the witnesses went to the island

magistrate who gave his permission and solemnized the marriage. Ali returned home and distributed wedding-rice to all his friends and neighbours. Sakeena was brought to the house on Friday morning after ten o'clock, her mother-in-law gave Sakeena all the keys to the locked places in the house. Ali's wife checked the valuables, rearranging things to her personal satisfaction, and began her new life as the owner of the home.

(Sadiq 1976: 9)

Here, we notice that, historically, marriages were not arranged by parents as in other parts of South Asia but initiated by the man. The woman, however, had to give her consent and had the ability to refuse, as in one instance described later in the story. The woman also named her dowry price and received her dowry personally, not through her family. Two people acted as witnesses to the wedding and traditionally it was a low-key affair, and the woman need not even be present.

After a magic curse on Raaveri Ali by a jealous island leader, his seven children and his wife Sakeena die suddenly, one after the other. Later, Ali finds himself another wife, Amina, on a different island and they have a son called Moosa. The conversation between the island chief and his daughter, Dhon Aisa, about Moosa's marriage proposal goes as follows:

'Moosa has come to this island to marry you, Dhon Aisa. What do you think about that?'
'I don't like Moosa Malin at all', she insisted.
'If you married Moosa, you would be allowed to wear the full veil and stay in your house.'
'Even if I'm allowed all that, he still doesn't tempt me at all.'
'If you married Moosa, you'd be allowed to wear shoes of gold with pommels made of fish teeth.'
'Even if I was permitted to wear such shoes, I couldn't just pretend to be interested in someone.'
'If you married Moosa Malin, you will be allowed to use a curtained parasol on the street.'
'Hmmm, then I would be very tempted by Moosa Malin.'
'Alright, accept the proposal, and give your dowry price.'

(Sadiq 1976: 27)

It is instructive to observe the strength and assertiveness of Dhon Aisa's character and other female characters in the story. Dhon Aisa had control over whom she married, which is reflective of women's position in the Maldives at the time. It is also evident that attraction and love were acceptable reasons for marriage at this time, as Dhon Aisa says that even with beautiful shoes she could not just pretend to be interested in Moosa Malin. It is also noteworthy that veiling and seclusion were very rare and seen as a sign of wealth and privilege for women, as in recent years veiling has become more common and associated more with religious beliefs than status. The seclusion of women is still virtually unheard of in the Maldives (Chapter 3 explores contemporary veiling practices in detail).

Dhon Aisa and Moosa get married and have a daughter called Dhon Hiyala – a girl of incredible beauty. On another island, Hulhudheli, a young man named Ali Fulhu is told in a dream that his future wife is in Buruni Island and so he travels there. After Dhon Hiyala sees Ali Fulhu for the first time she proclaims to herself that this will be her husband and pursues him. Hiyala washes and perfumes her body, adorns herself with jewellery and goes with a bundle of carefully prepared betel leaves, areca nuts, cloves, lime and tobacco to find Ali Fulhu.

> When she found him, Dhon Hiyala spoke to Ali in a very soft voice. 'Shall we go to your house and chew betel and areca nut, and smoke together?' He didn't answer so she cut off the limed part of the betel and areca preparations, and put it into Ali Fulhu's mouth with her hands. As he chewed, she fed him fine strands of extra tobacco. Ali Fulhu sat quietly, saying nothing. The first thing he noticed were Dhon Hiyala's fair round arms and her thin fingers with their graceful nails. He looked up into her radiant face, staring at her delicate neem leaf eyebrows and dark noddy bird eyes. Overcome by her beauty, Ali fainted, only recovering when Dhon Hiyala sprinkled some water on his face. She smiled and said,
> 'Is this a problem you've had since childhood?'
> 'My dear Hiyala, I have been working by the fire all morning without a drop of water. It's afternoon now. I have collapsed from lack of food.'
> Ali watched as Dhon Hiyala glanced at him again, and this time she passed out. He sprinkled some water on her face and when she revived, Ali asked, 'A childhood affliction, Dhon Hiyala?'
> 'No, it was the sight of your face,' she admitted.
> (Sadiq 1976: 76)

The romantic, playful and intimate interaction between these two characters illustrates that love and romance are not recent importations into the Maldives but have had a long tradition in literature and in real life. At the beginning of this chapter I demonstrated that arranged marriage was a statistically significant risk factor for partner violence in the Maldivian context. In other words, women who chose their own husbands are less likely to experience intimate partner violence in the Maldives. Therefore the fact that most women in the Maldives do chose their own partners appears to have a protective effect in this cultural context and may contribute to the overall low prevalence of violence in the Maldives.

The relatively egalitarian nature of household relationships in the Maldives is evident in the strength of the female characters in *Dhon Hiyala*. Similarly, in recent times, husband and wife are considered equal and decisions are generally made jointly, even though gender roles within the household are defined quite markedly. One older man explained to me that

> Women did the management of all the domestic work and the day-to-day caring of the children. Whilst raising children was shared by both husbands and wives in some ways, cooking, cleaning and washing seemed to be very much the domain of women, including the management of the domestic budget. Men generally did not enter the kitchen areas, which were quite separately located in homes in those days ... But I would say that in terms of decision-making, generally they were made jointly, whilst men and women would exercise greater or lesser say, depending on the domain of their influence.

In the Maldives individuals may reside with either paternal or maternal kin after marriage. Practicality, such as who has more space, is often the principal factor in decisions about residence. On the other hand, 'many new South Asian brides live with their in-laws, including their husband's siblings, so that they become answerable to many people' (Venkataramani-Kothari 2007: 15). According to Venkataramani-Kothari (2007), this extended family system where women live with their in-laws increases the acceptance of violence by South Asian women. The fact that Maldivian women often remain living with their own families, rather than in-laws, after marriage may act as a form of protection against partner violence, as Aishath Mohamed Didi, the then Minister of Gender and Family explained:

> My personal viewpoint is that [violence is less] on a small island because people know each other and also because we live in extended families and women don't go away from home, they will stay with their family, unlike in Bangladesh and India where women will go to strangers ... If the husband is living with the wife's family and he beats his wife the family wouldn't accept that.

Even when women do move to the husband's family they are not considered the property of the husband's family and generally maintain strong connections with their family of birth. This offers women protection because they have a greater degree of support. In fact, as explained above, one significant protective factor against violence in the Maldives is if a woman can count on her family of birth for support. Violence will likely be less prevalent where there is a low degree of social isolation or strong social support networks (Michalski 2004: 662). As Brown (1992: 12) explains,

> A wife is in a much more vulnerable position and there is a far greater likelihood that she will be ill-treated, if she is isolated from her family by rules for post-marital residence that compel her to move to her husband's distant community at marriage.

Communities in the Maldives tend to be small and close-knit. Maldivian society has even been described as a large extended family where individuals are linked through a network of bonds such as bloodline, religion and a community history (Misra 2004: 134). In fact, 91 per cent of women who participated in the survey reported that neighbours in their community know each other well; that if someone decided to undertake a community project most people would be willing to contribute time, labour or money; and that most people generally trust one another in matters of lending and borrowing things. Some 87 per cent said that if someone in their family suddenly fell ill or had an accident, their neighbours would offer to help. These strong family and community support networks that most women in the Maldives have access to may be one reason why violence against women is less than in other countries in the region.

As we saw in *Dhon Hiyala and Ali Fulhu*, dowry in the Maldives has long been requested by the bride herself and paid to her directly by her husband. In the Maldives, traditionally a woman's property remains hers and she is able to take her wealth or assets with her when and if she is divorced. These days, the amount requested in the Maldives is so small that it has become a token gesture. In other traditions in South Asia, the groom or groom's family demands a dowry from the bride's family. It is seen as the property a woman brings to her husband at the time of and during the marriage to compensate for the financial burden she places on her in-laws (Diwan 1990). While the dowry has become less significant in the Maldives, it has become more expensive in some parts of India, Bangladesh, Nepal and Pakistan, and can include money, gold ornaments, televisions, cars, refrigerators, furniture and land. Habiba Zaman (2005: 124) argues that the demand for a huge dowry can cause enormous psychological pressure on the prospective bride and her family. For example, disputes about dowry in parts of South Asia have been highlighted as instigating serious domestic violence incidents, including murder and suicide.

According to Rastogi and Therly (2006: 67), although the practice of dowry became illegal in India in 1961, it continues among all classes today. Umar (1998) suggests that there were 5,582 dowry-related deaths in India in 1993 but many more cases go unreported. In Bangladesh, in an attempt to reduce the number of brides killed because of dowry, an anti-dowry law was enacted by the parliament in 1980, and the Pakistan government enacted the Dowry and Bridal Gifts (Restriction) Rules in 1976. However, there were still 21,622 women who committed suicide between 1992 and 1993 in Bangladesh, and Zaman (2005: 124) suggests that these were mostly cases of dowry deaths, whereby women are murdered in a planned way and their husbands or relatives report that they have committed suicide. In contrast, in the Maldives, dowry disputes are unheard of and there has never been a recorded incident of violence related to dowry.

Current divorce practices: leaving abusive relationships

Divorce practices in the Maldives are relatively fluid. Pyrard (1619: 153–5) recorded the phenomenon of common divorce in the Maldives in the seventeenth century and noted that some men married up to 100 times throughout their lives. Ibn Battuta (1929) noted that from about 800 CE, sailors who got stuck on an island in the Maldives for months on end waiting for the wind to change would regularly marry local women for the duration of their stay, on the understanding that they would divorce them before their departure. He explained, 'When ships arrive, those on board take wives, and repudiate them on their departure: it is a kind of temporary marriage'. Temporary marriage practices in the early modern period, often between foreign traders and local women, have also been recorded in Southeast Asian contexts (Andaya 1998; Peletz 2009). My grandparents, as is very typical in the Maldives, were married and divorced many times. They were both married to other people before they met each other and my grandmother had two children in her first marriage but they both died at birth. My grandparents were then married to each other for approximately ten years and had four children. They later divorced because they were both having affairs. After the divorce they married their respective lovers and had a child each. After some time, both my grandparents divorced their new partners and eventually renewed their relationship, remarried and stayed together until my grandfather died.

In the Maldives, there has also been a common expectation that marriage may not last forever, and divorce is commonplace and acceptable. It is possible that this stems from the fact that Islamic law actually enables a fragility of marital bonds. Charrad (2001: 35) suggests that procedures to terminate marriage, the legality of polygamy and the absence of communal property between husband and wife in Islamic law serves to underplay the formation and continuity of independent and stable conjugal units.

Although divorce for women and men is still common and acceptable, staying single is considered relatively undesirable and therefore remarriage is very common. Research from 1980 shows that women married on average four times in their life (Siedler 1980). A survey conducted in 1991 showed that 63 per cent of women were married two or more times, with 37 per cent married only once (Ibrahim 1991). Many people I spoke to suggested that marriage has never been considered a permanent state; even today, it is almost accepted that a couple will eventually get divorced and remarry. As such there has been very little stigma associated with divorce, although this is changing (see Chapter 4).

Literature from South Asia and other Islamic countries indicates that parents often encourage women to stay in abusive relationships because of the shame associated with divorce, or because violence is considered to be an accepted part of married life (Idrus and Bennett 2003: 57; Shaikh 2007: 77–9). This is less common in the Maldives, meaning that women are, generally speaking, more easily able to leave an abusive relationship. Hawwa recalled that

> When I became pregnant, and when I was three months pregnant, my mother saw him being violent towards me. That time, my mother told him not to do that and to divorce me if he wants to be violent towards me.

A senior government employee proposed that domestic violence may be lower in the Maldives because 'we have a very high divorce rate, so women who experience violence can get divorced'. This is supported by Levinson's (1989) study of small-scale societies, which found that societal indicators of female autonomy – most notably a lack of divorce restrictions and more egalitarian household relationships – were important in protecting women from abuse by husbands. Heise (2012) has also confirmed through a study of macro-level influences on population prevalence of intimate partner violence that rates of partner violence are lower in settings that are more accepting of divorce and exhibit less discrimination against women in laws related to inheritance, marriage and child custody.

Maldivian women can chose their own partners, live with their own families, accept their own dowries and generally have equitable household relationships. These cultural components of family life create an environment where intimate partner violence is rare. Furthermore, the relatively flexible nature of divorce enables women to leave abusive relationships more easily when they actually do occur. The fairly equitable gender relations evident at the household level are also apparent in the public sphere or at the community level.

The community level: comparatively equal gender relations

The global prevalence of violence against women is rooted in a history of structural male dominance and is embedded in the dynamics of unequal gender relations (Dobash and Dobash 1980; Hunjan and Towson 2007; Wilcox 2006; Yllo 2005). The level of gender equality or inequality in a community inevitably contributes to the prevalence of intimate partner violence in the home. A UNIFEM report from 2010 clearly shows that in countries with greater gender equality the prevalence of violence against women tends to be lower. Heise (2012) has also confirmed a link between the geographic distribution of partner violence and various measures of gender inequality, including women's access to post-secondary education relative to men's, women's relative access to waged employment and gender inequality in women's access to land, property and credit.

In the Maldives there are a number of different sites of gender inequality, including structural, legalized discrimination against women, economic limitations on women's ownership and control over resources, and political and religious patriarchy, which collude to support ideals of gender inequality. For example, the Constitution barred women from the country's presidency until 2008, when the law was changed to give women the right to run for the highest office. Women also still face legal obstacles with regard to property rights, inheritance and the provision of legal evidence. A woman can only marry a Muslim man, while a man may marry any woman who belongs to a monotheistic religion (Christianity, Islam, Judaism). A man may also marry up to four wives, while a woman can marry only one man at a time, although the practice of polygamy has been very rare in the Maldives until recently (the increase in polygamous marriage is discussed in Chapter 4).

Maldivian law also discriminates against women when it comes to punishment under Shari'a. The law prohibits men and women from engaging in sex outside marriage, referred to as *zina* (any form of sexual misconduct including adultery and fornication), and punishment for fornication or adultery includes public flogging and banishment and/or house arrest. To prove such crimes there must be a confession by the parties involved or testimonies of two male eyewitnesses or four female eyewitnesses to the actual act (women's testimony is worth half that of men). This rarely occurs. However, women who become pregnant outside wedlock are often found guilty of fornication and punished while men are usually able to deny the crime. Furthermore, under Maldivian law, child sexual abuse requires a confession by the alleged abuser or testimony by eyewitnesses. Therefore, if a victim reports sexual abuse but the perpetrator denies it, the court can find the child (usually a female) guilty of fornication. The state would then wait for the girl to turn 18 before carrying out the sentence of flogging. Therefore the number of women punished for this crime tends to be greater than the number of men. This is reflected in the record of court sentences for *zina* in Malé and the islands. In 2003, 156 women were sentenced to flogging for sexual misconduct while only 50 men were convicted. In 2004, 178 women were punished compared with only 37 men; in 2005, 168 women and 23 men were sentenced for *zina*; and in 2006, 146 women were punished compared to only 28 men (Ministry of Justice 2006).[3]

Aishath Shujune, who was a senior employee at the Ministry of Justice at the time of interview in 2006, explained that if a woman reports sexual assault or rape by someone other than her husband they will also potentially face charges for unlawful sexual conduct:

> The onus somehow falls on her. And she will be lashed 100 times. It is still enforced; it is still done on the Justice Building porch by one of our staff. I find it disgusting but some people really go out to take a look, even people working at the Ministry, they go out and stare.

However, in April 2012 the Maldives Domestic Violence Act was ratified, which now defines domestic violence as a punishable crime and will hopefully provide more protection for victims.

Furthermore, girls are still expected to perform a range of household tasks whereas sons are not; there is still a protectiveness displayed by society towards women that impacts on their mobility; and women are still almost exclusively responsible for household work and caring for children and the elderly, despite the fact that they also often work outside the home (Razee 2006).

Despite the obvious gender divide, women have historically held a relatively high position in society compared to neighbouring countries. Deeply entrenched patriarchal values in many Asian countries – exacerbated, in some cases, by centuries of colonial rule followed by decades of political and economic instability and numerous recent natural disasters – have resulted in societies where both men and women view a 'good woman' as one who maintains the integrity, traditions and cohesion of the family, the community and the nation (Adamson 2007; Frisk 2009; Pinnewala 2009). Embedded within this image of a 'good woman' is often a social acceptance of male privilege and male aggression and an assumption that it is a man's right to have sex with his wife whenever he wants to (Hien 2008; Kassam 2010; Pinnewala 2009; Rani and Bonu 2009). The frequent reluctance on the part of police and policy-makers in Asia to take intimate partner violence seriously is symptomatic of this normalization of male dominance over women (Pinnewala 2009).

Bennett and Manderson (2003: 6) argue that for women in South Asia, 'The constraints on their movement, their limited access to education and work, and the absence of their rights as human rights, inhibit also their ability to name and to escape violence'. Hunjan and Towson (2007) also argue that South Asian culture is characterized by various norms that serve to maintain violence against women and silence those who experience it. They argue that

> from the time they are born, if they survive the abortion, infanticide, malnutrition, and femicide that result in a low ratio of girls to boys in most parts of South Asia, girls learn that they are valued less than boys but are duty bound to provide service, sacrifice, and devotion.
> (Hunjan and Towson 2007: 53)

In contrast to the general situation in South Asia, in the Maldives, girl babies or children do not face infanticide, malnutrition, femicide or abortion because they are girls; they are valued as highly as boy children. This is reflected by the equal sex ratio. One older man that I spoke to recalled that in his school days, 'I was never led to imagine that they [girls] were less in any way'. Furthermore, women have historically played a significant role in politics and society in the Maldives, and early Arabic records mention that before converting to Islam, the islands were ruled by a queen (Mittra and Kumar 2004: 4). Even after their conversion to Islam the Maldives had several sultanas, as noted by merchants such as Sulaiman and Al Masudi in the ninth and early tenth centuries. When Al Idrisi visited in 1150 CE, a king was on the throne; however, he noted that

> his wife administers justice, and speaks in public unveiled, after an established custom from which they never vary ... This Queen, on solemn feasts and other great occasions, appears in public along with her Maids of Honour, with great array of elephants, trumpets and flags. Her husband and the Vazirs follow her at a certain distance.
> (Quoted in Bell 1940: 17)

He continued to explain that the Queen 'acted as arbitrator among the people and did not veil herself from them. She issued many orders and her husband, although he was present, did not interfere. It had always been a custom with them' (quoted in Bell 1940: 17).

Women continue to play a significant role in society and the Maldives has the lowest Gender Inequality Index (GII) in South Asia, with a value of 0.533.[4] The Maldives also has equal primary and lower-secondary educational enrolment levels of boys and girls, no evidence of discrimination against girl children in terms of access to health and relatively equal life expectancy. The literacy rate in the Maldives of both men and women is also the highest in the region at 98 per cent. Education of women is valued as highly as the education of men. In fact, the ratio of female to male adult and youth literacy and primary enrolment is exactly equal at one. Secondary and tertiary enrolment rates are now higher for females than males (UNDP 2007: 335). Women are very visible in public life and are not segregated from men. While their mobility is slightly more restricted than men's, they are generally free to participate in all aspects of society and travel widely. Furthermore, the majority of Maldivians believe in gender equality as indicated by the results of a baseline survey on human rights awareness in the Maldives, conducted by the Human Rights Commission in August 2005. The survey found that 81 per cent of respondents thought 'the right of women to exercise/enjoy all human rights on the basis of equality with men' was 'very important' (Hosking 2006).

Bennett and Manderson (2003: 9) argue that 'the salience of notions of honour and shame, and the reverence for female virginity and sexual purity prior to marriage and chastity thereafter, is uniform' in the countries represented in their book *Violence against Women in Asian Societies*, including Bangladesh, Nepal, India and others. The notion of *izzat* or family honour is said to be a culturally specific patriarchal tool that is used to control women in parts of South Asia (Imam and Akhtar 2005: 73). According to Aylin Akpinar (2003: 426), the honour/shame complex is a means of controlling female sexuality and in particular protecting virginity, or 'the public effect of virginity'. In these contexts actions that can bring dishonour include associating with male friends, having a boyfriend, attending college or going to work without permission, violating dress codes, choosing one's own marriage partner and many others (Sen 2005: 47). The preoccupation with honour, shame and the sexual purity of women is said to be 'central in sustaining gender inequality, simultaneously justifying violence against women and depending upon such violence to reinforce hegemonic systems of gender differentiation and gender inequality' (Bennett and Manderson 2003: 9). According to Khan and Hussain (2008) domestic violence is extremely common; however, women are reluctant to speak openly because of harming the honour of the family. Regulation of behaviour may involve violence against women and in extreme cases 'honour killings'. Other forms of indirect, subtle control are exercised through threats of force or withdrawal of family benefits and security (Coomaraswamy 2005: xi).[5]

In contrast, notions of honour and shame in the Maldives function in a very different way. The honour/shame complex in the Maldives is not a strictly gendered phenomenon and is not used as a means of controlling female sexuality or protecting virginity. Associating with male friends and colleagues, having a boyfriend, attending school or work and choosing one's marriage partner are all normal and acceptable behaviours. It is expected that young men and women will have boyfriends and girlfriends and often date for years before getting married.

While sex outside marriage is unlawful, there is no importance placed on virginity before marriage. Despite a legalistic and modest attitude towards sex at the official level, individuals have an open attitude when it comes to practice. Maloney (1980: 367) reports, albeit in moralistic terms, that 'Dhivehi society combines a rigid legalistic and prudish attitude toward sex at the ideal level, with a remarkably open attitude at the behavioural level'. Research on adolescents and reproductive health as well as common knowledge reveal that young people commonly have sex before marriage (Rishana 2006), although it is rarely discussed publicly.

Reputation in the Maldives is important and for women this relates to dress codes, modest sexual behaviour and meeting wifely and motherly obligations. However, reputation is equally as important for men. Although notions of honour and shame exist in the Maldives, they do not dominate gender relations and are not used as a patriarchal tool to control women. Honour and shame would certainly never be used to justify violence. It is unheard of that a male relative would kill or harm a woman because of behaviour that supposedly brought shame on the family. I believe that a moderate honour/shame complex and reasonably equitable gender relations in the Maldives compared to other parts of South Asia contribute to an environment where intimate partner violence is less common.

The society level: geographies of non-violence

I acknowledge the problem of talking about the Maldives as a 'peaceful' place because it is reminiscent of discourses on the paradise island (Connell 2003; Jolly 1997). It could play on essentialized notions about paradise when in reality societies are never all violent or all peaceful. On the other hand, there are many essentialized notions that Islamic countries are violent and particularly oppressive towards women and challenging this misconception is also important.

Unlike many other developing countries, the Maldives has never experienced the oppression of long-term colonization, has not been recently at war and has never experienced any significant ethnic or civil conflict, despite a number of attempted coups. Until very recently, murder and rape were unheard of and theft was rare. People virtually never raise their voices, let alone physically fight in public, and generally there is (or at least was until the early 2000s) an air of calm in the islands. This is not to suggest that there is no violence in the Maldives – as we have seen there is a history of political violence and flogging. However, historically, day-to-day, social violence between citizens has been very rare. There is strong cultural emphasis on maintaining harmony and unity at the family, community and national levels. In the 1970s, Maloney (1976: 659) commented that 'Maldivians are non-violent people ... Murder is practically unheard of, except for a few historical political murders. Infanticide, abortion, and suicide are rarely acknowledged and seem to be genuinely rare'. Maldivians themselves understand their country to be a peaceful place and expressing anger and violence is considered highly inappropriate. Razee (2006: 53), a Maldivian ethnographer, explains this well:

> In everyday life people present an outward appearance of being calm, quiet and contented. They usually speak in a mild voice and avoid gesticulating and showing emotion. Gentleness, self-control and discretion are generally observed and considered virtues, especially in women. The outward appearance of being in control is a sign of being brought up well and being a good Muslim. Direct violence is very rare and when it happens is considered a serious crime. Verbal fights and public expression of emotions such as anger are usually perceived as signs of being uncultured and uneducated. As children we were taught not to express anger by raising our voice or throwing a tantrum. Whenever we heard verbal fights my parents would remind us that educated or well-brought up people would not behave in that way.

In fact, according to Maldivian popular wisdom the worst sins are greed, arrogance and *anger*, and one of the gravest insults is to call someone *rulhi gadha* (short tempered/anger-prone) (Razee 2006; Romero-Frias 2003). Many Maldivians find the recent political conflicts and increase in violent crime (discussed in more detail in the following chapters), particularly disturbing. A government employee explained: 'Now we are having crime problems and social problems, however, even now the majority of people don't support violence ... so generally I think that Maldivians don't like violence, they would rather try to resolve things peacefully.' This is partially why many

58 *The protective factors*

Maldivians were shocked that 20 per cent of women aged 15–49 reported experiencing some form of physical and/or sexual partner violence. While this is low compared to other countries around the world, it seemed incongruous with their understanding of the Maldives as a non-violent place.

It is likely that the relatively non-violent nature of Maldivian communities contributes to a relatively low rate of partner violence. Cross-cultural research suggests that family violence is more common in societies in which other forms of violence are also common (Levinson 1989; Torres and Han 2003). Partner violence against women has been found to be associated with high rates of personal crime, theft, aggression, suicide, homicide, feuding and warfare (Browning 2002; Koenig *et al.* 2003; Masamura 1979; Straus 1994.). Others suggest that a high level of violence in larger society, reflected in rates of murder, assault, rape and war, lead to cultural norms that legitimize violence as a way of dealing with problems (Straus *et al.* 1990). Heise (1998: 282) says, 'in short, where interpersonal violence is tolerated in the society at large, women are at greater risk'.

Likewise, violence against women has been found to be more prevalent in societies that are in conflict, or in post-conflict situations. For example, the United Nations now clearly acknowledges that the general breakdown in law and order that occurs during conflict and displacement leads to an increase in all forms of violence (Swiss and Giller 1993; UNHCR 1995). Furthermore, the tensions of conflict and the frustration, powerlessness and loss of traditional male roles associated with displacement may be manifested in an increased incidence of domestic violence against women.

It can be expected that those who are raised in environments that are more conducive to violent means of conflict resolution may be more likely to engage in violence later in life (Mahajan 1995; Widom 1989). Katz and Chambliss (1991: 270) conducted an in-depth review of the research on the relationship between biology and crime and concluded that 'an individual learns to be aggressive in the same manner that he or she learns to inhibit aggression'. Similarly, British psychotherapist Roger Hottocks (1994) argued that certain societies are much more likely to teach violence to men than others. The 2006–8 Maldivian Gender Minister, Aishath Mohamed Didi, argued that violence against women is not easily accepted in Maldivian society because Maldivians generally do not approve of violence. She said,

> Some people say we are timid. But I don't think we are timid, I think we are by nature peaceful. If we have options we will not go into violence … So people do in general respect law and order and people in general do not like violence and I think we do everything to avoid violence.

She links this back to Maldivian history, which has involved little violence.

> And if you think about it I think it shows in the Maldives because we have never experienced violence for ourselves or had to resort to

violence to get anything. It has been difficult in some islands but people don't resort to violence they just talk about it and they try to get it by talking, not by shouting and screaming.

The level of acceptance of violence in a community is often strongly associated with the rates of intimate partner violence. In the Maldives, violence is not considered to be an acceptable part of intimate relationships. However, research suggests that in many other countries in Asia physical partner violence is often justified as a form of discipline or admonition for women who transgress gender norms (Hassan 1995; Jejeebhoy 1998; Schuler *et al.* 1996). Counts (1999) suggests that in Kaliai, Papua New Guinea, the somewhat frequent nature of partner violence is associated with its relative acceptance.

This was a strong theme observed in the Kiribati Family Health and Safety Study (Secretariat of the Pacific Community 2010). The research indicated that women are expected to be obedient, faithful, perform household chores, defer to their husband on decision-making and to bear children. Physical punishment is often used as a form of disciplining women who are seen as transgressing prescribed gender roles and is often considered justifiable or acceptable (Secretariat of the Pacific Community 2010). Both female victims of violence and male perpetrators often directly blamed violence on women's disobedience. One Kiribati woman who had experienced partner violence said, 'I found that whenever I disobeyed him, he just hit me' (Secretariat of the Pacific Community 2010: 92). In interviews with victims of violence, women consistently blamed themselves for the abuse and advised other women to obey their husbands at all times to prevent violence. One woman suggested, 'If I really love my husband then I should allow myself to give in and be obedient to him at all times' (Secretariat of the Pacific Community 2010: 92). Another respondent advised women who were also facing violence: 'To be obedient, to prepare food for the husband and to wash his clothes and prepare his bathtub before he comes home from fishing. He must be made happy' (Secretariat of the Pacific Community 2010: 176). This was consistent with the results from interviews with male perpetrators, who also blamed their violence on their wife's behaviour, insisting that their wives should do what they say to stop the violence. One male perpetrator of violence said that in order to prevent problems in their relationship, 'She must obey me at all times'. Another male perpetrator articulated, 'She must be patient and obedient to what I say' (Secretariat of the Pacific Community 2010: 176).

Intimate partner violence in the Maldives does not reflect this pattern. Very few, if any, women spoke of obedience or discipline with regards to the violence they were experiencing. In the Maldives, women experienced a high level of uncertainty as to when, where or why their partner would act in a violent or controlling way. Women who reported physical violence were asked if there were any particular situations that tended to lead to violence and the most common response from women was that there was no particular situation that tended to lead to violence. One woman, Shehenaz, explained:

> There are no particular times or reasons which lead to his violent behaviour. He is just bad. When he feels like it he just does whatever he wants to do. Some people have different personalities; some things about a person may be good, while other things may be bad. But everything about him is bad. So I haven't noticed anything which indicates why he was being violent.

Here violence is not defined as culturally condoned behaviour or justified as a form of discipline or admonition. Shehenaz accepts no responsibility for the violence. Rather, the violent behaviour is blamed on the perpetrator who is defined as simply a bad person. For most Maldivians violence is seen as the practice of 'bad' people. In fact, most women expressed shock and surprise when the violence started. They had not expected it and had never been led to believe that violence was part of married life, quite probably because it is relatively uncommon. Hawwa recalls how the violence she experienced was totally unexpected:

> I was a very independent person [when I married him] and I didn't expect any of these things that I had to face from him. But from the beginning of the relationship ... He was very violent. For small things he gets angry ... When he acted this way at first, I was very shocked and didn't say anything.

Similarly, Aishath Mohamed Didi explained that 'Here in many ways, it [violence against women] is not very easily accepted. It happens but it is not accepted that this is how a woman should be treated'. People in the general community also suggested that violence within relationships was not normal or justifiable. One Maldivian man explained in a private interview:

> Violence is not used as a way of resolving conflict within families and between individuals. I also know there are exceptions to this. However, the general understanding is that overt violent behaviour is not commonly used by individuals or families ... In terms of conflict, generally we avoid it in the first place, letting it go until it becomes a glaring issue of concern, then raising the issue gently with whom one is having conflict, whilst treating him or her with dignity. This is the ideal.

Clearly violence exists in the Maldives and its recognition should not be minimized. Nevertheless, the fact that it is generally considered unacceptable by the community and indeed victims themselves, unlike in other countries such as Kiribati, helps to explain why the prevalence rate is relatively low.

Maldivian masculinity

The non-violent nature of Maldivian society is also reflected in gender norms and notions of masculinity. While there are always multiple masculinities, which vary across time, space and cultures (Connell 1995), hegemonic masculinity in the Maldives has historically been associated with calmness and rationality, rather than any form of aggression or violence. Violence in the Maldives is likely lower than in other countries because of this.

Michael Kimmel (2007) identifies some common ideals around masculinity that anthropologists have isolated as leading towards interpersonal and social violence. These ideals include: manhood is associated with the fierce and handsome warrior; public leadership is associated with male dominance; women are prohibited from political participation; boys and girls are systematically separated from an early age; during initiation of boys they are separated from women, taught male solidarity and endurance, and trained to accept the dominance of the older groups of men; emotional displays of male virility and sexuality are highly elaborate; male economic activities and the products of male labour are prized over female ones (Kimmel 2007: 109).

This is an interesting and useful list as it serves to underline the contrast between Maldivian and other notions of masculinity. While men have dominated public leadership in recent years, the public is not only a male domain and historically women have played a significant role in all aspects of Maldivian society. Public interaction between men and women is normal and there is no segregation of boys and girls or men and women. They go to school together, work together, have friendships together and date openly.

Maldivian ideals of manhood have nothing to do with ferocity or being a warrior. One older Maldivian man explained that the ideal qualities of manhood are: 'Steadfastness, courage, determination, inner strength, cool-headedness and behaving rationally. Having arguments, being defiant and violent were not part of what I was led to believe as the ideal masculine qualities.' Recall from the previous chapter that Aishath described her husband as a very 'quiet' and 'respected' person when they met, indicating that quietness is connected to respect for men in the Maldives. However, when Aishath's husband first became abusive she said that 'The whole person changed, the way he talked changed; he was louder'. Being loud is a negative personality trait in the Maldivian context and Aishath herself links his change from quiet to loud with his violent behaviour. Also, reflecting on the story of *Dhon Hiyala and Ali Fulhu* we see that 'Ali spoke softly and Sakeena agreed to marry him', again indicating that speaking softly is a desirable attribute in a husband. A good husband is not simply defined as providing financially for the family, but more important is the emotional care and commitment provided. According to Razee's (2006) research with Maldivian women, having a husband who was loving, caring and faithful to his wife were considered the most important aspect of an emotionally well-balanced married life. A good husband was defined by the women as someone who showed he loved and cared for his wife, and was kind and considerate to her when she was sick (Razee 2006).

In fact, notions of masculinity appear to be similar to notions of femininity in the Maldives. Ideals of kindness and gentleness are more prominent for women. Women are taught to 'care' for the family while men are expected to 'provide' for the family; however, characteristics of being softspoken and calm are qualities that are sought after in both men and women. One older Maldivian man in his sixties explained that 'the ideal qualities for a woman are being soft spoken, clear-headed, rational and well-groomed. They should not appear to be aggressive, outspoken or callous. Rather, femininity is associated with being kind, gentle and sensitive'.

In the Maldives there is no initiation of boys into manhood; however, there is a celebration surrounding circumcision, which happens at between five and nine years of age for all boys. The same man explained:

> Through the circumcision ceremony one becomes aware of reaching an important age in becoming a member of society, a Muslim, a part of the culture, a readiness to grow into adulthood. It is the first time one becomes aware of being acknowledged by adult relatives, adult neighbours and by implication the greater society.

The qualities that are instilled in young boys to be ideal men tend to promote respectful relationships. Boys are taught 'To demonstrate resilience, courage and a willingness to face challenges ... To seek ways to resolve conflict, to improve one's own life and help others and to acquire the means to support one's family and to be self-reliant'. By a western hegemonic definition of masculinity, men in the Maldives could be described as somewhat effeminate. Generally speaking, they are softly spoken and gentle, especially the older generation. Many men in high-level positions are considered to be masculine because they are able to stay calm in stressful situations, are quiet and dignified. My father explained to me that this is how Maldivian men show masculinity, and shared a historical example:

> When I was at school I knew that Nasir [the first President] was negotiating with the British seeking complete independence, as Maldives was a British Protectorate at the time. Based on what I was told I know that he was firm, yet courteous and completely rational in his manner of dealing with the British. This example had a deep impact on the young minds of the time in terms of what it meant to be a man.

The significance of notions of masculinity in relation to intimate partner violence is highlighted when we recall from the previous chapter that if a woman's partner had been involved in physical fights with other men it was a serious risk factor for intimate partner violence. Physical fights between men are very rare in Maldivian society, with notions of masculinity actually encouraging the opposite behaviour – rationality and respect. This no doubt contributes to the relatively low prevalence of partner violence in the Maldives. Other studies of societies where intimate partner violence is rare, such as among the Wape and the Nagovisi of Papua New Guinea, also suggest that people keep emotions, especially those that might lead to violence, under control. Mitchell (1992: 91) argues that among the Wape aggression is embarrassing and non-rewarding, and Nash (1992: 108) suggests that among the Nagovisi pride is taken in the ability to control the expression of emotion.

In contrast, according to research by the International Center for Research on Women, Indian men reporting violence were more likely to define masculinity in terms of power and control (ICRW 2002: 66). According to Hien (2008), Vietnamese men are seen to enhance their 'manliness' through dominance, aggression and violence whereas the ideal womanhood is defined by self-restraint and passivity. Qualitative research on masculinities and domestic violence in Cambodia reveals that men are expected to manage and financially support the family, make critical decisions and embody characteristics such as bravery, strength and discipline. The widely held codes on masculinity and femininity are perceived as sanctioning and propagating gender inequality and an environment conducive to violence (Gender and Development Cambodia 2010; Kingdom of Cambodia 2009; Lilja 2010). A number of recent studies outside Asia on men, masculinity and violence also indicate that men's perpetration of violence is associated with notions of masculinity linked to dominance, toughness, control and honour; however, more research is needed in this area (Barker *et al.* 2011; Dunkle *et al.* 2004; Ford and Lyons 2012; Naved *et al.* 2011; Seedat *et al.* 2009).

Unfortunately, the elements discussed in this chapter that have served to protect women from partner violence in the Maldives are being eroded with the impact of globalization. In the following chapters I will discuss how this is contributing to an increase in women's vulnerability to violence.

Notes

1 The outcome variable for the logistic regression analysis is whether an ever-married woman had experienced physical and/or sexual violence by a partner within the last 12 months (current violence). This risk-factor analysis is based on the group of women who have ever been married rather than a broader definition of partnership, because many of the questions that relate to the characteristics of the respondent's partner were only asked of women who had ever been married. In all, 1,409 women in the survey had been married. All data on the husband's characteristics are obtained through the reports of the female respondents. Those who had ever experienced partner violence but had not experienced it in the last 12 months (i.e. only prior to the last 12 months) were not included in this analysis so as not to dilute observed associations with putative risk factors. This is because much of the relevant 'partner' data was only collected for the respondent's current

64 *The protective factors*

or most recent partner. In all, 212 women were excluded from the analysis for this reason, leaving a total sample of 1,195 women for the analysis.
2 Toddy is a drink made from the sap of the coconut tree. Toddy collectors climb coconut trees and collect the sap by fastening containers to the stumps of the cut flower on the tree.
3 Some other crimes such as not fasting during Ramazan may also be punished by flogging, although sexual misconduct is a common crime for which flogging is a sentence. The issue of flogging and the gender-asymmetric nature of sentencing was being debated in 2012 in the Maldives (see Chapter 5).
4 The GII is a composite index measuring loss in achievements in three dimensions of human development – reproductive health, empowerment and labour market – due to inequality between the sexes and 2008 is the most recent data. See http://hdrstats.undp.org/en/indicators/68606.html.
5 We must be wary of only associating this type of violence with the 'uniqueness of Asian cultures, with irrational communities and aberrant and archaic patriarchal practices refusing to modernise' (Chakravarti 2005: 309). Concepts of honour are evident in western societies as well and honour crimes fit within the broader context of violence against women and patriarchy and are not simply a problem of 'the other' (Narayan 1997; Sen 2005; Welchman and Hossain 2005).

3 'A good wife obeys her husband'
The changing nature of the family

> Studying social transformation means examining the different ways in which globalizing forces affect local communities and national societies with highly diverse historical experiences, economic and social patterns, political institutions, and cultures.
>
> (Castles 2001: 18)

In focus group discussions conducted with Maldivian boys and men in 2004, more young men (aged 15–25 years) than older men (aged 26 and over) agreed with the statement, 'a good wife obeys her husband even if she disagrees'. Furthermore, many of the young male participants argued that a man was justified in beating his wife if she disobeys him or is unfaithful. One 18-year-old boy said, 'If a wife is being disobedient and if her behaviour is uncontrollable, it is stated in the religion that a husband can hit the wife'. In contrast to this, many older men articulated that violence was not acceptable under any circumstances.

As demonstrated in the previous chapter, one of the primary reasons why partner violence is lower in the Maldives than in many other countries in the region is the relatively flexible and fluid nature of marriage and divorce. This chapter maps the changing nature of the private sphere: the family level of the ecological model, examining the impact of global flows of people and ideas on the shifting ideologies of love, romance, marriage and divorce and how these changes impact on women's experiences of partner violence. The changing structure of houses, increasing social and legal restrictions on divorce and marriage and more conservative gender dynamics within the family are making women more vulnerable to abuse and less able to leave violent relationships.

The new 'private' sphere: violence behind 'closed doors'

In the 1970s human geographers started looking at the micro-space of the home as a key place of human experience and identity and feminist geographers tried to make the patterns and experiences of women in the home more visible and to deconstruct the notion of the 'home as haven' (Warrington 2001: 369). Family homes in the Maldives used to be spacious and open. My family compound in Malé, for example, was quite large, with an outdoor toilet (*gifili*), a big wooden swing (*undholi*), mango and papaya trees in the backyard and plenty of space for children to run around. No one locked doors and friends and neighbours would walk in and out of houses without even knocking. Everyone knew everyone and individual privacy was not an applicable cultural concept in the Maldivian context. My father recalled,

> Especially when I was a teenager, people would visit you, you would never have met them before but they knew you or had heard of you. So they would just walk in, wouldn't even knock on the door most of the time.

Many Maldivians I spoke to suggested that in the past the shroud of secrecy surrounding domestic violence would have been difficult to maintain with the open nature of homes. There used to be no clear divide between public and private in terms of women's roles in the Maldives. While women took primary responsibility for the home, they were also active in the public sphere. Furthermore, many domestic activities were undertaken outdoors, such as drying fish, making *rihaakuru* (fish paste), grating coconut, grinding spices, hand washing and weaving mats.

With economic development, internal migration and urbanization in the last few decades, the style and structure of houses have been reconfigured and the kind of private sphere associated with western modernity is now evident. This is particularly visible in Malé where there has been a substantial increase in the population. After my grandfather's death the family home was split among his children into five small blocks. Now each block has a small home supporting each of his children, their children and their children's children. In 2004 I lived in one of these houses with my aunt and extended family. My aunt and uncle have four children, two boys and two girls who are now married and have children of their own. At the time, two of my cousins were overseas undertaking tertiary education so there was enough room for me to stay. With my grandmother, who is now in her nineties, there were 15 of us spread across four generations living in a small house.

On the one hand increased crowding may have reduced individual privacy within the home, however, there is now a more clearly established distinction between public and private, insider and outsider. Now large brick walls run along most roads, preventing people from seeing into houses or compounds. These walls are broken up with brightly painted doors of red, green and blue, with placards above indicating the name of the house that lies behind them. Down a laneway behind a brightly coloured door may be a whole apartment building with storey upon storey of people living there.

Another door may lead into a more traditional house with a concrete corridor running down the centre and a number of small rooms off each side of the path, sleeping whole families. Alternatively, other doors in Malé reveal expensive cars and expansive houses filled with imported furniture and the latest technology. However, the commonality that all places now share is that their doors are locked. Malé has become a small city, domestic activities no longer take place outdoors and people do not freely enter each other's houses.

The privacy and seclusion of homes today enables intimate partner violence to take place more easily than before. As Brown (1992: 13) suggests,

> The isolation of a wife is also determined by the degree of privacy a society traditionally assigns to the domestic sphere. In general when domestic activities take place almost entirely out of doors and in full view of the rest of the community, or when domestic activity is audible through thin house walls, it is less likely that women will be battered because others will step in. There is greater danger that wives will be abused when the domestic sphere is veiled in privacy.

With a greater degree of privacy being accorded to the domestic sphere, even if people do hear or see a woman being abused, they may be less likely to intervene because the home has become more restricted to outsiders. For example, one woman explained: 'Even though he keeps on aggressively beating me to death, the neighbours never try to stop him. They just stay there and listen to the commotion. If I got any help from them my injuries would be smaller.' Warrington (2001: 371) says that in the home, 'once the doors are closed, what happens behind them, particularly if it concerns adults, is seen as being of no concern of anyone else'.

The increasing distinction between insiders and outsiders may encourage women to stay silent about their victimization. The Maldives Survey revealed that the majority of women agreed with the statement that 'family problems should *only* be discussed with people in the family' (Fulu 2007c). A number of other scholars have also shown that South Asian culture generally prevents people from discussing intimate problems and emotional difficulties with anyone outside the family (Das and Kemp 1997; Kallivayalil 2007; Tewari *et al.* 2003). With reference to South Asian communities, Venkataramani-Kothari (2007: 14) argues that 'family boundaries are clearly defined and a strict distinction is drawn between insiders and outsiders. Each individual is made aware of the prohibition regarding exposing family information to the outside world'.

The fact that women are now more spatially constrained and isolated from friends and family is of concern because a woman being able to count on her family of birth for support was found to be a protective factor against violence in the Maldives. Similarly, Joseph Michalski (2004) argues that having a low degree of social isolation or strong network support contributes to a low rate of domestic violence. As we saw in Chapter 2, partner violence often involves spatial constraint and the increasingly closed structure of the family home makes such constraint possible. For example, Hawwa explained: 'my partner kept me at home with no food and didn't give me anything'. In an open home where neighbours walk in and out without even knocking and share produce from their garden and food from their kitchen with their neighbours, this would have been less likely.

The rise of white weddings: changing expectations of marriage

Marriage is a central part of Maldivian life. According to the 2006 census, 84 per cent of females were married by the age of 30–39 and 89 per cent of males were married by 50–54 (Republic of Maldives 2008a). In a review of 20 years of gender and development in the Maldives, Razee (2000: 10–1) argued that

> Culturally, marriage is an important aspiration for both men and women but especially for women ... Women tend to get married at an earlier age than men and often to older men indicating the need for security and stability, which men are culturally expected to provide.

Within this aspiration for marriage there has been a high degree of flexibility. Historically marriage in the Maldives has been based on love and attraction rather than being arranged. I recognize that there is a problem with divisions of love versus arranged marriage, as love can be accommodated into an arranged marriage model (De Munck 1996: 698), arranged marriages can become love marriages and many so-called arranged marriages have been found to begin with desire (Inhorn 2007: 142). However, there is an important distinction to make between the practices of marriage in the Maldives compared to other South Asian countries. Generally speaking, in the Maldives choosing a mate has not been a social or economic decision. The choice is most often based on personal attraction and feelings rather than family alliance or land. However, the nature of marriage and divorce in the Maldives is becoming more restrictive. I observed that ideologies of love and relationships are being influenced by the global spread of western-style white weddings and Bollywood love stories have become part of the Maldivian 'ideo-scape' and 'media-scape' (Appadurai 1991). This has started to challenge the fluid institution of marriage with heightened expectations that marriage should last forever.

Modern-day wedding practices are useful in exploring changing expectations about marriage because 'images of weddings, then and now, offer reassuring visual shorthand for fundamentally different premises of matrimony' (Kendall 1996: 92). In the Maldives, weddings used to be low-key affairs, as described in *Dhon Hiyala and Ali Fulhu*. While marriages were based on attraction or love, the wedding ceremony was not used as a public display of these emotions. One middle-aged Maldivian man explained to me that weddings used to be small events because the marriage was not necessarily expected to last forever. Marriage was not considered to be such a serious matter because inevitably one would marry a number of times in one's lifetime. Anthropologist Maloney (1980) contrasts the low-key weddings in the Maldives to the elaborate affairs in other Muslim communities in South Asia such as Sri Lanka and India. In these regions Muslims seldom divorce and so marriage links two families and is considered an important rite of passage. On the other hand, Maloney (1980: 341–2) explains that

> In the Maldives, divorce is so acceptable that marriage is hardly a rite of passage and getting married means no change in status for the groom. Marriage can be dissolved at will. Hence, in the Maldives, an elaborate wedding ceremony would be dysfunctional.

However, in recent years weddings have become much more elaborate and important – a place where love is demonstrated and consumed. Early one evening, on an auspicious day in mid-November 2005 as the light turned grey outside, the women of my family gathered in a small, poorly lit room in front of a mirror adjusting my cousin Yasmeen's white, beaded headscarf.[1] The mood was frivolous and joyous. She was nervous and her sisters were teasing her, laughing. She wore an intricate, white gown that her mother, a talented seamstress, had made. The beads had been sewn on by her sisters. Yasmeen and Mohamed were both 25 years old at the time and had been dating for a number of years. As in most marriages in the Maldives, they were marrying for love. In another bedroom in the house a table had been set up for the ceremony. The imam arrived and was offered food and drink before taking a seat at the table along with the bride and groom and their respective parents who were acting as guardians and witnesses.

The atmosphere at the ceremony was dignified and serious. As the imam recited the Qur'an the family sat in respectful silence, heads bowed slightly. He told them of their responsibilities in marriage and they exchanged simple vows. The imam publicly defined marriage as 'a contract prescribed in the Shari'a to maintain human lineage' and a contract that 'joins the lives of two persons of opposite sex and binds them to one life together'. He instructed the couple to love each other, to be honest with each other, to be faithful to each other, to willingly help each other and to live in peace and friendship. The ceremony highlighted the importance of love, caring and friendship in Maldivian marriage. The imam emphasized the equality of men and women at the beginning of his speech; however, he also set the terms of the marriage along traditional gender roles with men and women occupying different power positions, the wife obeying the husband and the husband treating the wife with kindness.

The elaborate reception party held two days later at a local primary school stood in stark contrast to the minimal affairs described in earlier accounts of marriage. The hall was ornately decorated and filled with iconic romantic trimmings: flowers, lace and love hearts. The rise of the white wedding is evident not only in the Maldives. Hirsch (2007: 101) reports that it has spread to many countries; however, there is diversity in local interpretations of these global ideologies of love. Padilla *et al.* (2007: xviii) argue that love is now something that people strive for and that it has become a strategy for affective mobility and a technique for framing oneself as a modern subject.

Until fairly recently the Maldives remained somewhat isolated from external influences and maintained its open practice of marriage and divorce. However, with the introduction of cable television, imported DVDs, music and the Internet, people have access to a much more diverse range of materials and ideas. The ways in which people interact with, and are affected by, different forms of media is changing. For example, research suggests that Maldivian teenagers now get most of their information about sex from the Internet, romantic novels and movies as well as pornography (despite the fact that it is illegal in the Maldives) (Saeed *et al.* 2003: 77).

Indian films have become the primary contemporary reference point for words, tunes, stories and images of love in South Asia (Dwyer 2006; Orsini 2006). As Rao (2007) points out, globalization is not simply Americanization and the expansion and influence of Bollywood is the perfect example of this. Indian films and TV soap operas give insight into the local reworking of transnational media flows that take place within and between non-western countries, disrupting the dichotomies between west and non-west, modernity and tradition, foregrounding instead the ability of media to create parallel modernities (Larkin 1997: 407).

In the Maldives, Hindi love songs are borrowed and the words are changed into Dhivehi and released by Maldivian pop singers. Posters of Indian movie stars adorn shops and pirated DVDs of Indian movies are far more popular than their American counterparts. In the evening on the islands, through the dark night you see the crackling light coming from televisions where Indian soap operas are playing in almost every house. And when Indian stars come to the Maldives they draw huge crowds. The influence of Indian popular culture is so strong these days that even though the medium of education is English, most young people understand Hindi more fluently just from watching television.

It is understandable that Bollywood has a stronger influence than Hollywood because of the Maldives' geographical proximity to India and the similarity of cultural patterns. Brian Larkin (1997: 406, my italics) argues, with regard to Indian films in Nigeria, that they have entered popular culture by offering 'men and women an alternative world, *similar to their own*, from which they can imagine other forms of fashion, beauty, love and romance'. The influence of soap operas across borders is also evident in Azerbaijan where Latin American soap operas are very popular because women relate to values of purity and virginity for girls, and self-sacrifice for wives and mothers (Heyat 2006). According to Larkin (1997: 410), Indian films offer images of modernity that parallel the west, exploring the changing nature of social life, but rooted in conservative values. In Indian television and cinema there is a strict division between the sexes and love songs and sexual relations, while sensuous, are kept within firm boundaries (Larkin 1997: 413). Kissing is rare and nudity absent. Similarly, public displays of affection such as kissing are inappropriate in the Maldives, and sexually explicit material is banned from television. As such, Hindi music and media are more easily appropriated and hybridized because they fit neatly with Maldivian sensibilities. While similar values are important in this cross-cultural exchange, the Islamic island culture of the Maldives is very different from Hindu culture in India. However, Larkin (1997: 414) says 'the coexistence between likeness and dissimilarity is important because it is in the gap that the narratives of Indian film allow the exploration of social relations'. Love and romance are two of the major themes in Indian films, television dramas and songs. In Hindi films romance is traditionally set in paradisiacal settings such as gardens, parks, valleys and mountains, drawing on aesthetics developed in Urdu and Sanskrit/Hindi poetry and calendar art (Dwyer 2006: 294). Maldivian video clips mimic the style of love and sexual interaction found in Indian films and music drawing on the beauty of the Maldivian landscape; the white sand beaches, the turquoise water and the swaying palm trees on the islands. Malé, the crowded, concrete city, is virtually never shown. Interestingly, some Indian film clips have recently been filmed on the beautiful beaches of the Maldives, where space is remote and paradisiacal.

The consumption of these images and ideologies of love and romance in the Maldives has in some sense changed people's expectations about marriage. Many young people have embraced the fairytale romance of 'happily ever after' encompassed by white weddings and Bollywood. There is now an assumption that marriage (as a reflection of love) will last forever, when this used not to be the case. A number of people of my generation spoke negatively of the high divorce rate in the Maldives. They saw divorce as a failure of love. Interestingly, many young people criticized the high divorce rate in the Maldives as a result of westernization or modernization, failing to recognize the long-standing history of this practice in their own country. This expectation, combined with conservative state and Islamic discourses and the new Family Law, is challenging the flexible nature of marriage, which had served as a protective factor against partner violence.

Islamic revival and the family law: increasing divorce restrictions

Islamization has been widely interpreted as a response to rapid and disruptive social change, and to the dislocation and alienation produced by modernization (Stivens 2006: 357).

The Maldives has often been described as moderate or liberal in its practice of Islam, particularly with regard to women. Historical records indicate that women never wore headscarves, chose their own partners and that marriage could be easily annulled if both parties so desired (Maloney 1980). When Ibn

Battuta, an Arab judge, arrived in the Maldives in the fourteenth century he tried to change the law to address the relaxed attitude of Maldivians towards daily prayers and women's dress (Battuta 1929). Ibn Battuta reported in 1344 that 'their womenfolk do not cover their heads, not even their queen does so … Most of them wear only an apron from their waists to the ground, the rest of their bodies being uncovered' (quoted in Mittra and Kumar 2004: 3). In applying a civil law based on Shari'a, Maldivian courts have generally been lenient, and punishments such as amputation and capital punishment do not exist. However, flogging (with a *durra*, a taut leather strap with flat copper studs), house arrest and banishment to another island are common punishments for crimes such as adultery and fornication. In 2011 and 2012 the practice of flogging was being debated in the Maldives with some calling for a moratorium on flogging while others argue that it should continue.

In 1997 the Constitution was changed, making Islam the official state religion with the implication that non-Muslims cannot be Maldivian citizens. The 1997 Constitution also designated the president as the supreme authority to propagate the tenets of Islam. Islam is integral to the Maldives and woven into many aspects of daily life. In particular, Islam has been intimately connected to politics and the running of the state. While the education system is based on the Cambridge system and the medium of instruction for most subjects is English, Islam is taught to all children from an early age both in school and in the home. Every island has a mosque, which is usually the geographical centre of the village and often the centre of village life. Celebrations are based around religious events and holidays, particularly the fasting month, Ramazan.

With increasing global cultural flows influencing, among other things, beliefs about marriage, there has been a discourse of resistance to outside influences in the Maldives. This is evident primarily in an Islamic revival. The Maldivian Islamic revival in part reflects a backlash against globalization; however, it is also a global movement in itself. Islamic Revival or Islamic Awakening (*al-Sahwa al-Islaamiyya*) has spread around the Muslim world since the 1970s (see Ahmed 2004; Hefner 1997 on Indonesia; Mahmood 2005 on the urban women's mosque movement in Egypt). Abaza (2001: 118) says that Egyptian society has witnessed a growing Islamization in political and everyday spheres of life and that 'public religion' has gained visibility.

The contemporary practice of Islam in the Maldives is in many ways a creation of President Maumoon Gayoom, an Islamic scholar who studied at al-Azhar University in Egypt and was in power from 1978 to 2008. He took it upon himself to revitalize Islam, attempting to create a unified national identity based on a moderate and modern Muslim society. President Maumoon Gayoom used the discourse of resistance to westernization and Christianity in the promotion of his Islamic revivalist policies and called on the discourse of national unity in his leadership more generally. In his biography, *A Man for All Islands*, he is reported as saying,

I thought it was very important to preserve the religious and cultural unity of the country. Without a strong identity of their own, it would have been difficult for Maldivians to resist the influences encountered within their country [from tourism] or on their travels abroad.

(Cited in Ellis 1998: 136)

When in power, Gayoom regularly warned the public of foreign Christian elements or missionaries that he said were trying to undermine the independence and unity of the Maldives. In his speech in 2003 on Victory Day, which commemorated the failed coup attempt of 3 November 1988, the president stressed that 'the people must always remain alert against any external influence or interference that could threaten the independence, the sovereignty and identity of the nation' (quoted in Jory 2005: 17). He portrayed himself as the 'defender of the faith' and often used religion as a means of discrediting his political opposition. For example, on 19 May 2005 President Gayoom said that the Maldives Democratic Party (MDP) was made up of 'communists and Christians' whose sole purpose was to destroy Islam. This approach is not unique to the Maldives and Islamism is often explained as an expression of resistance against western politico-cultural domination (Mahmood 2005: 24).

Gayoom made considerable efforts to prevent the contamination of Islamic values and culture by outside influences, particularly from the west. For example, no foreign organizations of a religious nature were allowed into the country, even after the tsunami. In addition, non-Islamic religious items are banned, including bibles and idols. Alcohol is also banned and inaccessible on inhabited islands (although available to tourists on resorts). Gayoom also strictly controlled what was shown on state television. Sex scenes in movies and non-Islamic religious references such as footage of the Pope were blocked. Television programmes are also suspended during the five daily calls to prayer.

The significant increase in tourism over the past 20 years has opened the Maldives up to the outside world; however, continued effort is made to keep tourist resorts separate from local Maldivian life. Tourists only stay on resort islands, which are not inhabited by Maldivians, and they must have a permit to visit one of the local islands. Many tourists will never meet a Maldivian apart from those that work on resorts. Even then, there are few Maldivians working on the islands and the majority of workers on resorts are from neighbouring South Asian countries because of the stigma associated with working in an environment where people dress immodestly and drink alcohol.

When Maumoon took power he began sending students to Islamic schools abroad (particularly in Egypt), made Islam a compulsory subject in all schools with an emphasis on the teaching of the Qur'an and opened hundreds of mosques and Islamic schools around the country. The first Arab/Islam-based religious schools were opened in Malé in 1983. In his study of Maldivian popular culture, Romero-Frias (2003: 290) argues that these schools discredited local cultural and religious practices.

> In those schools the first thing a Maldivian child is taught is that his father is a fool because he can't understand the Qur'an as he does not know Arabic, the second that his grandfather was a lunatic because he held on to many folk beliefs that were un-Islamic, the third that his mother was shameless because she does not cover her hair, the fourth that his grandmother was a whore because her form of dress revealed too much of her body, the fifth that all the old Maldive books and stories are lies, and the sixth that Dhivehi courtesy is rude because Maldive Islanders do not go around saying all the time 'Assalam alaykum' as polite Arabs do.

While Maldivians would perhaps not be as scathing as Romero-Frias in their judgement of the Arab/Islam-based religious schools, there has been a shift away, at least at a public level, from the folk beliefs of previous generations to a more institutionalized form of religion. While the Islamic revival under President Gayoom was relatively moderate ideologically, it was strictly controlled by the government.

For example, in November 1996 President Gayoom appointed the Supreme Council of Islamic Affairs, which is responsible for providing guidance on religious matters. The functions of the Supreme Council also included centrally drafting sermons and certifying Imams, as well as building and maintaining mosques. Members of the council were appointed by the government for unlimited terms.

President Gayoom introduced the Protection of Religious Unity Act in 1994 to supposedly 'safeguard' Maldivian Muslim identity. Under the Act, both the government and the people must protect religious unity, and any statement or action contrary to the law was subject to criminal penalty (US Department of State 2010b). This allowed the president to deem illegal any form of Islam that did not conform to his own interpretation. For example, it stipulates that women are not allowed to wear a veil that covers their face and until recently this has been strictly enforced. Women have been arrested for having their face covered in public and men have been arrested by the National Security Service and had their beards forcibly shaved off (Human Rights Council 2007). This law also required all religious teachers and preachers to obtain written permission from the president prior to starting their work. For example, in 2006 a man named Ali Jaleel was charged with and found guilty of 'teaching Islam without the permission of the Supreme Council of Islamic Affairs' (Minivan News 2006d). Sheikh Fareed, a popular religious figure, was arrested in 2007 on the grounds that he was an extremist who held dangerous religious views, although the specific charges were not revealed. Chief government spokesman at the time, Mohammed Hussein Sharif, said, 'Religious unity is becoming a key issue. It is a matter of concern for us that individuals like Fareed get a platform to press their very concerning views to the public'. But the MDP, of which Fareed is a member, argued that the government was deliberately portraying him as an Islamic terrorist in order to justify their heavy-handed approach towards him and other political opponents (Minivan News 2007).

The new family law

As part of this revivalism, state and religious groups claim that Maldivian families are in crisis due to the high divorce rate, children born out of wedlock, drugs, crime and sex work. In response to this 'crisis', a National Conference on Strengthening the Family was held in the Maldives in November 1995 during which President Gayoom proposed a seven-point national plan to strengthen families that included 'Introducing legislation on marriage, divorce and bringing up children, as not every individual knows the Islamic principles on marriage and divorce, and codifying Family Law and presenting it in black and white would enable everyone to look at it' (quoted in Velezinee 2004). In contrast to the previously flexible practice of marriage and divorce, the state wanted to redefine the institution of marriage within the stricter confines of Islam and legislate on family life. It was within this socio-political discourse on disintegrating families that the new Family Law was enacted in 2001 to consciously and systematically bring down the divorce rate (Velezinee 2004). Although the divorce rate has always been high in the Maldives, it was now being defined as a problem, both socially and in terms of Islam. Even the most recent census reported that 'divorce is a common *social problem* in the Maldives' (Republic of Maldives 2008a: 187). The family and particularly women became the site for producing new versions of purer Islam and, as Stivens (2006: 358) describes of Malaysia, 'parents, especially women, within it carry large responsibility for securing an Islamic future'.

The Maldivian Family Law (2001) recognizes three types of divorces, *ruju*, *khul* and *faskh*. A *ruju* divorce is a pronouncement *talaq* by the man, which automatically results in an extra-judicial divorce. Although this has been made illegal under the new Family Law, the act is still deemed valid and the divorce is accepted and registered by the court but the man is fined (not exceeding 5,000Rf).[2] In a *khul* divorce the wife offers the husband compensation in return for a divorce regardless of the reasons she desires a divorce. And in a *faskh* divorce, the court orders a dissolution of the marriage based on a woman-initiated petition and may order the woman to return the dowry. A wife may petition a divorce from her husband based on the following four grounds: he acts in a way that demeans the sanctity of the wife; he treats the wife with cruelty; he forces the wife to perform an act that is prohibited in Islam (*haram*); he refrains from conjugal relations with the wife for a period of over four months without valid reason (Article 24).

According to Velezinee (2004: 29), *khul* and *faskh* divorces 'appear to offer the possibility for a woman to "buy" her way out of a marriage; but, it is not so simple and is a rather complicated, and often lengthy process'. When it comes to wife-initiated divorce where the husband is not willing to grant divorce, the burden of proof lies heavily on the woman.

The new law has proved successful in reducing the divorce rate, but in the process has made women particularly vulnerable to ongoing abuse. According to Velezinee (2004), a review of the court records revealed that there were an average of 28 divorces per week in 1999 in Malé, which dropped to 15 per week in 2002, after the application of the law. More recent data from the 2006 census reveals that the proportion of women marrying multiple times has decreased since the introduction of the Family Law and the proportion of women marrying only once has increased (Republic of Maldives 2008a: 72). In 2000, 48 per cent of women aged 50 and above had been married four or more times; however, in 2006 this had dropped to 23 per cent. Similarly, in 2000, among ever-married women aged 15 and above, 38 per cent had been married only once and that increased significantly in 2006 to 47 per cent (Republic of Maldives 2008a: 72). Women seem to be less likely to remarry than men. The proportion of the population (15 years and over) currently divorced is 3.5 per cent for men and 6.2 per cent for women. There are 176 divorced women for every 100 divorced men and this sex ratio has been increasing since 1990, which can be attributed to the decreasing number of remarriages for women. This is likely because the stigma associated with divorce and remarriage has increased, particularly for women.

Wife-initiated petitions for divorce are the ones being denied by the courts. In 2001, following the application of the Family Law, Velezinee (2004) conducted a review of cases where the court refused divorce. She found that 71 per cent were wife-initiated petitions, and in all these cases the husband had not agreed to the divorce. Aishath Shujune, a senior staff member at the Ministry of Justice who was appointed as the first female magistrate in the Maldives, explained that under the new Family Law magistrates make judgments and also provide 'counselling' to couples. She said that magistrates often order the couple to reconcile, particularly if the wife initiated the divorce:

> It happens often that the judge orders the husband and wife to reconcile even if there has been violence. The male is asked not to hit her and the woman is asked to go back and live with the husband even if she has sought refuge with a friend or whatever and she goes back and most often it is worse. So long as they are not divorced they are supposed to live together.

Previously a *ruju* divorce resulted in an extra-judicial divorce; however, now divorce is only possible through the court system and it is only granted if efforts to reconcile undertaken by the arbitrators have failed. This is of particular concern for women living with violence who are forced to return to abusive relationships. The Minister of Gender and Family from 2005 to 2008 explained that currently under the Family Law if a woman is not granted a divorce she must return to her husband if he tells her to come home, even if he is abusive:

> At the moment if a woman comes being beaten up I can't put her anywhere, I can only put the case to court but she has to go back to her husband if he tells her to come home. If she is strong enough she can request not to come home but he can drag her on the street and force her to come home. The magistrate can tell her to go home and the magistrate can even arrest her for not going home to her husband. There are many cases where women are house arrested in an abusive situation.

For example, Ahalam, a 37-year-old woman who escaped to Malé from an outer island, has been trying to get a divorce for five years. When she came to Malé her husband reported to the Island Court that she had left him and the children. She was put under house arrest for 15 days because she did not attend the Island Court as she was in Malé trying to get a divorce. She has written to the Island Court three times, the Family Court five times, the Ministry of Justice and the Ministry of Gender and Family and she has still not been able to get a divorce.

Furthermore, while it is now unlawful under the Family Law for men to divorce their wives by pronouncing *talaq*, 'I divorce thee', it is still considered a valid divorce, and the man simply has to pay a fine. This makes the situation confusing for many women and can increase their vulnerability. Mariyam, a 35-year-old woman from the Southern atolls, has lived on her island all her life. She has been married three times, has three children and experienced emotional and physical violence by her most recent husband. The physical violence was particularly severe, including slapping, punching, kicking and choking. Mariyam explained:

> Once he [my husband] was mad at me and said something that would indirectly divorce me. So, after that I believed that he is not my husband any more. But later he said that he didn't divorce me, however, I refused to have sex with him after that. He got very angry about that. One night while I was pregnant, he tried to have sex with me. He strangled my neck when I refused and as I tried to escape I scratched him with my nails. He got so angry that he kicked my lower stomach with his full strength and I fell down.

While women never had *equal* access to divorce, they are now more restricted due to the concerted effort by the state to challenge the flexibility of marriage and lower the divorce rate. The state has used the family as a site for producing a purer version of Islam and this has indirectly put more women at risk of partner violence. The Maldives Survey found that women who were separated or divorced reported a significantly higher prevalence of all forms of violence than currently married women (45 per cent compared with 19 per cent). This suggests that violence is likely to be an important cause of marriage breakdown in the Maldives. If accessing a divorce becomes more difficult, either because of social stigma or legal restrictions, women are more likely to be trapped in violent relationships and will likely contribute to an increase in violence. In fact, cross-cultural research suggests that one of the strongest predicators of domestic violence is women's ability to get a divorce (Hajjar 2004; Levinson 1989).

The tsunami, democratization and the rise of Islamism

In recent years Islamic revivalism has shifted from being a state-controlled moderate political/religious discourse to a widespread fundamentalist movement strongly influencing family dynamics. The rise in conservative Islamism has been instrumental in creating a more patriarchal family ideology in many homes. Islam the religion is extremely important to Maldivians and has, generally speaking, not been oppressive of women.

While in power President Gayoom was instrumental in revitalizing Islam as a state religion in the Maldives; however, he strictly controlled the 'type' of Islamic practices, promoting a relatively moderate interpretation. For many years Gayoom tried to control the rise of Islamic extremism, which he saw as a threat to his leadership. On the occasion of Ramazan in 2002, Gayoom cautioned people about the dangers of fundamentalism, arguing that it threatened the Maldives' cohesive and homogeneous society. In 2004, in an interview given to *The Hindu*, an Indian newspaper, he said that fundamentalists in the Maldives

> do not have a critical mass, but I think this is a potential threat we have to be very careful about. These could infiltrate into the country gradually and all of a sudden you are faced with a situation when you see that there are a lot of these people around and they become violent. Before that happens, you have to nip it in the bud; you have to control the situation.
> (*The Hindu* Online 2004)

In 2006, conflict on the island of Himandhoo highlighted the tension between religious conservatives and the government's attempt to maintain control over the practice of Islam in the country. The dispute was between supporters of the Island Chief (a government representative) and religious conservatives who make up most of the island's population. At the centre of the tension was a government-built mosque in which most locals refused to pray, citing that it was erected on a former cemetery and therefore defied the Prophet's teachings. A group of islanders built another mosque, which was closed by the government for being in breach of the Religious Unity Act, which requires all mosques, imams and preachers to be approved by the president. It was reported that a 16-year-old boy was beaten by the police and eight others were arrested on Himandhoo for reportedly 'threatening to fragment the religious harmony of Himandhoo Island' (Minivan News 2006a). In December that year, Ibrahim Shaheem, a 27-year-old government official who had overseen the destruction of a building that the religious conservatives were using to hold meetings, was found dead on the beach under suspicious circumstances.

It is possible to read the rise of Islamism in the Maldives in part as a resistance to western influence, for example from tourism, one of the reasons for the establishment of the Religious Unity Act. However, it is also evident that the increase in religious conservatism stems in part from resistance to the authority of the dominant norms and structures set by President Gayoom and his government. Gayoom's oppression of alternative interpretations of Islam contributed to its radicalization as a form of resistance. Talking about dramatic changes to the way people dress in the Maldives and how it relates to politics, an opinion article published in *Minivan News* states that 'every extra hijab and every extra beard is a symbol of rebellion against the present regime [the Gayoom government]' (Rasheed 2006a). Similarly to what Ayubi (1993: 225–6) argues with regard to religion and politics in the Arab world, resistance to state power in the Maldives has taken on a more conservative religious form because marginalized groups naturally adopt an ideology that is in stark contrast to the official state ideology that has taken on the language of liberalism and modernization. Fundamentalism has become a popular vehicle to register protest in the Maldives, and indeed around the world because of what people see as a failure and unavailability of other options (see Euben 1999). At the same time it is necessary to recognize that political resistance is only part of the story, and the dimension of religious belief is also important.

With the lack of educational facilities in the Maldives during the 1970s and 1980s many students went to study overseas in countries such as India and Pakistan. Aishath Mohamed Didi stated that:

> In Maldives in late 1970s early 80s very young boys, between age of ten, twelve and fourteen were taken to some institutions in Pakistan, in Medina and it is in these institutions that they were given a certain kind of religious training and education. So they came back in the late 80s, early 90s and it is this group of people, I personally think, are the people behind this whole transformation. So for them rather than seeing Islam as a moderate religion where there is flexibility and personal opinions I think they see very fundamental, very strict ways of physical behaviour.

Many of these graduates from Middle Eastern universities returned to the Maldives and became Islamic teachers, introducing a more conservative Islamic interpretation than had previously been practised in the Maldives. Greater flows of information through media, satellite television and the

80 *'A good wife obeys her husband'*

Internet have increased the influence of international Islamic movements (Fealy 2005; Lahoud and Johns 2005; Pottenger 2005). Furthermore, funding from the Middle East to build mosques and madrasas has contributed to the spread of what Maldivians refer to as Wahhabism in the country, as in other countries (see Williams 2004).[3]

The Indian Ocean tsunami and democratization

While the seeds of conservative Islamic thought were planted in the minds of young men sent abroad to study in the late 1970s and early 1980s, and further fuelled by then President Gayoom's oppressive control over religion, it was the Indian Ocean tsunami that in many ways became the catalyst for a sudden shift in the practice of Islam in the Maldives. The Indian Ocean tsunami struck the islands on 26 December 2004, injuring and displacing thousands of people, destroying homes, infrastructure and livelihoods. In the immediate aftermath of this tragedy, some groups suggested that the tsunami was a result of Allah's wrath due to immorality. In many cases in the Maldives, the mosques, which are usually the largest and strongest structures and built in the centre of islands, were the only buildings left standing after the tsunami. This seemed to support the argument that the tsunami was a message from God.

Women's bodies in particular became the target, with a number of people blaming the tragedy on women not wearing the *buruga* (Aniya 2007).[4] This message was conveyed through multiple sources. For example, a well-known Maldivian pop singer released a song along such lines. Aishath Mohamed Didi suggests that 'a lot of people went around to these islands where the tsunami had affected most and told them this is because you were behaving badly; it is God's punishment'. Following a mission to the Maldives, the UN Special Rapporteur on Freedom of Religion and Belief, Asma Jahangir, reported that on one of the islands she visited, the women informed her that they had begun to wear the headscarf after programmes on the media said that the tsunami had been the result of Maldivians failing to live in accordance with Islam (Human Rights Council 2007: 15).

Blaming women for the tsunami was not unique to the Maldives; examples from Aceh, Sri Lanka and Southern India indicate that similar representations of women's immorality were used to explain the tsunami (Salim 2007). For example, many Acehnese saw the tsunami as a spiritual test or a punishment from God and also an opportunity for accelerating the application of Shari'a in Aceh. Following the tsunami, Aceh witnessed increased crackdowns by religious police on women's dress and on men and women associating together in public (Donnan 2006; Salim 2007; *The Jakarta Post* 2006; Williamson 2006).

While the tsunami fuelled the fear campaigns of conservative preachers from the Wahhabi movement who had funding from Saudi Arabia, western donor money for emergency relief was accompanied by pressure to democratize. Some Maldivians had been pushing for the introduction of democratic processes for a number of years, although reform was taking place at a very slow pace. The tsunami meant that for the first time the Maldives was thrust into the international spotlight and the United States and the European Union expressed serious concerns over the lack of democracy and freedom under President Gayoom. This sped up the political reform process and the introduction of multi-party democracy in 2005. The promotion of democracy by international agencies, especially under the George W. Bush administration, is a prominent feature of globalization. The introduction of a multi-party system enabled the MDP to come out of exile in Sri Lanka and also opened up the political space for other parties. Perhaps not surprisingly, conservative religious groups also formed political parties and the Adhaalath Party in particular rallied popular support using Islam as its vehicle. The Adhaalath Party promotes strict adherence to Islamic law and wants to implement full Shari'a and institute an Iranian-style scholar's council with supreme power over the country (Minivan News 2006c).

Global ideologies such as democracy are often assumed to be positive and offer potential gains for women. Although, on the other hand, a number of scholars have suggested that the negative impacts of modernization, colonization and unequal and arrested development have contributed to a cultural crisis favourable for the development of Islamism, 'the return to religion as a source of solace and even more so as a compass and a solid anchor provide[s] a sense of stability and meaningful orientation, and coherent identity' (Moghadam 2003; Sahgal and Yuval-Davis 1991: 23). A number of women in the Maldives have been critical of the process of democratization, which they believe has enabled fundamentalist Islamic discourses to spread in the Maldives through parties like Adhaalath. A senior government employee said,

> Because there are political parties there is now a forum for such groups to spread their message. There are a lot of people in the Adhaalath Party and people in that party are following that and spreading it in the atolls. That is helping get the message across more than it would if there weren't political parties.

The ex-president Nasheed, in an op-ed in the *New York Times* following his ousting from government, said that

> New laws guaranteeing freedom of speech were abused by a new force in Maldivian politics: Islamic extremists. The former president's cabinet members threw anti-Semitic and anti-Christian slurs at my government, branding as apostates anyone who tried to defend the country's liberal Islamic traditions and claiming that democracy granted them and their allies license to call for violent jihad and indulge in hate speech.
> (Nasheed 2012)

During a by-election held in 2006, the Adhaalath Party contested in three different areas but failed to secure a single seat. However, although they were not successful in terms of obtaining votes, I believe that they were quite effective in influencing the political debate and pushing the previous government to compromise on certain issues. One of the first campaigns that the party undertook, and won, was against massage parlours and spas in Malé. When Adhaalath first emerged as a political party, massage parlours had been on the increase in Malé and gained notoriety for being places of prostitution. Some parlours were no doubt facades for brothels but a great number were legitimate beauty salons that offered manicures, facials and massages to women. In various rallies the Adhaalath Party gave fierce religious sermons threatening those who ran and frequented such places with hellfire. Eventually the government closed all massage parlours and spas in Malé, including those that were used by women exclusively. The spaces where many women went to relax and spend time with other women had been shut down under the guise of immorality.

The Adhaalath Party is also known to have played a key role in convincing some government departments to drop their ban on wearing the *buruga* with uniforms. Previously departments such as the Department of Immigration had not allowed women to wear a headscarf with their uniform and had discouraged male staff from growing their beards too long. However, in August 2007 they announced that a uniform with a headscarf had been introduced because of numerous requests from staff (Haveeru News Service 2007b). They were also instrumental in promoting a resolution by parliament to ban Israel's El Al airline from flying to the Maldives (Keck 2012). The concessions that the MDP government made to the Adhaalath Party despite the fact that they have never received enough votes from the Maldivian public to hold a seat in parliament highlights their political power. In this exact manner, Marcotte (2005: 75) suggests that the power of Islamist's moral discourse, as a political tool, 'is illustrated by the various concessions that many governments throughout the Muslim world have made' to these religious forces. Lahoud and Johns (2005: 2) similarly suggest that while Islamism in its radical form only inspires a minority, 'it exerts a wide influence in many Muslim countries and across the globe, even among those who do not realize its implications or understand its principles'.

More recently, the Adhaalath Party has achieved greater power and influence. When the first democratic elections were held in the Maldives in 2008, the MDP did not win an outright majority and had to form a coalition with the Islamic Party and the Adhaalath Party in order to take power. With the restructuring of the government, a Ministry of Islamic Affairs was created and Sheikh Mohammed Shaheem Ali Saeed, a member of the Adhaalath Party, was appointed as the State Minister. In May 2010 the Ministry of Islamic Affairs unveiled extensive new amendments to the 1994 Religious Unity Act. The amendments included setting the criteria for imams to qualify for preaching licences, approving the curriculum for religious education in schools and authorizing the deportation of foreigners who propagate religions other than Islam.

As mentioned earlier, the Adhaalath Party now supports current President Waheed and Islamic conservatism continues to assert its influence, not only at a political level, but also on family life. Ali Rasheed, a documentary filmmaker in the Maldives, believes that while the Adhaalath Party does not have any elected Members of Parliament it holds a lot of sway in communities and is having a big impact on women's lives. Among the examples he cites are husbands who refuse to allow their wives access to reproductive health services and insist that women give birth in the home rather than at a health centre for supposedly religious reasons. Rasheed told me,

> I always thought that the majority of people would see these people for what they really were and wouldn't really support them, but now there seems to be a lot of support. And at the family level there is more acceptance.

'A man should show his wife who's boss': an increase in patriarchal family ideologies

The influence of Islamism at the family level has meant that more and more women are expected to take responsibility for the home, be obedient to male authority and be sexually available to their husbands. As we know, partner violence is more prevalent within relationships that have a more unequal gender dynamic, or a strong patriarchal family ideology (Dobash 1996; Levinson 1989). Smith (1990) suggests that the ideology of familial patriarchy usually includes obedience, respect, loyalty, dependency, sexual access, sexual fidelity and ownership and finds a positive association between the degree to which a woman's husband believed in familial patriarchy and their approval of using violence against women.

The belief that gender transgressions such as not obeying one's husband, refusing sex or committing infidelity can be legitimately disciplined and controlled through violence appears to be increasing in the Maldives, particularly among young men. My field research revealed that younger women tended to advocate for gender equality and women's rights. They expressed more gender-equitable views than older women about women and men's roles within marriage in both the Maldives Survey and focus group discussions. However, young men tended to support patriarchal family values and used religion to justify such beliefs.

In focus group discussions, most men in the 15- to 20-year-old age group expressed much more conservative patriarchal ideas than older men, suggesting that these views are becoming more acceptable. Many men in the youngest age group also argued that Islam states that women should stay in the home and that husbands had the right to use violence against their wives. They justified such beliefs by referring to the following verse from the Qur'an (4:34),

> To those women on whose part you fear wilfulness, admonish them first, then abandon them in beds and last hit them with a single strike: and if they obey you, seek not against them means (of annoyance or harm) for God is most high and Great above you all.

One young man in secondary school said, 'Women are less intelligent, and less mature, and men are better at thinking about practical issues. Women are easily provoked so it is important to keep them inside'. However, older men offered very different views about women and their roles. Reflecting what many older people articulated, one man in his forties said,

> A couple in a marriage are two independent people. They should each understand that they have separate interests and the wife should be allowed to have her own personal interests. And if he doesn't like what she does that doesn't mean he can just beat her up.

This view reflects what has been a common understanding of marriage in the Maldives, where husband and wife have relatively equal positions and decision-making power. However, the teenager's view suggests that the subordinate position of women within the marital relationship is becoming more normalized among the younger generation.

According to Ayyub (2007: 31) and other Islamic feminists (Moghadam 2001, 2003; Moghissi 1999), Islam takes a very strong stand on violence against women and categorically condemns it. The verse quoted above has been repeatedly translated to justify beating of wives (Ayyub 2007). However, some Islamic feminist groups, such as Sisters in Islam in Malaysia, are challenging this translation, pointing out a long list of other meanings that can be ascribed to the word *idribuhunna*, which is traditionally translated as 'beat them with a single strike', such as travel, set up, take away, ignore, condemn and explain. Furthermore, Al-Hibri (2003) explains that the word *nushuz* (wilfulness), which traditionally meant any defiance of the will of the husband, has been shifted to mean obedience to Allah by both men and women. Ayyub (2007) also argues that this selective preference of one verse from the Qur'an over many others that speak about kindness and justice towards women has created an atmosphere that tolerates violence against women.

Polygamy and early marriage

Conservative state and Islamic discourses are eroding the flexibility and fluidity of marriage and divorce in the Maldives, and early marriage and polygamy appear to be on the increase. The practices of early marriage and polygamy have been very rare in the Maldives until recently and have not been widely accepted. The legal age of marriage is 18 and the mean age for first marriage for women has increased from 18 in 1985 to 23 in 2005 (Republic of Maldives 2008a). There are few formal statistics on polygamy;[5] however, only 2 per cent of ever-married women in the Maldives Survey reported that their husband had another wife while being married to them. Nevertheless informal accounts attest to a rise in these practices. The Committee on the Elimination of Discrimination against Women (CEDAW) wrote in their concluding comments to the Maldives CEDAW report in 2007 that they were concerned about the recent reports of early marriage and the practice of polygamy in the Maldives (CEDAW 2007: 7). These phenomena were also reported at a 2012 meeting of the Asian Forum of Parliamentarians on Population and Development, Standing Committee on Male Involvement in Ending Violence against Women that I attended in Colombo.

Although the legal age for marriage since 2001 is 18, some people are reportedly marrying their daughters at 14 or 15 in religious ceremonies outside legal channels. In fact, it has been suggested that a number of people are functioning completely outside the formal legal system, not registering marriages or divorces, arguing that because the government is not sufficiently Islamic they do not have a responsibility to abide by the laws.[6] The CEDAW shadow report stated that since 2006 there have been a number of marriages of children under the age of 18. The report showed that all minors married were girl children and the authors related this to the recent sociopolitical changes that have influenced the enforcement of the Family Law Act. For example, the report explained:

> The Adhaalath Party has published statements and publically criticized the Family Law as being anti-Islamic. They argue that Islam permits marriage at puberty and that it is 'unnatural' and goes against Islam to prohibit marriage until the age of eighteen.
> (Hama Jamiyya 2006: 12)

The new Child Sex Abuse Act (2009) categorizes child sex offences for the first time in the Maldives;[7] however, under Article 14, if an adult is legally married to a child under Islamic Shari'a, none of the offences specified in the Act will be considered a crime. Following public condemnation of Article 14 by human rights activists and the Resident Representative of UNICEF Maldives, this contentious article is being reconsidered. However, the State Minister for Islamic Affairs insists that the article is not in conflict with the law and that underage marriage is legal in the Maldives (Naish 2009).

While there are few official statistics on polygamy, a number of people indicated to me that the practice is on the rise. One friend confided to me that a male friend of hers who was married had asked her if she would become his second wife. She explained that being a second wife was not something she had ever imagined, as it was so uncommon in the Maldives until recently. A senior government employee also reported in a personal interview that some men were pressuring their wives to find them a second wife, telling them that this will help them reach heaven:

> There are specific reasons in Islam why you take a second wife whereas here it seems that now men just get married because they find someone younger and more beautiful, they don't actually think about the real reasons. This is something that I heard today, that some of the wives of the extremist groups go around looking for younger wives for their husbands because they have been told that they will get rewards in heaven if they provide a younger wife. It is just brainwashing.

Aishath Mohamed Didi described polygamy as a form of emotional abuse.

> People who have been in this area of counselling and who have had years of working with people know that it exists and we know how awful it is, especially with emotional or psychological abuse, [for example], men who are married to two or more women and the kind of suffering they live through.

Similarly, some women we interviewed described how their husband would threaten them with getting another wife or being with another woman as a means of controlling or humiliating them. Ainthu, a 31-year-old woman who lives in the northern part of the Maldives, married Moosa approximately seven years ago and he works as a fisherman and is often away from the island. They have three children, two boys and a girl. Moosa is very controlling and tries to restrict Ainthu's contact with her family. He often insults her, belittles and humiliates her in public. He threatens her and she says she often feels scared and intimidated by him. He has been having an affair and now he says that he is going to take the woman as a second wife. 'He hits me when I question him about it', she said. Ainthu said she does not want to be a co-wife; 'I want a divorce and I went to the courts but he refused to divorce me and the court refused my petition'. Hunjan and Towson (2007) in their research on partner violence in a South Asian immigrant community in Canada also found that some husbands used the idea of being with another woman to control, humiliate or neglect their wives. Abraham (2000) has labelled this form of abuse as the 'use of the sexual other'. Nurmila (2009) also provides a detailed account of women's lived experiences of polygamy in Indonesia and argues that it has been a source of injustice for women and children and that it goes against Islamic teaching.

The Ministry of Islamic Affairs itself recognizes the growing extremist ideologies in the Maldives and has recently unveiled new regulations governing religion in the Maldives. According to the Ministry, the purpose of the regulations was 'to protect the country and Maldivian society from brutal and harsh practices, divisions and antagonism in the name of Islam and from practices that contradict Islam and Islamic culture'. State Minister for Islamic Affairs, Sheikh Shaheem Ali Saeed, also noted that the regulations would be instrumental in curbing extremist ideologies in the country. The regulations also state that 'the Ministry of Islamic Affairs shall be responsible for enforcement of the regulations and shall be the highest authority to propagate Islam and dictate its principles'. In 2008 the Ministry of Islamic Affairs replaced the Supreme Council for Islamic Affairs. The Ministry mandated Islamic instructions in schools, funded salaries of religious instructors and certified imams, who were responsible for presenting government-approved sermons. By law no one may publicly discuss Islam unless invited to do so by the government, and imams could not prepare sermons without government authorization; but some in the country complained that newly found freedom of expression had led to foreign speakers giving lectures promoting more conservative styles of Islam than that espoused by the government ministry (US Department of State 2010b). The new rules require private organizations or civil society associations to seek the Ministry's approval before organizing sermons by foreign scholars, and are particularly strict concerning the issue of *fatwas* by individuals. In recognition of the fact that new conservative discourses are promoting gender inequality and putting women at increase risk of violence, the new regulations states that it will be illegal to either telecast or broadcast sermons that 'encroaches on the rights of a person based on gender' and that sermons should not contain language that 'encourages violence' (quoted in Robinson 2010b). However, while the Ministry expresses concern over the rising number of privately held, unsanctioned congregations (Nazeer 2010), the sermons that it sanctions continue to promote gender inequality and fail to recognize violence against women.

The Ministry of Islamic Affairs has previously reported that one way of addressing the issue of religious fundamentalism in the Maldives is by inviting moderate scholars to preach in the country. In May 2010 they invited controversial Islamic scholar and popular public speaker Dr Zakir Naik to speak at an event that the Ministry claimed would be 'the biggest event ever held in the Maldives' (quoted in Aniya 2010). However, it is debatable whether this scholar can be considered moderate – in one particular appearance Dr Naik says, 'If he [Osama Bin Laden] is terrorizing the terrorists, if he is terrorizing America the terrorist ... I am with him. Every Muslim should be a terrorist' (Naik 2008a). Naik has argued that these comments have been taken out of context. However, his relatively conservative beliefs, compared to Maldivian practices of Islam, are evidenced in his observations that being an air hostess is not a respectable profession for women and that there should be no dating before marriage (Naik 2008b, 2009).

During this event the Ministry of Islamic Affairs hosted a women's night at the Islamic Centre with a lecture by the wife of Dr Zakir Naik. To a congregation of more than 6,000 women, Mrs Naik argued that girls who wear the headscarf rightly portray the message that they are 'prohibited', while girls who wear skirts give the message 'you are invited' (Aniya 2010). She also said that if all women wore the *hijab* then there would be no crimes such as harassment, rape or abuse of women. Such statements stand in direct contradiction to the Ministry's own law that requires sermons to respect both men and women. It is clear that the new Islamic Unity policy will not prevent the ongoing promotion of women's subordination under the guise of Islam in the Maldives.

The extremely violent reactions that now seemed to be associated with Islam in the Maldives were also observed at this event. At one of Dr Naik's speeches, a Maldivian man described himself as 'Maldivian but not a Muslim', and he was escorted from Maafaanu Stadium by Islamic Ministry officials into police custody for committing apostasy. Several officers were attacked for trying to protect him when members of the crowd turned violent and called for his death. The following day the Islamic Foundation NGO issued a press release calling for the man to be executed under Islamic law if he failed to repent. Then after two days of counselling in custody the man gave *Shahada* – the Muslim testimony of belief – during a press conference held at the Islamic Ministry. He also apologized for causing 'agony for the Maldivian people' and said 'major misconceptions I had regarding Islam have been clarified' (quoted in Robinson 2010a). He further requested that the community accept him back into society. Such extreme and violent reactions are difficult to reconcile with the descriptions of peaceable Maldivian masculinity of the past. Islamization has shifted notions of masculinity and gendered power dynamics on both the domestic and global scale. Violence has become an element of a system of power and inequality, which is enacted by individuals and institutions.

Conclusion

As in the Maldives, globalization and the influx of discourses from the west and south have greatly impacted on gender dynamics in other Asian societies. Recent literature on women and Islam in Asia testifies to ongoing transformations, cultural exchanges, frictions and negotiations (Sharify-Funk 2008). According to Heyat (2006), gender norms in Azerbaijan are now complicated by a growing gap between rich and poor, the impact of western consumerist ideology, Islamist projections of feminist ideals and various post-independence destabilizing socio-political forces. Lindberg (2009) highlights that the effects of globalization on women's lives in South India have been multiple, contradictory, inclusionary and exclusionary. Globalization has brought higher social status and standard of living to some groups, but others have lost freedom of movement as women's confinement in the home becomes more prevalent.

As in the Maldives, globalization in Asia more broadly has led to a resurgence of various religiously defined fundamentalisms, partly in response to the threat of outside values (Derichs and Fleschenberg 2010). There has been an increasing influence of transnational Islam from the Middle East, with emphasis on piety and more strict adherence to religious practices (Rinaldo 2008). Gerami (2005) also suggests that new ideas of Islamist masculinity are a product of fundamentalist resistance movements and media and there has been a focus on reinstating an earlier 'pure' Islamic society. This increased leverage of religious fundamentalist groups affect women disproportionately. In South India, women are experiencing greater isolation due to strengthening of religious dogmas, and men returning from working in the Gulf often enact a selective Islamization to legitimate patriarchal control (Lindberg 2009). In Malaysia, amendments to make many laws more gender egalitarian are denied to Muslim women and many recent *fatwas* reduce Malay Muslim women's rights (Aziz 2010).

Like the post-tsunami experience in the Maldives, there has been pressure to democratize in other Asian post-conflict and post-disaster settings, but Kandiyoti (2007) rightly points out that democracy 'by design' can legitimize social forces that are likely to resist gender equality. For example, in Indonesia, 'The concern continues to be that, while democratic reform might occur in the government, social values concerning women's roles in conjunction with increasing expressions of Islamic faith threaten to become increasingly restrictive' (Adamson 2007: 6).

In the Maldives, and elsewhere in Asia, it is not only the gender dynamics within the private/family realm that are shifting; women's public roles are being challenged and gender inequality at a community level is also increasing. This ultimately impacts on intimate relationships, as we will see in the following chapter.

Notes

1 Yasmeen is a pseudonym.
2 US$1 = 15 Rufiyaa.
3 Followers of Muhammad Ibn Abd al-Wahhab (d. 1207/1792) are referred to as 'Wahhabi'; however, the followers refer to themselves as 'unitarians' or followers of the way of the 'righteous earliest Muslims'. Wahhabism or the Wahhabi movement started in Saudi Arabia and called for the strict observance of the Shari'a, and 'highlighted a "return to pristine Islam", calling for a strict observance of and adherence to the teachings associated with the idea of unity of God' (Saeed 2006: 132).
4 *Buruga* is the Maldivian word for headscarf, and usually refers to a scarf that covers a woman's hair but not her face.
5 The 1995 Census found that 1 in 11 married men reported having more than one wife; however, this question was not asked in the consecutive censuses.
6 This has been discussed on a number of Maldivian blog sites. Given the restrictions on freedom of religion and expression in the Maldives, blog sites have become spaces where some of the more contentious social issues are being discussed. See www.mymaldives.blogspot.com and www.maldivesdissent.blogspot.com.
7 The Act has not redressed the requirement of having at least two witnesses or a confession to prosecute cases of rape, and flogging is still a legal punishment for sex outside marriage, although only for those over the age of 18.

4 'For the love of women'
Increasing gender inequality

> What I'd like to say to Aneesa on her proposal is that men love women more than women do and therefore men will seek what's best for women. Just leave it to us.
>
> (Quoted in *Adduvas* 2006: 11)

This quotation is a response by the Member for Faadhippolhu, Hussein Ibrahim, to a proposal made in November 2006 to introduce a female quota into parliament to try to reduce the significant gender disparity in the political sphere. At that time women held just 6 out of 50 seats in parliament. The proposal was rejected, with most male parliamentarians voting against it. The paternalistic tone of the quotation, implying that women, like children, do not know what is best for themselves and should therefore let men, as the wiser sex, decide on their roles, reflects the contradictory processes of globalization being played out on the ground in the Maldives. We see that while women's rights are being promoted on the one hand, there has been a backlash against gender equality on the other, with some groups reconstructing the idealized woman as a domesticated, dependent wife and mother.

While partner violence takes place in the private sphere, women's experiences of violence are also influenced by what takes place in the public sphere. At the same time as examining the internal and interpersonal dimensions of women's experience of the gender order, it is also important to consider the institutional and ideological dimensions of its workings. We need to understand the ways in which violence against women is reproduced by the policies and cultures of political, economic and social institutions and legitimated by ideologies that sanction hierarchies based not only on gender but other axes of inequality, including sexuality, class, race/ethnicity, caste, faith and age.

This chapter examines the impact of globalization on women's roles in the public sphere, their work outside the home and their involvement in politics and positions of authority. I have shown in Chapter 3 that intimate partner violence in the Maldives is lower than in other countries in the region partly because of more equal gender relations, reflected in women's active involvement in all aspects of public and private life. But political and social change processes are changing the gender order and women's experiences of violence.

Women's economic marginalization

Since the 1970s the Maldives has experienced rapid economic development and transformation. It has shifted from a small-scale subsistence economy to a service and export economy, driven primarily by the tourism and fishing industries. While this has increased GDP and reduced overall poverty, economic development has, in many ways, marginalized women's economic position in the Maldives.

Today women have significantly less access to financial resources than men. The female labour force participation rate used to be one of the highest in the region at 60 per cent in 1978, but fell to one of the lowest in the world, 21 per cent, in 1995 (Republic of Maldives 2005c). This is because until a few decades ago, men and women had relatively equal participation rates within the fishing industry, with men going fishing and women processing and preparing the fish. However, with the shift in the Maldivian economy towards the service and tourism sectors, together with the technological modernization of the fishing industry, the fish processing activities undertaken by women have decreased substantially. Although the tourism sector has become the largest single contributor to economic development in the Maldives, only 4 per cent of its employees are women (Republic of Maldives 2005c). This is primarily because of cultural and social restrictions on women's mobility; working in tourism involves living on islands away from their family and with large groups of unknown males.

Over the past decade, the female labour force participation rate has started to increase again with women moving into the education, health and welfare sectors. Their employment in government has also expanded. However, there is still considerable gender disparity, with men comprising 73 per cent and women 37 per cent of the workforce (Republic of Maldives 2008a). Furthermore, the proportion of women in senior and managerial positions remains low (10 to 20 per cent, depending on the industry) (Republic of Maldives 2008a). Unemployment is widespread among females and is particularly profound in the atolls with 27 per cent of women unemployed compared to only 8 per cent male unemployment, according to the 2006 Census (Republic of Maldives 2008a). Razee (2006: 60) suggests that women are, in principle, free to pursue outside occupations; however, socially determined restrictions on the movement of some young women, combined with limited employment possibilities in most of the islands, inhibit women from achieving financial independence.

The shift in the economy has also increased the number of female-headed households in the Maldives. According to the 2006 Census, 44 per cent of Maldivian households are headed by women, one of the highest rates of female-headed households in the world (Republic of Maldives 2008a). This is primarily because men are often away working in Malé, at resorts or fishing at sea. Without a man in the home, women may be more vulnerable to abuse from outsiders. For example, one woman told us:

> My next-door neighbour gave me a difficult time. I couldn't sleep. My husband was out of the island working. It made me cry, but it's okay now. I hope no one else has to face this kind of thing.

A number of gender critiques of development have highlighted that women in developing countries have been especially negatively affected by the development process (Kabeer 1994; Sparr 1994). It has been suggested that sex and gender biases in mainstream development policies have increased women's unpaid work and created oppressive and exploitative conditions (Barker 1998). In development policy women's issues are often considered peripheral to the main concerns. The western stereotype of women as mothers and wives rather than economic actors means that they are regarded only as potential beneficiaries of development policies, even though in most developing countries women play a pivotal role in economic life. Roces and Edwards (2000: 1) suggest that social changes in women's place in society in Asia are often expressed as 'progress towards modernity'; however, not all change is 'progress' and not all 'modernity' enhances women's status. Such critiques are still relevant in the Maldives, and were highlighted recently by the response to the tsunami, which contributed to the ongoing economic marginalization of women.

The Maldivian government's National Recovery and Reconstruction Programme (NRRP) clearly stated that the government was committed to ensuring gender equity in recovery priorities and women's participation in the recovery work (Republic of Maldives 2005b: 3). However, a closer look at the NRRP reveals that the rhetoric was not supported by practical measures to enable these pro-gender goals to be achieved. There was no single programme area in which any of the intended outcomes, indicators or outputs addressed the specific needs of women. Similarly the United Nations Development Programme (UNDP) livelihoods project initially did not allocate any resources to women's lost livelihoods. Following pressure from the United Nations Population Fund (UNFPA) and the Ministry of Gender and Family, the UNDP incorporated a component into their livelihoods project to address women's lost livelihoods by replacing items such as sewing machines and fish-processing equipment. Nevertheless it should be noted that only US$150,000 was dedicated to replacing women's lost livelihoods, from a total of US$5 million for the whole project. This focus on male breadwinners and heads of households valorizes a particular kind of masculinity; it ignores women's significant contribution to household income and the fact that there are so many female-headed households in the Maldives (Fulu 2007b).

The Tsunami Impact Assessment (World Bank *et al.* 2005) showed the particularly negative impact that the tsunami had on women's livelihoods, which can be attributed, at least in part, to the relative disregard of the importance of women's economic roles in the response. The sectors most affected by the tsunami were agriculture and manufacturing, which tend to employ more women than men. For the populations displaced externally (to other islands) women were replaced in the manufacturing labour force by men, while among populations displaced internally (on their own islands), it was only women who lost manufacturing jobs (Republic of Maldives 2006a: 91). In contrast, sectors such as fishing, construction, trade and transport actually boomed after the tsunami, benefiting certain groups of men in particular. There was a notable increase in the unemployment rate for women, from 10 per cent in 2004 to 15 per cent following the tsunami. In 2005, in absolute terms, the number of women looking for work increased from about 6,000 to 15,500, while the number of unemployed men went from only 4,000 to 6,500. Overall, a significant factor that influenced whether a household fell into poverty after the tsunami was the proportion of female household members (Republic of Maldives 2006a: 83).

Gender inequality, including unequal access to economic and political resources, increases the likelihood of abuse in societies. Generally, women who have some level of financial autonomy are found to have more say over financial and other household matters and be able to leave abusive relationships more easily (Kishor and Johnson 2004b; Sev'er 2002). One woman interviewed who was experiencing partner violence said, 'Please get me a job. I don't want to live with this man. I am only living here because I can't support my children'. Many other women also disclosed that they felt trapped in a violent relationship because of a lack of financial resources.

However, earning a wage is not an indicator of empowerment by itself and needs to be understood in a larger context. In societies where women have historically had little economic autonomy, attempts to promote women's economic empowerment can have the unintended consequence of increasing the risk of partner violence. Microcredit schemes in South Asia have mixed results, with some research indicating a protective effect while others suggest it may provoke violence (Schuler *et al.* 1996). In Bangladesh it was found that women who contributed significantly to the household income were at increased risk of violence (Bates *et al.* 2004). Research in South India indicated that efforts to help women with vocational training, employment opportunities and social groups put women at increased risk of domestic violence (Rocca *et al.* 2009). Jewkes *et al.* (2002: 1612) argue that 'violence against women is normalized as men lash out at women they can no longer patriarchally control or economically support'. Counts *et al.* (1992) have also suggested that in societies where women's status is in transition, violence is used to re-enforce male authority. This does not mean that no attempts should be made to promote women's economic empowerment; however, the specific cultural context in which such programmes take place must be considered and efforts must be made to ameliorate any potentially negative consequences.

Interestingly, in the Maldives we see a number of elements at play. Historically women had a comparatively strong economic position; however, this has been eroded by processes of globalization, which makes leaving abusive relationships more difficult. At the same time, attempts to regain women's economic empowerment and further enhance gender equality in areas that have been unequal, such as in the legal and political spheres, have been met with patriarchal resistance. Even attempts to protect women from violence have been met with opposition under the guise of Islam and arguments that men have God-given rights to use violence against their wives.

A 'god-given right': justification of violence against women and a backlash against gender equality

The Maldives used to have the highest gender empowerment measure (GEM) in South Asia, which measures empowerment based on the percentage of seats in parliament held by women, the percentage of female legislators, senior officials and managers, the percentage of female professional and technical workers and the ratio of estimated female to male earned income. However, between 2008 and 2011 the Maldives GEM value has fallen from 0.437 to 0.429 and now ranks 90 out of a total of 109 countries (UNDP 2008, 2010). This is particularly significant in relation to women's experiences of violence because, as we saw in earlier chapters, relative gender equality has been a protective factor against violence in the Maldives. This section explores how gender equality and women's status is now being challenged.

Transnational feminist and international human rights discourses have influenced gender policy in the Maldives. In fact, research on violence against women came about, at least in part, because of such discourses. However, the promotion of gender equality has come from within as much as from without. Former President Maumoon Abdul Gayoom proved himself to be relatively progressive and moderate on women's issues. While addressing the closing ceremony of the second meeting of the DRP Women's Council on 5 December 2006, President Gayoom said,

> The government pays high regard to gender equality. Some might question it on the grounds that men and women are physically and biologically differently but that's beside the point ... Islam doesn't stop women from interacting with the society, working, running businesses, and playing their part in nation building.
> (Quoted in Haleem 2006: 55)

During Gayoom's administration, religious discourse was employed to validate the promotion of gender equality. This is reflected in the National Gender Policy, where the first guiding principle is that Islam recognizes that men and women are equal. The policy states that 'Islam promotes and protects the rights of women, and there is no differentiation between spiritual and virtuous men and women in the eyes of Allah' (Republic of Maldives 2006b: 6).

Since 2008, the Maldives has undertaken a number of legal reforms that promote gender equality. In 2009 the Special *Majlis* (Constitutional Assembly) passed a provision on non-discrimination on the basis of sex for inclusion in the new Constitution, which was introduced in 2008. The new Constitution also enables women to become president for the first time, and allows children of Maldivian mothers to become Maldivian citizens (Republic of Maldives 2008b). There have also been a number of other bills recently submitted to parliament for adoption, although as of March 2012 they have not yet been passed. The Labour Bill contains a prohibition of direct and indirect discrimination, a provision on equal pay for equal work and paid paternal/maternal leave. The Evidence Bill provides for forensic and scientific evidence to be used in courts and the Penal Bill includes a provision that criminalizes marital rape. Since 2006, as political spaces have opened up and regulations relating to civil society organizations have been relaxed, a number of women's human rights NGOs have been established and have been actively involved in promoting women's rights.

Shaarif Ali, a filmmaker in his early thirties, believes that 'women are becoming more involved in the workplace and in political affairs but they do bear the brunt of domestic duties even in our generation.' A number of other men in their twenties and thirties suggested in personal interviews that child rearing and domestic duties were the responsibilities of both men and women. One man said, 'exposure to higher education and living in different countries has meant that many men of a younger generation today are more aware of gender equality and the negative impact that "culture" sometimes has on women'.

Nevertheless, there are currently conflicting trends being played out in Maldivian society. Some women are taking a more active role in the public sphere while others are being influenced by more conservative ideals around women's role within society. Shaarif Ali explained to me,

> Recent developments are changing the way we, especially women, fit into the society. While many women are succumbing to Islamic fundamentalism, covering up more and staying home, others are becoming more involved in the day-to-day affairs of the country. For example, although only a few women are represented in Parliament a large number of women ran for it with vigorous campaigns. We never saw it before. More women are taking up opportunities to grab an equal footing with men. Women are extremely active in NGOs as well.

While a number of women and men are attempting to enhance gender equality, this is being met with some social opposition, partly because they destabilize the existing power relations and threaten those in positions of dominance (Bennett and Manderson 2003: 11). As we saw in the previous chapter, conservative groups aim to instil a more rigid gender hierarchy in the Maldives. Zahra, a government employee, explained:

> I think the younger generation is more accepting of women's rights. I think I definitely see fathers playing a more supportive role in raising children and a more supportive role in women working. But at the same time, probably because of religion, there seems to be a conflict. In recent years, there is a threat to what has been achieved in women's rights so far, there are groups saying women shouldn't be allowed to work ... this is not something that people should assume will go away, I think it is getting more, even at the regional conference for MDP, when we talk about women's employment, people say that women's role in the Qur'an is very clear, I think that is coming back from fundamentalism.

Interestingly, those trying to constrain women's sexual and social autonomy, as the above quotation explains, also employ Islamic discourse to support their position. Shadiya Ibrahim from UNFPA agrees that attempts to improve the status of women are met with challenges by conservative Islamic discourses, while other social changes do not meet the same resistance. She said,

> Even in Islam, the only thing they debate is women's position, what women wear, what women do, instead of talking about the substantial Islamic issues. They only talk about issues related to women. Even in passing laws or doing policies, when it comes to giving a better life to this vulnerable group [women] then Islam is a big obstruction, but if you are doing anything not related to that then Islam will not come in your way.

In response to the promotion of women's rights some conservative Islamic groups are trying to push women into the domestic sphere even though historically Maldivian women have played a strong role in all aspects of society. This has been particularly evident in responses to two contentious attempts to promote gender equality. The first was a proposal for a female quota into parliament that I introduced at the beginning of this chapter. Mulaku Atoll Member of Parliament (MP) and former Women's Affairs and Social Security Minister Aneesa Ahmed introduced a bill to reserve ten seats for women in the People's *Majlis* (parliament). Other female MPs such as Rashidha Yoosuf, the first ever Minister for Women's Affairs (a presidential appointment), supported the bill, saying that the few number of women in the People's *Majlis* indicated that the notion of women enjoying equal opportunities in the Maldives was only a claim rather than a reality. 'Women are deemed incapable of carrying out these responsibilities. We need more women represented in the People's *Majlis* to change that mentality', she said (quoted in Kulsum 2006: 6).

However, the bill was rejected, with virtually all male MPs voting against it. Many of the comments made in parliament in response to the bill were not simply against positive discrimination but condemned women being in parliament altogether. For example, Adam Zahir, the South Huvadhu Atoll Member, said,

> I do object to having special seats for women ... They are not supposed to go out and campaign and play an active role in politics or anything else. The Almighty asks them to stay home, bring up their children and serve their husbands well, and they can't evade these responsibilities. From a religious point of view women who take up seats here are offenders.
>
> (Quoted in Adduvas 2006: 10)

As in other Islamic societies we see how religious discourse is co-opted to serve ideals of gender inequality (see Idrus and Bennett 2003: 41). The notion that a woman's place is in the home was a common theme among comments made by MPs. Hussein Ibrahim, the Faadhippolhu Atoll Member, said,

> It's unnatural when women leave their true responsibilities of staying home to look after children, serving their spouses and performing other domestic duties, to mingle with society. This would have disastrous results such as promiscuity and disintegration of families ... God created two genders and vested two main responsibilities on them: Men to work hard and earn a livelihood for the family and women to undertake all domestic duties.
>
> (Quoted in Adduvas 2006: 11)

While more and more women are moving back into the paid workforce after being marginalized by the processes of economic development, the rise of Islamism has reinforced a conservative gender narrative that has raised women's domesticity as an ideal. As the above quotation shows, women are blamed for all moral and social ills of society and virtually shamed into domesticity. Zahra, a senior government employee, agreed. She said,

> What I hear mainly about is women not wearing the *buruga* or not staying at home to look after the children. Even from people generally, the drug problem and problems with child abuse is because women go to work, that they can't look after their family or children like they are supposed to do. Everything is always targeted at women. They never talk about what men are supposed to do and not do. Even when you get into taxis driven by Wahhabis, they put on a CD that provides a sermon on how women are supposed to live. Women, women, women ... I think they have planned the whole thing according to their own agenda.

This is not just the case in the Maldives. Blackwood (1995: 126) argues that in Indonesia mainstream Islamic discourse on womanhood portrays women as wives and mothers above all else and Stivens (1998: 60) suggests that domesticity is a powerful ideology endorsed by culture, Islam and the state even in the midst of the desire to become 'modern'.

In the previous chapter, I discussed changing idioms of love in the private sphere in relation to marriage. Ideologies of love are also being articulated in the public sphere. As stated in the quotation at the beginning of this chapter, a number of MPs articulated their opposition to quotas for women in parliament based on their love for women. Likewise, Ibrahim Khaleel Abdullah, from North Huvadhu, made the comment that

> Women are adored and respected. Indeed, one of the wonders of the world, the Taj Mahal, is a token of love for a woman. Hence, if we bring more women in here I'm afraid our attention may shift to them rather than our duties as MPs. It is simply wrong for women to be part of such an institution.
>
> (Quoted in Adduvas 2006)

Ibrahim Khaleel Abdullah emphasizes men's love for women; however, he focuses on sexual attraction and the distracting effect that women have on men. In this example, women are reduced to sexual objects who are unable to contribute positively to the institution of parliament but only detract from the role that men play.

In the second example I want to discuss, the Judicial Service Commission appointed two female judges for the first time in June 2007 in an attempt to promote gender equality. This evoked a public backlash, with calls for women to be relegated to the domestic sphere. The two major parties, the DRP and the MDP, both endorsed the appointment of female judges. DRP Registrar, Ibrahim Shafeeu, said, 'this would open up more opportunities for women in the political scene. DRP would back women's progress by all means' (quoted in Ahmed 2007: 34). On the other hand, the Islamic conservative Adhaalath Party leader, Hussein Rasheed Ahmed, condemned the appointment of women magistrates, arguing that it was prohibited in Islam (Ahmed 2007: 34).

Unlike the quota proposal, the decision to appoint female judges was made by the government and did not require approval from parliament. However, the response from many people was one of outrage, again in the name of Islam. A number of letters to local newspapers indicated that the two major political parties' support of the appointment did not necessarily reflect public opinion. One letter to the editor of Haveeru Newspaper said, 'Women should be concealed (kept hidden) in Islam but the government is attempting to reverse it. I was surprised and disappointed that the two main parties endorsed the idea of appointing women judges' (Haveeru News Service 2007a). The notion that women should be kept hidden is a recently imported ideal reflecting traditions of segregation and seclusion that are common in some parts of the Islamic world. In the Maldives, women have never been segregated or secluded and have, for the most part, never worn the veil. In another letter to the editor, one reader wrote:

> Looks like this country is willing to do just about anything in the name of reform. Have we forgotten how much of a responsibility serving justice is in Islam? Yes, bring on reform: follow the West! What misery! God, please enlighten us.
>
> (Haveeru News Service 2007a)

This emotional response suggests that women do not have the same capacity as men to carry out roles of high responsibility like serving justice. The writer sees this reform as a threat stemming from 'western' ideals. Algerian feminist Helie-Lucas (1987: 13) suggests that defending women's rights is always criticized as a betrayal 'of the people, of the nation, of the revolution, of Islam, of national identity, or cultural roots, of the Third World'.

In contrast to the above point of view, Aishath Shujune, one of the first female magistrates whom I interviewed before her appointment, argued that having a female judge was not in conflict with Islamic law and that many Islamic countries have female judges:

> There is no legal bar to women being magistrates; however, there has not been a single appointment. What has happened over the years is that whoever comes back with a law or a Shari'a degree, if he is male, is admitted to the bench even though they have had no previous experience ... Females go in as legal officers, with the same qualifications, with a huge difference in pay, maybe even five, six, or seven fold ... It is not part of Shari'a law [that prevents female judges]. It is apparently an interpretation. And we have looked at so many different countries, even Afghanistan has female judges, Pakistan has female judges, Iran has female judges.

Shujune suggested that comments that use 'Islamic principles' to justify women being prevented from taking on roles as judges are not based on Shari'a law but an apparent translation. She argued that Islam is being misused to stifle debate and support ideals of gender inequality. A recent UN report on women in public life in the Maldives concluded that there has been a reduction of important public entities for women that suggests a withdrawal of support for women's rights and influence in the public sphere. Respondents who had been involved in the study suggested that 'a shift towards a more conservative interpretation of Islam is resulting in women's role in the public domain becoming increasingly difficult' (UNDP Maldives 2010: 24).

When it comes to violence against women, during this period of rapid social change a similar conservative religious discourse has been used to maintain women's subordination. For example, the issue of flogging as a form of punishment has been debated in the Maldives since 2009. A number of Maldivians, including the Foreign Minister, Dr Ahmed Shaheed and the Maldives Ambassador to the United Kingdom, Dr Farhanaz Faisal, have challenged the practice that disproportionately punishes women, many of them victims of sexual abuse (see Chapter 3). Dr Shaheed said that Shari'a has only been enforced in the Maldives in the last 20–30 years. 'The traditions we follow have been very very moderate', he said (quoted in Omidi 2009). However, in July 2009 a group of approximately 150 religious conservatives protested in Malé, arguing that writings that questioned public flogging were 'anti-Islamic', calling for a ban on the newspaper *Minivan News* and the deportation of its writer Mariyam Omidi (9 July 2009). They rejected the suggestion that DNA testing on males should be introduced to ensure that both parties involved in *zina* crimes were equally punished. A Maldivian blogger suggested that 'They want to continue to punish women and girls but are happy to absolve men of their part in the crime. And, when they feel the status quo is threatened, they always look for a female to vilify' (Maldives Dissent 2009). Then in 2011, following a visit to the Maldives, the UN High Commissioner for Human Rights, Navi Pillay (quoted in Doherty 2012), defined flogging as 'one of the most inhumane and degrading forms of violence against women' and urged that the practice be abolished. Conservative Muslim groups protested outside the UN building in Malé with signs that read 'Flog Pillay' and 'Islam is not a toy' (Keck 2012).

The relationship between increasingly conservative Islamic discourse and domestic violence is made clear in some of the responses to the Maldives Domestic Violence Bill. The bill was drafted in 2009 in direct response to the findings of the Maldives Survey – it criminalizes domestic violence and allows victims of violence to gain emergency protection and improves woman's access to divorce. While many from both sides of government supported the bill, it stalled in parliament for over a year because of a number of objections from MPs, often under the guise of Islamic law. For example, during a debate on the bill in late 2010, Thimarafushi MP Mohamed Musthafa said, 'Do not to call upon us to make *haraam* [forbidden] something that God's law has permitted us to do. It is when we try to forbid things that God allows us to do that problems begin.' He continued, 'We are being swayed by non-Islamic people and their beliefs' (quoted in Naseem 2010). Another MP, Ibrahim Muththalib, was concerned that the bill would become an impediment to the practice of polygamy, which he said was 'a right accorded to every man by Islam' (quoted in Naseem 2010), even though it has been a very rare practice in the Maldives. Muththalib also suggested that the punishments outlined in the bill would mean the criminalization of a man's rightful actions against his wife's infidelity.

Covering women in public

In the writings which view the veil as a tool of empowerment, the element of choice is taken for granted, while, more often than not, the

element of coercion, be it in the form of using brutal force or intimidation, or social, cultural and political pressure, is not even mentioned.
(Moghissi 1999: 42)

One of the most visible manifestations of increasing religious conservatism in the Maldives is the increase in the number of women wearing the veil and black robes. Werbner (2005: 25) suggests that the rise of Islamic fundamentalism in Europe has been tangibly signalled by an increase in women and girls wearing the veil. While the veil cannot be defined simply as a form of oppression, one must question the reason for, and impact of, the dramatic increase in veiling and the lack of choice that many women now feel with regard to wearing the headscarf. The current practices of veiling in the Maldives reflect, at least in part, an attempt by certain groups to subordinate the position of women, which indirectly makes women more vulnerable to intimate partner violence.

The increase in veiling is perhaps another indicator of the new public/private dichotomy in the Maldives that I discussed in Chapter 3. Veiling has often been interpreted as extending the private space into the public. Given the little distinction between public and private in the Maldives, perhaps it is not surprising that women have rarely veiled. However, the new separation of spheres and the increasing Islamic conservatism has been accompanied by an increase in veiling.

Historically, wearing a headscarf has been uncommon in the Maldives. Maldivian women traditionally wore a skirt called the *feyli* without covering the top half of their bodies. Ibn Battuta (1929) observed of the Maldives in the fourteenth century:

> Their womenfolk do not cover their heads, not even their queen does so, and they comb their hair and gather it at one side. Most of them wear only an apron from their waists to the ground, the rest of their bodies being uncovered. When I held the courtship there, I tried to put an end to this practice and ordered them to wear clothes, but I met with no success.

Apart from a short period of enforcement of the veil in the seventeenth century there is no further record of veiled women in the Maldives until the twentieth century. In the 1980s the simple headscarf, which covered women's hair but not their face, started to become slightly more common; however, it was not until after the tsunami in 2004 that there was a dramatic increase in its use.

When I returned to the Maldives in 2006 after only eight months away from the country, I struggled to find any women who were not wearing the *buruga*. In some islands all women are now wearing the headscarf and loose fitting dark robes. When addressing the people of Kulhudhuffushi on his official visit to Haa Dhaalu Atoll in 2007, the then President Gayoom also noted that the number of women veiling and wearing black for religious reasons had risen dramatically. Trying to discourage the practice, he said that 'Neither the Holy Qur'an nor Prophet Muhammad preached it and hence it cannot be attributed to religion' (quoted in Moosa and Shareef 2007).

Wearing the veil has previously been a free choice for women in the Maldives and has had multiple meanings. For example, some women wear the veil because of religious beliefs and their desire to demonstrate piety. However, other young women may start wearing the veil to protect themselves from certain judgements. A friend once explained that Maldivian women could break social rules like smoking or having sexual relationships outside marriage more easily if their public image is of a 'good Muslim woman', defined by wearing the veil. Similarly Mona Abaza (2001: 118), describes how 'Islamic attire becomes a protective mechanism, allowing youth to smoke cigarettes or water pipes in public, and allowing flirtation in the intimate spaces of the coffee houses' in Egypt. Newcomb (2006: 299) also found that in Morocco, 'The practice of veiling ... is one tactic that many younger women have begun to employ in public spaces', and Rinaldo (2008) writes with regard to Indonesia that compliance to religious 'rules' or practices may allow women to participate more fully in the modern public sphere. Veiling in the Maldives, as elsewhere, could also be described as a fashion statement. It is not uncommon to see women in tight-fitting jeans and T-shirts wearing a headscarf wrapped firmly around their head and neck.

Aishath Mohamed Didi explained that women in their late forties usually only put on the veil after they have been on Hajj or as a form of etiquette:

> It used to be because you had become a grandma or elderly you put it on. It was more like an etiquette, beautifying thing, when you start going grey you put this on to cover your head and you wear it in a decorative kind of way with a pin, really nice. Even now, my grandmother, that's how they wear it.

For many educated, modernist Muslim women like Aishath Mohamed Didi, their grandmother's veiling is seen as an innocent act while the new veiling phenomenon is seen as threatening. Likewise, Göle (2002: 181) says that in Turkey 'many will say they are not against their grandmother's headscarf, that on the contrary they remember it with affection and respect', but that today they view the headscarf as being deliberately appropriated rather than passively handed down from generation to generation.

Some would suggest that there has been a concerted fear campaign in the Maldives targeting women's attire. Men who support Wahabbism now have a strong public presence in the Maldives, identifiable by their ankle-length pants and long beards. They argue that women's place is in the home and pressure women to wear the headscarf. According to one government employee I interviewed, they use various tactics to promote their agenda:

'They have leaflets, with titles such as "Cover yourself before it is too late", and regular meetings and I understand that they are using Islamic teachers to preach their message.'

The free choice to veil that Maldivian women and girls have always enjoyed is being eroded. Aishath Mohamed Didi agrees that Islamic teachers are being used to instil fear and pressure women to veil. She explained:

> For my daughter, my eldest daughter, it's school pressure. Her Islamic teacher's pressure forced her to wear it. And I say forced her because she came home one day and said that 'we are wearing it, all of us in class, none of us can stay in class without wearing it'. I asked her why. She told me how for three days the teacher had been giving them lectures on why they had to cover themselves and the last thing they were told was to go home, light a candle, put their finger in the flame and see how much you can bear it. If they can't bear it how will they bear hell? This is what I mean by fear.

Marcotte (2005: 76) argues that Foucault's idea that dominant discourses 'write' the body is useful in understanding the increased veiling phenomenon throughout the Muslim world. The new scripts being written on women's bodies in the Maldives advocate a new veiling, a new segregation of public and private, a new domestication of women and a conservative moral order. While this veiling is new to the Maldives, many other countries in the Muslim world are undergoing a re-veiling, where veiling was once common, became less common and is now experiencing a resurgence in popularity. For example, during the 1940s–1960s, the dominant discourse in countries like Turkey and Egypt was around modernization, secularism, westernization and, by extension, unveiling (Marcotte 2005). However, the emerging Islamist discourse focuses on a rejection of anything foreign. According to Marcotte (2005: 76), the veil is a symbol of resistance and women's bodies now take on the burden of a new type of nationalist marker (see also Kandiyoti 1991; Mir-Hosseini 1992; Newcomb 2006).

'Who speaks for Islam?': silencing the moderate voice

Islamism in the Maldives is manifesting an increase in veiling, a backlash against gender equality, a reconstruction of the idealized woman as a domesticated, dependent wife and mother and justification of domestic violence. However, the increasing fundamentalism that has so many direct and indirect negative consequences for women's position in society is rarely a topic of public discussion.[1] In this sense, the question of 'who speaks for Islam' has become significant.

The majority of Maldivians do not hold fundamentalist Islamic views. As Shaarif Ali, a man in his early thirties, explained, 'However much fundamentalism is taking root, they are a minority and our generation is basically moderate'. Nevertheless, a conservative and politically extreme rendition of Islam is taking centre stage in the public arena. The visit of Asma Jahangir, the UN Special Rapporteur on Freedom of Religion, to the Maldives in 2006 illustrates how religious debate has been silenced. The Gayoom government invited the Special Rapporteur to the Maldives and the president welcomed her and thanked her for accepting the government's invitation. Many people found it strange that Jahangir had been invited to the Maldives because the Constitution states that a non-Muslim cannot be a Maldivian citizen and the government openly acknowledges that it denies freedom of religion.

In a statement delivered at a press conference following her visit, Jahangir reported that 'open and honest discourse on the question of freedom of religion or belief is vigorously denied and the few that dare to raise their voices are denounced and threatened' (Jahangir 2006). She called for the establishment of freedom of religion and belief. Immediately, the then Justice Minister, Mohammed Jameel, lashed out at the Special Rapporteur, accusing her of trying to undermine the Islamic unity of the Maldives. He said,

> For a people that have accepted Islamic Shari'a as their law, to try to bring in freedom of other religions by talking rights, is a challenge to the freedom of Islam and respect to Islam. It is not permitted in Islam. Looked at in this way, it is compulsory for Maldivians to stop this.
> (Quoted in Minivan News 2006b)

A senior member of MDP, Hamid Abdul Garroor, argued that the Justice Minister was 'just trying to score political points. He is trying to turn himself into a budding politician by taking pot shots at the Special Rapporteur' (quoted in Hameed 2006b: 17). In the end there was a public outcry over Jahangir's visit, and it became clear that her invitation to the Maldives and subsequent demonization had likely been a tactic to garner support for the government as the 'protectors of Islam' in the lead-up to an election.

While President Gayoom previously maintained strict control over religious discourse for decades, globalized conservative Islamic rhetoric has become common in recent years. In one sense we see a pluralization of Islamic authority as Mandaville (2007) suggests, in that people are gaining different understandings of Islam from countries like Saudi Arabia, Egypt and Pakistan. Furthermore, there has been a shift from former President Gayoom as the central Islamic authority to other figures in the Maldives and abroad. There are also new texts such as leaflets being distributed on the streets, and unauthorized preachers are drawing large followings. In this sense globalization processes have disrupted and destabilized the traditional system of knowledge production in the Maldives in terms of both the ontological status and spatial location of authority.

However, rather than leading to multiple voices, we see that a singular but more conservative discourse still dominates the political and social landscape of the Maldives. The public, and political parties in particular, have been extremely hesitant to respond publicly to conservative rhetoric or challenge the deteriorating position of women. This is because Maldivians have been taught to never question religion and they are afraid of being seen as 'un-Islamic'. Religious discourse has always come from above in the Maldives; from the likes of the president, who is defined under the Constitution as the 'Protector of Islam', or Islamic scholars from the Supreme Council of Islamic Affairs. Lay people are taught to believe what they are told by the authorities and not to question religion themselves. Hamza Latheef (2006) says that religion is one of the most taboo subjects in Maldivian society and fear about speaking on such taboo subjects is instilled from an early age.

When Aishath Aniya, the Secretary-General of the MDP (in opposition at the time), challenged fundamentalist discourse with regards to the 'woman-question' she was absolutely vilified. In March 2007 Aniya wrote an article entitled 'Are women the germs that spread social ills?', which was published in *Minivan News*. This thoughtful but daring article was the first of its kind in the Maldives. She questioned the message that the tsunami and other social ills were a result of women not wearing the *buruga*. She criticized the conservative 'scholars', whom she called the 'newly self-appointed prophets', for demanding that people unquestioningly believe what they advocate and called for people to think for themselves as the Qur'an commands, and rely on one's own sound reasoning. She argued that women should not be held responsible for men's inappropriate actions and thus should not be required to veil.

Aniya highlighted how the taboo of talking about religion had enabled Islamic fundamentalism to prosper in the Maldives. She explained that the mere thought of questioning the religion leads to 'fear of paralysis of the mouth and limbs and of contracting a disease' (Aniya 2007). The teaching of not questioning Islam is so deeply embedded in the Maldives that to go against it leads to the fear of disease and even, quite conceivably, the disease itself. In Dhivehi, thinking and feeling are not separated as in English: 'heart' and 'mind' are the same word – *hith*.

There was a public outcry in response to Aniya's article. A number of people, including women, criticized her, reinforcing the belief that only religious scholars can comment on such issues; others resigned from the MDP in protest. High-level members of the MDP even called for Aniya's resignation to spare the party any further damage (Makan 2007). Eventually Aniya was forced to resign from her position as Secretary-General of the MDP and went into hiding after receiving threats against herself and her family. She was later arrested and taken to the Supreme Council of Islamic Affairs for questioning, where she was told that the article was 'against Islam' and 'against Islamic principles' (Jordan 2007; Makan 2007).

The outraged religious conservatives barely engaged with Aniya's contentions. Aniya writes from a relatively secular position, taking the language of rationality, equality and modernization. But as Euben (1999: 51) explains, attempting to understand Islamic fundamentalism through a rationalist epistemology is problematic because the practices and ideas are 'guided by and defined in terms of belief in divine truths unknowable by purely human means'.

One person wrote, 'Aniya's article is an insult to religion and she needs to be punished' (quoted in Saman 2007: 6). Another wrote, 'Aniya, do you understand Islam? If so you would not have questioned it ... If you believe in the Holy Qur'an do not dispute the scholars who preach *true Islam*' (Haneez 2007: 2, my italics). Similarly, a female member of the same party argued, 'No one has the right to assess religion without sufficient knowledge of it' (quoted in Saman 2007: 6). This clearly ignores the fact that Islam is debated and interpreted differently around the Muslim world. However, fundamentalists like Sayyid Qutb, whose 'books have become the staple of the new generation of Islamist university students' (Marcotte 2005: 77), generally shun interpretation as a mode of understanding because it is not appropriate in grasping self-evident truths (Euben 1999). The 'true Islam' that Haneez refers to reflects Qutb's argument that there is only one 'true Islam' and Islamic society is not one in which people follow their own interpretation (Euben 1999: 60). Marcotte (2005: 70) says of Islamism in Egypt that 'The claim to authenticity is the "backbone" of Islamism with its return to Islam and its moral rectitude, epitomized by proper Islamic female attire and behaviours'.

In an article entitled 'Freedom of expression without boundaries', published in *Haveeru* in April 2007 in response to Aniya's piece, Moosa Latheef argued that

> The insulting language and the sarcastic tone show just how much a Maldivian has denigrated an important aspect of Maldivian life. She has taken her hatred towards those who preach Islam out on an Islamic obligation that is wearing the headscarf ... Maldivians are influenced by western individualism. We are at liberty to wear whatever we wish.
> (Latheef 2007: 8)

In a letter to the Editor, Saman (2007: 6) said, 'We are spoiled by western influences. Western education and western-style upbringing created anti-Islamic sentiments'. The threat to Islam is articulated as stemming from western ideals. This narrative is reminiscent of Qutb's argument that 'when Muslims struggle to imitate alien models, they inevitably replicate the ills of western society in the Islamic world ... and it is precisely when the threat to Islam comes from within that the danger is greatest' (quoted in Euben 1999: 60).

In another letter to the editors, Ali Rasheed (2007b)[2] condemned Aniya for being a single mother: 'may I also caution Miss Aniya against hasty action while reminding her that whatever decision she takes is bound to affect the lives of her children.' According to fundamentalist narratives, one of the most obvious examples of western moral bankruptcy is the deterioration of the family unit, emphasizing that women should not work outside the home and that her role as caretaker of children within the home defines her identity (Euben 1999: 64–5).

Examining these reactions to Aniya's article and women's position more generally, it is evident that a fundamentalist Islamic ideology has taken hold in the Maldives. It has taken hold very quickly. Until 2005, veiling was relatively rare in the Maldives and face coverings were illegal. Now to question its dramatic increase is tantamount to apostasy. It is particularly concerning that this Islamist discourse has become so dominant because, as Marcotte (2005: 75) argues, 'dominant discourses determine the nature of truth and knowledge. Whichever explanation "wins" becomes knowledge and, therefore, "truth"'.

Even though there has been a powerful attempt to silence all debate on Islamism in the Maldives, there are some subtle yet evident forms of resistance by women and men. Islam as a religion remains extremely important to most Maldivians; however, they are challenging discourses that they see as curtailing women's personal freedoms and position in society. Those who have spoken out publicly against Islamism or the increase in veiling have been vilified. In response, many Maldivians are carrying out rigorous debates and discussions in more anonymous forums such as blogs and other social networking websites.

When the results of the Survey on Violence against Women were released to the public, a small booklet including some of the statistics and findings was published. On the front cover were some photos of men and women participating in the 'hands campaign' for the 16 Days of Activism against Gender Violence. In the pictures I originally selected for the front cover, all the women were wearing a headscarf. This was not a conscious choice; it just happened that most women in the photographs were covered. A senior staff member of the Ministry of Gender and Family at the time noticed this and made the decision to change the photos to show women who were not wearing the headscarf. By changing the photos on this publication that would be distributed widely she was making a subtle political statement to promote the image of Maldivian women not wearing the headscarf.

Another example comes from when I was presenting the findings of the survey to the media. I had shared a quotation from the *Untold Stories* documentary where a woman reported that her husband had beaten her when she had refused sex because she was menstruating. One young man stood up and said that this was an example of why more men should practise polygamy. He argued that if the man had another wife then he could have had sexual relations with her and would not have beaten up this woman. For him the violence was justified and could be prevented if men were never denied sex. As a partly foreign, western-educated outsider, I could respond by arguing that violence was not acceptable under any circumstances, although I could not legitimately argue with him on religious doctrine. However, another female staff member from the Ministry of Gender and Family who was present immediately stood up and strongly challenged his pro-polygamy argument on religious grounds. She wears the *buruga* and, interestingly, this visible manifestation of religiosity gave her a legitimate voice with regard to the practice of Islam. The young man listened carefully to her and apologized for his comments.

Conclusion

We saw in the previous chapter how migration and urbanization have contributed to the creation of a more separate private sphere. So, too, globalization has resulted in an increasingly demarcated public sphere and a dichotomization of the public/private. The processes have had complex and contradictory effects on women. Rather than women taking on greater roles in the public sphere, economic development and Islamism has meant that women are being pushed into the private sphere. The idealized woman is being reconstructed as a domesticated, dependent wife and mother, whose purpose in life is to serve her husband and family. Furthermore, violence against women is being justified as a God-given right of men, and attempts to prevent violence (including domestic violence and flogging) are being met with outright hostility under the guise of Islam.

The complex and contradictory experience of globalization in the local context of the Maldives offers a space for both positive and negative readings of globalization on the ground. The shifting gender order and the localized manifestation of the global discourse and practice of Islamism provides a theoretical and empirical basis for understanding the intersection between the global and the local in the Maldives and also in Asia more broadly.

Globalization has contributed in part to economic growth but also to the economic marginalization of women in the Maldives. Various scholars have argued that globalization has disproportionately negatively affected women (Bahramitash 2005; Rege 2003). In a process that many scholars have referred to as the feminization of labour, neo-liberal economic policies and the movement of sites of mass production to Asia in the 1970s and 1980s led many women to leave their homes and families to work in large factories in New Economic Zones in Asian cities (Rege 2003: 4557). While this process has expanded many Asian women's employment and education opportunities and increased their independence from their families, working conditions are often very poor and women rarely enjoy benefits in casual labour arrangements (Bahramitash 2005). The complexities of the gendered impacts of globalization are apparent, for example, in the South Indian province of Kerala. As many men from Kerala migrate to the Gulf States for work, their wives who remain in India often gain higher social status with remittances from their husbands and also have increased freedom of movement in their husband's absence. However, an intensification of religious dogmas in Kerala, partly in response to the perceived imposition of globalization, has also resulted in greater restrictions on women's clothing and movement (Lindberg 2009). Likewise, in urban Azerbaijan increased costs of living continue to widen the gap between rich and poor but, in lower-income communities, this has also necessitated the relaxation of restrictions on women's interactions with men so that women can also contribute to supporting the family (Heyat 2006).

In other parts of Asia, struggles over women's rights have been also been influenced by transnational discourses and movements, especially democracy, Islamization and human rights (Hajjar 2004). Gender equality has been promoted at political and institutional levels, leading to greater awareness of and response to violence against women. However, in the Maldives and elsewhere a conservative Islamic backlash is asserting a more rigid gender hierarchy and women are being pushed into the domestic sphere. Kandiyoti (2007: 505) argues that women's rights have also become 'implicated in the geopolitical manoeuvrings of powerful global actors', for example, the United States' instrumentalist use of women's rights in *Operation Enduring Freedom* (Afghanistan invasion). The belief that international standards for women's rights are un-Islamic has reinforced male power over women as 'authentically Islamic'. Islamist movements have mobilized in many countries to demand a (re)turn to Islam and a commitment to preserve patriarchal family relations.

Furthermore, while in and of itself the veil is not a sign of oppression, within the global climate of Islamism, the dramatic increase in veiling represents another example of women's marginalization from public life. Adamson (2007) argues that in Java morality is seen as being threatened by consumer goods, globalization and influx of western values. However, the Shari'a-inspired legislation, including laws that restrict women's mobility and mandate their dress, that has been adopted to counter this particularly targets women and restricts women's rights. In Malaysia, there appears to be a trend towards rejecting diversity and secularism in favour of state regulation of behaviour, faith, identity, etc., and recent *fatwas* are reducing Malay Muslim women's rights (Aziz 2010). In Bangladesh there has been a recent backlash by fundamentalists against progress on women's rights. In April 2011 there was a shutdown ordered by the leader of the Islami Ain Bastabayan Committee (IABC; Islamic Law Implementation Committee), in response to the National Women's Development Policy (NWDP) 2011, which includes equal share for women in property and employment and business opportunities. Fundamentalists have called for scrapping of the NWDP, calling it anti-Islamic and anti-Qur'an (Bhattacharya 2011).

As discussed, the increasing fundamentalism in the Maldives is rarely a topic of public discussion. At the time of writing, a singular conservative discourse dominates the political and social landscape. Despite subtle signs of resistance, the majority of moderate voices on the interpretation of Islam have been silenced. Questions about who speaks for Islam are also being raised in other parts of Asia. For example, what Islam means and who represents the imagined Islamic community remain highly contested in Indonesia and, similar to the Maldives, there are two divergent tendencies regarding women's political participation: one promoting participation of women and one seeking to impose limits on women in the public sphere (Machrusah 2010). In Malaysia as well the state has become the sole interpreter and protector of Islam and there are diminishing spaces in which civil society can discuss issues related to gender and Islam (Aziz 2010).

This silence surrounding religious fundamentalism and women's increasing marginalization in the Maldives and in other parts of Asia sadly echoes the silence that has historically kept women's experiences of domestic violence hidden. The manifestations of globalization inevitably bring changes in women's lives and not least in the private sphere and in relation to their intimate relationships. Given that partner violence is both a consequence of gender equality and used to sustain gender inequality, these transformations at the political and institutional levels have the potential to increase women's vulnerability to violence in the home.

Notes

1 Similarly, Wieringa (2005) says that the process of Islamism in Indonesia is rarely a topic of discussion.
2 This is a different Ali Rasheed from the documentary filmmaker I interviewed and quote throughout this book.

5 A social crisis in the Maldives

> Intimate partner violence will be highest in societies where women are in a state of transition.
>
> (Krug *et al.* 2002: 99)

Maldivian communities were, until recently, generally cohesive, crime was rare and prevailing cultural norms did not legitimize violence as a way of dealing with problems. These were significant factors in keeping the prevalence of partner violence low. However, economic and social inequality, a lack of physical space and opportunities for the young and sheer boredom have led to what many Maldivians are calling a 'social crisis'. Symptoms of this crisis include an epidemic of heroin addiction, an increase in violent crime and a shift in notions of masculinity. Once-cohesive communities are becoming fragmented and the Maldivian geography of non-violence is being called into question. We are already witnessing an increase in women's risk of violence as a consequence of these changes and I argue that the prevalence of domestic violence will inevitably increase if things continue on the current trajectory.

In this chapter I first examine how some elements of globalization have contributed to the fragmentation of communities and a state of social disorganization. I show that economic development, while increasing GDP, has also created growing wealth disparity. In addition, mass internal migration has led to increased urbanization, housing problems and high rates of youth unemployment. Second, I explore how these factors have led to a social crisis. Finally, I consider how the symptoms of this social crisis are potentially impacting on partner violence. I argue that the drug epidemic in the Maldives has serious implications for women's safety at home and on the streets. The increasingly violent nature of society creates a situation in which people are more likely to learn that violence is an acceptable means of dealing with problems, putting women at increased risk. Furthermore, I suggest that many men feel a sense of powerlessness that is leading to a reconstruction of masculinity away from notions of calmness and rationality towards ideals of power, dominance and control.

112 *A social crisis in the Maldives*

In the context of globalization, social transformation affects all types of societies, in both developed and less developed regions (Castles 2001: 18). As Avtar Brah (2002: 30) argues, globalization is a complex and contradictory phenomenon with diverse impacts across distinct categories of people, localities, regions and hemispheres. This book therefore aims to humanize the large-scale economic and social transformations and thereby provide a means for both positive and negative readings of globalization on the ground.

On the one hand, global cultural flows in the Maldives have led to increased freedoms. Global ideologies of democracy and human rights have enabled greater freedom of expression, freedom of assembly and free and fair presidential elections. However, in 2012 we have seen some major steps backward in these gains. Global feminist discourses have promoted gender equality and initiated the discussion of gender-based violence. However, perhaps inevitably, such rapid and dramatic change has also created a sense of uncertainty and social disorganization. Many Maldivians refer to this as a social crisis.

One man I interviewed spoke thoughtfully and eloquently about the possible causes of the social crisis Maldivians are facing:

> There could be numerous reasons for the increase in violence and the so-called social crisis, such as Malé being so congested these days. People are living under very stressful conditions, sharing rather small spaces, having little or no privacy in some cases, not being able to sleep or rest adequately and in some of the extreme cases more than one person having to take turns to sleep on the same bed ... Paradoxically in such crowded situations we feel a sense of alienation from ourselves, from who we are, when people are constantly surrounded by people without any respite and at the same time being subtly but powerfully influenced by religious dogma and political rhetoric through the media.

In the media there has also been extensive discussion of these issues. Journalist Fathimath Musthaq (2006: 11) said that 'Malé became a population magnet a long time ago, and the ever increasing numbers are causing a number of social problems.' Ali Rasheed (2007a: 23), in an opinion piece published in *Minivan News*, explained that 'When the population itself is so tiny and so many factions have sprung up within factions, it is like an edifice rotten and hollow on the inside with no real strength'. In another newspaper article, Afrah Rasheed (2006c: 16) suggested that

> Once peaceful and quiet, the streets of Malé have now been transformed into wrestling compounds where the contestants engage themselves in battles so fierce that it only ends when the weaker part gets a severe beating, sometimes even causing them fatal injuries.

Economic development, urbanization and youth unemployment

The Maldives has experienced rapid economic development over the past three decades and now has the highest GDP per capita in South Asia. There has been an overall reduction in poverty and a significant rise in social indicators related to health and education. However, economic development has also been accompanied by a widening gap in the distribution of wealth, with some individuals profiting significantly from the tourism industry while others live in cramped conditions and relative poverty. In the Maldives, as Castles (2001: 18) argues with regard to development more broadly, uneven growth and social polarization are increasing the disadvantages and marginalization of significant groups.

Income distribution in the Maldives is now relatively unequal compared with neighbouring countries (Republic of Maldives 2006a: xx). The 2006 Vulnerability and Poverty Assessment shows that almost 21 per cent of the total population lives on less than 15 Rufiyaa a day (US$1 = 15Rf) (Republic of Maldives 2006a). Disparities between Malé and the atolls in terms of wealth and access to services such as health and education are particularly evident with a Gini coefficient of 0.41 recorded in 2006 (Republic of Maldives 2006a).[1]

Monetary wealth has become the defining character of status in recent years, creating a new class system in the Maldives. Although Maldivian society does not have a strict caste system as in India, it was stratified at the beginning of the twentieth century into royalty, upper class, middle class and local class. Traditionally, the upper classes were close friends and relatives of the sultan and his family. The English word 'class' does not easily translate in the Maldives, having no equivalent word in Dhivehi. Royal class (*beifulu*) is related to birth; however, middle class seems to be defined by the qualities a person demonstrates: by their education, wealth, service to the country and level of respectability. The lower classes include working-class people, such as fisherman, or women who carry out fish processing or handicrafts, boat builders, farmers and tradesmen. Nowadays these distinctions are breaking down, and wealth and education have become markers of status. As such people who have become economically marginalized feel particularly powerless. One man I interviewed suggested that

> People tend to place much emphasis on material wealth to enhance their self-image. Related to this are also the profound cultural changes that have taken place at a rapid rate in the Maldives, particularly in Malé. They suffer from status anxiety. They want power for its own sake generally rather than for the service of others.

With development opportunities centred in Malé there has been a mass migration to the capital city from all other parts of the country. Due to rapid urbanization the housing index for Malé deteriorated sharply between

1997 and 2004 (Republic of Maldives 2006a: xi). Food security in Malé also deteriorated over this period due to a dramatic increase in the cost of living because of the increasing population. As discussed earlier, the cost of housing is exceptionally high with many people having to share small rooms and rotate sleep times. Ibrahim Hameed (2006a) reported in the *Evening Weekly* that the number of beggars has also increased in Malé despite the overall increase in the development of the country.

Furthermore, according to the Vulnerability and Poverty Assessment (VPAII) there has been a substantial deterioration in the employment index over the last few years. Labour-force participation rates have increased but there are rising problems of unemployment, particularly among the youth (Republic of Maldives 2006a). In Malé, unemployment rates among 20–24 year olds increased from 6 to 10 per cent for males and from 10 to 18 per cent for females between 2000 and 2006 (Republic of Maldives 2008a). In the atolls it increased from 7 to 10 per cent for males and for females it was substantially higher at 34 per cent in both 2000 and 2006.

The Maldives has a young age profile with 32 per cent of the overall population aged between 18 and 34 years (Republic of Maldives 2008a) and the unmet expectations and aspirations of young people seem to be contributing to a 'social crisis'. Economic development has enabled more students to undertake tertiary education overseas. However, a number of Maldivians note that those who have high levels of education often feel underutilized and somewhat 'lost' when they return to Malé. Inaya Shareef wrote in a feature in the *Evening Weekly* about feelings of hopelessness among young people in the Maldives. She shared an example of a young man returning to Malé to work for the government after studying overseas:

> The same young man sits in a fluorescent-lit, poorly air-conditioned room ... there is no hope in his eyes. His shoulders are drooping and he sits hunched over his table. He's not doing anything, but then he isn't given any work. He had ideas to make things better ... He had come into the cramped cubicle of a government department all full of innovation and a desire for service ... He has been shot down so many times, there is no fight left in him.
>
> (Shareef 2006: 18)

Another person explained to me that the impact of spending so many years overseas means that young Maldivians have lost their cultural connection and sense of belonging:

> Young people, particularly teenagers are being sent overseas to study in their most formative years, quite often with the best of intentions. But it has a huge influence on their sense of belonging. They are extracted

from their cultural roots and placed on foreign soil and they have to establish new roots which means having to redefine their identity. They generally live isolated lives overseas. I think that they experience a sense of inadequacy, a kind of hollowness, which can never be overcome easily.

I have personally witnessed this problem among many highly educated Maldivians of my age who studied overseas. Returning to the confines of an overcrowded two-square-kilometre island can be extremely challenging. This is especially true for young women who are returning to an increasingly conservative society where they feel that their freedoms have been curtailed.

This is perhaps aggravated by the fact that beyond promoting a religious identity, the state has done little to preserve and promote Maldivian cultural traditions as the country has opened up to global cultural flows through tourism and industrialization. There is only one small museum in the Maldives that most Maldivians have never seen – only a few tourists visit it. There is little value placed on arts, dance and literature, and history before Islam is ignored altogether.

Political divides and social disorganization

As discussed in the Introduction, the process of democratization and political reform has also created many divisions in the Maldives and an increase in violence. This has been most visible recently in 2012 with the resignation of President Nasheed and the mass protests by both Islamic hardliners and those calling for new elections. Amnesty International and human rights activists have condemned the heavy-handed response of the police and army. There were important gains made in the democratic process given that only a couple of years ago public assembly was deemed illegal and protests and demonstrations of any kind were virtually unheard of. However, the current state of political tension reflects greater ideological, religious and political divisions within communities. Maldivian ethnographer, Razee (2006: 49), suggests that the riots in 2003 in the capital island were an example of these increasing tensions and that kind of rioting and public expression of dissatisfaction was 'only the second such incident in the entire history of the Maldives'.

Post-tsunami democratization in the Maldives has taken place very rapidly. There was no programme of civic education leading up to the introduction of a multi-party system in 2005, and many people are still struggling to understand what it all means. Despite assumptions that introducing democracy will always benefit the people, many Maldivians I spoke to were not in favour of establishing a multi-party political system. They felt it would bring instability to the country and create tension in what they described as a relatively unified nation. Some say islands have been virtually split down the middle by the new political party system: those who support the DRP on one side and those who support the MDP on the other. A magazine article entitled 'The great divider' discusses how party politics has divided families and friends, and one person is quoted as humorously saying, 'I don't mind a wedding party or a birthday party. I don't like political parties' (Didi 2006: 19).

The establishment of a multi-party political system in the Maldives has also enabled increasingly conservative religious discourses to take hold, undermining women's position in society. It is possible that the rise in Islamism also stems in part from the high level of uncertainty caused by so many other social changes taking place in the Maldives. It has often been suggested that religion gives purpose to those who need or desire certainty. One Maldivian explained to me: 'There are tens of thousands of Maldivians who are aimless and lost, living on two square kilometres. They are unoccupied and jobless ... They dream of better times and religion grants them an eternity of it.'

Islamism is taking place side-by-side with a greater influence of international human rights discourse, new communications technology, as well as American and Indian culture, which has challenged the social cohesion of Maldivian communities. Opinion writer Aminath Shauna (2008) says,

> As the country has changed dramatically over the past few years, the way people practice and perceive religion has also been subjected to change. The divide was seen at its starkest with the Maldives' first extremist bomb attack last year.

On 29 September 2007, a homemade bomb blamed on Islamic militants exploded in Malé's Sultan Park, injuring 12 tourists. A number of men were arrested and charged over what was determined to be a terrorist attack. In 2009 religious conflict had become a matter of such concern that the new Ministry of Islamic Affairs formed a 17-member committee to address it.

While globalization, migration and urbanization have brought positive changes to Maldivian society, they have also challenged the integrity of local communities and created a sense of uncertainty and fragmentation. While on each island everyone used to know everyone, people are becoming more faceless. Increasingly neighbours in Malé in particular do not know each other and families tend to keep to themselves. This is of particular concern because of the association that has been established between social cohesion and violence against women. For example, Frye *et al.* (2008: 1473) found in the United States that 'the effects of macro-level processes such as industrialization, urbanization, and immigration alter a neighbourhood's social structure and weaken its cohesiveness', which increases the risk of violence against women.

This social disorganization in the Maldives has contributed to what many in the Maldives are referring to as a social crisis, including a drug epidemic and a rise in crime and violence. In recent years, drug use (cannabis, hashish, glue, cologne as a substitute for alcohol which is illegal and difficult to access, and heroin) has become a serious problem, especially among the youth populations. Injecting drug use has become more widespread and 'brown sugar' (unrefined heroin cut with impurities) is now the most common drug in the Maldives. UNICEF says that up to 30 per cent of young people on some islands are now using banned narcotics. In 2006 Ken Maskall, the then head of UNICEF in the Maldives, reported that 'the average age of first use of drugs in the Maldives is twelve years, but some children are known to have started using as young as nine' (*Haveeru News Service* 2006). The National Narcotics Control Bureau (NNCB) estimates that 10,000 to 20,000 people are addicted to drugs in the Maldives, but others put the likely figure closer to 30,000 (Evans 2008). According to the Rapid Situation Assessment of Drug Abuse in the Maldives conducted in 2003 by the Narcotics Control Board, 90 per cent of drug abusers are male and approximately 20 per cent are less than 20 years of age (NNCB 2003). However, according to the Society for Women against Drugs, there are more than 35,000 known drug addicts in the country and among them a large percentage are minors and young girls (Mohamed 2007).

Drugs have become readily available and relatively cheap. In an article in *Minivan News*, a young man on Gaafu Dhaalu Atoll explained that 'There is nothing to do here. If you don't use drugs, you go crazy. There's nothing to do on this island ... most people use because we get so bored' (quoted in Rasheed 2008). Others say that most people start using drugs because of curiosity and peer pressure, enhanced by the small island population and even smaller youth population who all know each other (*Minivan News* 2005). 'Brown sugar' is also highly addictive and rehabilitation services are extremely limited. There is only one rehabilitation centre in the Maldives; it has a long waiting list and is acutely under-staffed and under-resourced. As a result, the majority of drug addicts end up in prison. In fact 80 per cent of the inmates in Maafushi Prison are drug addicts. A methadone programme was launched in the prison for the first time in 2008 (Evans 2008).

According to Frye *et al.* (2008: 1473), social cohesion is a key component in the ability of a community to informally control violence and social and health problems. In the Maldives, too, a breakdown in social cohesion is connected to an increase in violence. Numerous articles have appeared in the media questioning what has happened to the 'peaceful' nation of the Maldives. Hursheed (2006: 12) says, 'not long ago, even the concept of gang wars in the Maldives would have been a ridiculous one ... [but] the sudden increase in incidents ... have proved without a doubt that street gangs are waging all out war'. In another newspaper article, Rasheed (2006c: 16) indicates that while violent behaviour used to be unacceptable it has become more normalized and people are less likely to intervene in violent incidents than they used to be. Rasheed (2006c: 16), like many other Maldivians that I spoke with, laments 'How did our loving community become so vindictive and malicious over the years?' A government employee said that while Maldivians generally have not supported violence as a way of resolving things, 'Now because we have such a huge drug problem there are people who are exploiting those people, because they can be exploited very easily, so they are taking advantage of gangs and these people to push violence.'

The Maldives has witnessed a recent spate of attacks against Bangladeshi expatriate workers in the Maldives, which reflects a rise in racism and xenophobia. Expatriate workers now face almost daily attacks and one foreign worker was brutally murdered in 2007 and another was found imprisoned by his employer inside a house in Malé shackled in iron chains. In August 2007, four South Asian embassies wrote a joint letter to the Maldivian Foreign Ministry pressuring the government to step up security measures (H. Rasheed 2007).

The general increase in crime and violence in Maldivian society has been accompanied by an increase in violence against women in particular. Prior to 2005 sexual assault or rape cases were virtually unheard of; now they are reported in the newspapers almost every day. It is likely that this is due in part to greater reporting of violence against women, stemming from increased awareness of this issue. However, there has also been a tangible increase in the number of violent crimes against women committed in recent years (CEDAW 2007; Hama Jamiyya 2006).

A 'social crisis' and women's experiences of violence

Increasing levels of economic inequality and economic hardship faced by many families are of concern because of the consistent associations found around the world between inequality and low socio-economic status and intimate partner violence. According to conflict theory, any form of inequality is a risk factor for violence, with societies that have a high degree of economic inequality having higher rates of violence (Blau and Blau 1982; Williams 1984). Although violence against women occurs across all socio-economic classes, there is evidence that it is more common in families with low incomes and unemployed men (Andersson *et al.* 2009; Garcia-Moreno *et al.* 2005; Hoffman *et al.* 1994; Hotaling and Sugarman 1986; Nelson and Zimmerman 1996; O'Campo *et al.* 1995). It is not clear, however, how low socio-economic status and unemployment operate to increase the risk of abuse. It may be not just the lack of income but crowding or hopelessness that is significant, generating stress and frustration, increasing marital conflict, or a sense of inadequacy in men for failing to provide economically (Heise 1998: 274–5).

The breakdown in the social fabric and close-knit nature of communities leads to social isolation that also makes women more vulnerable to abuse. In Chapter 2 I explored how social isolation can be a common element in violent relationships as controlling men prevent their wives from seeing family or friends, or even leaving the house, in some instances. However, social isolation can also contribute to the likelihood of intimate partner violence occurring because socially isolated people lack the support networks of close kin, friends and neighbours. As Brown (1992: 12) explains, 'A wife is in a much more vulnerable position and there is a far greater likelihood that she will be ill-treated, if she is isolated from her family'. Nielsen *et al.* (1992) found that isolation of the woman and her family preceded battering, although isolation tended to increase as a relationship became more violent. In the Maldives Survey we found that women who lived close by and had regular contact with their family of birth were less likely to experience intimate partner violence. For example, Hawwa explained that living with her family offered a form of protection: 'My family didn't bring me up by being violent, so they don't want that to happen to me from him either. And as I live with him in my family home, he hesitates to get violent.' However, Hawwa explained that when she moved away from her network of support the violence became worse. She said, 'He asked me to go with him to his island. He took me there and was more violent than before. He even kept me at home with no food and didn't give me anything.' When Hawwa became socially isolated by moving to her husband's island where she did not know anyone she became more vulnerable to abuse as well as increased isolation, with her husband forcing her to stay in the home.

Fathimath shared a similar story. One day during Ramazan, Fathimath saw her husband eating and when she asked him not to he became angry and shoved her and pushed her onto the floor. 'My arms were bruised and I was badly hurt and reported the matter to the police on the island', she explained. He was banished to another island for three months for not fasting; however, he was not punished or charged for abusing Fathimath. She said, 'I went to live with him on the island he had been banished to and the violence became more and more intense. We moved to another island and still the violence continued to escalate'. Other non-western research examples also suggest that the shift in family structure from three-generational households to nuclear families 'may precipitate a form of family isolation and a lack of kin and social support that may be vital to reducing wife abuse' (Hoffman *et al.* 1994: 143).

The drug epidemic in the Maldives has the potential to increase women's exposure to violence in a number of ways. The association between intimate partner violence and drug abuse in the Maldives is extremely significant. As in other countries, women who have a partner who uses drugs are at much higher risk of experiencing intimate partner violence. In fact, we found that Maldivian women are nearly *11* times more likely to experience domestic violence if their partner has used intoxicating substances than if he has never used intoxicating substances.

Women and young girls who are drug addicts are at increased risk of violence in the home and are more likely to enter into sex work or sexually abusive situations. The NNCB report (2003) revealed high-risk sexual behaviour among drug addicts. An article in *Adduvas* magazine supports this finding, telling the story of a young couple where the girl has sex with a different man each day in return for enough money for a 'hit' for them both (Ali 2006). A former drug dealer in Malé who is now part of an anti-drug campaign also admits to having sexual encounters with countless young girls (some as young as 14) in exchange for drugs (Ali 2006).

The impact of increasing violence and shifting masculinities

The general increase in violence discussed above also has significant implications for women's experiences of intimate partner violence. As I demonstrated in Chapter 3, social violence in the Maldives has historically been rare, with a low crime rate and murder and rape virtually unheard of. This helps to explain the comparatively low prevalence of intimate partner violence. However, with violence and crime on the rise, there is cause for concern. For example, according to the Maldives Survey, women whose partner had been in at least one physical fight with another man were significantly more likely to experience partner violence. In fact, women whose partner was violent with other men were nearly *eight* times more likely to report partner violence than women whose partner had never been violent with other men.

The increase in violence in part reflects a shift in Maldivian masculinities, which has further implications for women's exposure to violence. As discussed in Chapter 2 Maldivian notions of masculinity associated with calmness and rationality have contributed to a lower rate of partner violence compared to other regional countries. However, as Marchand and Runyan (2000: 18) point out, globalization entails reworkings of the boundaries between and meanings of femininity and masculinity.

In the Maldives, some young men are now involved in gang violence and violent crime. It appears that manhood is now being performed by physically fighting in the street, riding a large motorbike, sexually harassing women and being muscular and tough. Shaarif Ali, a young man in his early thirties, said, 'It seems as if violence has even become fashionable among the youth as the best way to demonstrate their authority and to settle scores. Gang rivalry is largely believed to be behind the majority of fights'. In contrast, notions of femininity related to domesticity and seclusion are being emphasized. Shaarif Ali explained, 'The growing Islamic fundamentalism does have an influence on determining masculinity and femininity for those who conform to such beliefs. Women become passive by covering up with head scarves and full veils and many are staying home'. Men are also learning new notions of masculinity through the global reach of television, film, music and the Internet. In the Indian and American action movies that Maldivian young men tend to watch violence is valorized as manly.

Typically, violence against women has been theorized as an expression of men's power, domination and control over women, and we certainly see elements of that in Maldivian women's experiences. However, Kimmel

(2007) has rightly pointed out that men, as a group, may be in power but individually they often feel powerless. One man explained to me in a personal interview that in the Maldives,

> The general population also experiences a sense of powerlessness and many individuals do not have any sense of control over their own destiny. As a result of the huge cultural changes people are facing, individuals often do not have any idea of their place or usefulness in society.

Similarly, in a feature article in the *Evening Weekly*, Inaya Shareef wrote 'An equation for rebellion', outlining a number of stories of everyday Maldivians who have lost hope. She wrote,

> While bureaucracy sprawled unchecked across the nation, the common people stood by silently, wondering how it would help them. Frustration at this failing system, desperation at being helpless all boiled close to the surface, waiting and waiting for a release.
>
> (Shareef 2006: 19)

Similarly, Gerami (2005) suggests that, contrary to expectations, in countries in the Middle East implementing Shari'a law, men are not faring better in terms of money, education and standards of living.

As society changes, violence is becoming a means by which men construct a new form of masculinity: a compensatory method of exerting control when they feel that their authority has been called into question. Many men are unable to fulfil their role as breadwinners due to socio-economic changes and shifting gender roles. Others live in cramped conditions and feel isolated and bored in the concrete jungle of Malé. It is possible that violence has become a means by which men can perform masculinity to compensate for their disempowerment. In fact the survey data showed that women who were earning more money than their husband were more likely to experience intimate partner violence. Kimmel (2007) suggests partner violence becomes 'more about getting the power to which you feel you're entitled than an expression of the power you already have'.

It should also be noted that a number of young Maldivian men, especially those who have been in more privileged positions and had access to tertiary-level education, do not associate masculinity with violence or aggression. Many men in their late twenties and early thirties told me that 'there is no excuse to be violent' and suggested that they would not tolerate violence against women. For example, one man said, 'If one of my friends showed violence towards his wife or girlfriend, then I would advise him to stop it and if he doesn't then I will not hang around with him any more.' Perhaps those who have not been as exposed to symptoms of the social crisis or a growing sense of powerlessness have had less need to take on alternative models of masculinity. Rather they maintain notions of masculinity associated with independence, confidence, education and rationality similar to what men of an older generation spoke of (see Chapter 3). As Gerami (2005) suggests with regard to Islamist and Muslim masculinities in the Middle East, despite presentations in western media, Islamic fundamentalism does not have wide appeal for these young, urban men.

Conclusion

Maldivian society has changed radically since the late nineteenth century. The Maldives has shifted from an isolated small island culture based primarily on subsistence to an overcrowded, industrialized country, open to various global cultural flows. The sheer speed at which life has been transformed, particularly since 2000, is hard for many Maldivians to believe. While a number of positive changes can be noted, it is perhaps inevitable that various elements of the social change that I have discussed throughout this book have led to a heightened level of social disorganization, where social bonds have been weakened. Some groups in particular have been more negatively affected than others by the processes of globalization and have experienced increasing poverty and marginalization.

We are currently witnessing a social crisis in the Maldives with a drug epidemic, high levels of youth unemployment, increasing crime and violence, and political instability. All of these symptoms combine to increase women's vulnerability to intimate partner violence. Increasing levels of economic inequality and economic hardship faced by many families are of concern because of the consistent associations found around the world between inequality and low socio-economic status and intimate partner violence. The breakdown in social fabric and close-knit communities leads to social isolation that also makes women more vulnerable to abuse. Furthermore, the heroin epidemic puts women at increased risk of partner abuse, as well as increased risk of entering into sexually abusive situations to support their own drug habit.

It appears that marginalized groups of young men in particular are expressing their feelings of powerlessness through drugs, gang culture and violence perhaps in a desperate attempt to regain control and power. For some, ideals of masculinity are shifting from notions of calmness and rationality to a focus on power, control and aggression. Overall, the non-violent nature of Maldivian society that has helped protect women from intimate partner violence in the past is disappearing. The dramatic increase in crime and violence in the Maldives is potentially creating a cultural ethos that condones violence as a means of dealing with problems.

Such negative manifestations of globalization are evident far beyond the Maldives. Pateman (2008:4) argues that globally neo-liberal economic doctrines have led to a rapid increase in social inequality and economic insecurities both within and between communities. Similarly, Castles (2001: 18) points out that globalization is leading to polarization between rich and poor as well as social exclusion at national and international levels. According to Bahramitash (2005), the market economy in Southeast Asia has increased women's employment but exacerbated poverty. There has been an inflation in the prices of basic goods and services, a decline in male employment, a shift towards less-skilled, low-wage and casual employment for women and an increase in women's burden of work in the family and community (Bahramitash 2005).

The influx of global socio-cultural and religious flows, as well as information from the Internet, is inevitably impacting on gender roles among Asia's population. Gerami (2005) suggests that this population's masculine identity will be influenced greatly by hegemonic global economic and cultural forces. Steve Derné (2008) suggests that cultural globalization, in particular the proliferation of cable television and foreign movies, may be intensifying men's attraction to violent masculinities in India. He says that cultural globalization gives men new ideas about how to act out oppressive gender hierarchies (Derné 2008: 137).

As in the Maldives, examples from other Asian countries indicate that the shifting gender norms and the marginalization that men may experience can contribute to an increase in violence against women. Research indicates that men often initiate violence against women when they feel a loss of power or are unable to fulfil hegemonic masculinity (Eves 2007; ICRW 2002; Jewkes *et al.* 2002; Josephides 1994). In India, Papua New Guinea and East Africa, it has been found that partner violence is linked to failed masculinity and a backlash against changing gender roles (Eves 2007; ICRW 2002; Silberschmidt 2001). According to large-scale surveys in Eastern India and Pakistan, women being in paid employment or making a greater contribution to family income was found to be a risk factor for partner violence (Andersson *et al.* 2009; Babu and Kar 2010). Spark (2011) found that in Papua New Guinea educated women are particularly vulnerable to partner violence because of strong class tensions and labelling of university-educated women as symbols of 'all that is wrong with contemporary PNG society'. According to Eves (2007: 53), 'helping women to gain greater financial independence and to be more assertive of their rights seems to bring more rather than less domestic violence'.

But it is also important to remember that, as in the Maldives, globalization has also encouraged cultural tolerance and political liberalization and Muslim masculinities are also responding to this (Gerami 2005). For example, Iranian liberal masculinities are anti-Islamist and anti-*shahid* and are an attempt to design an Islamized modernism compatible with pluralism, reformation and dismantling of religious jurisprudence. Progressive Muslim men are also reinterpreting the Qur'an to espouse new constructions of Muslim identity focusing on tolerance and gender equality (Gerami 2005).

Historically the Maldives had a relatively low prevalence of partner violence. However, the Maldives is changing. We only have prevalence data on domestic violence in the Maldives from 2006 so it is difficult to conclusively prove an increase in prevalence, either from before 2006 or after 2006. However, all the factors that have historically kept domestic violence low in the Maldives are being challenged. Therefore, it is almost inevitable that this will lead to an increase in such violence. Looking more closely at the data from the Maldives Study by age we see that the prevalence of lifetime and current (experienced in the 12 months prior to interview) intimate partner violence is highest among women aged 25–29 years, which is also the age when most women marry for the first time. In contrast, in most other studies from other countries, there is an expected pattern of a higher prevalence of lifetime violence by an intimate partner among older women because they have been exposed to the risk of violence longer than younger women. While not conclusive, it may suggest that partner violence is becoming more common and accepted among the younger generation in the Maldives. This is supported by qualitative and ethnographic data that I have presented, particularly with regard to changing attitudes, norms and expectations about masculinities, femininities and gender roles. According to the Ministry of Gender there has also been an increase in the number of cases of domestic violence reported in 2008 and 2009, and the United States' 2009 Annual Country Report on Human Rights expressed concern for increased violence against women in the Maldives (US Department of State 2010a). Furthermore, a coalition of Maldivian NGOs and the Human Rights Commission Maldives recently condemned the rise in crime, including sexual violence and rape, and the failure of the state and authorities to hold perpetrators accountable (Ortega 2010). I suggest that domestic violence is increasing and will continue to do so if the various risk factors discussed in this book are not addressed.

Notes

1 The Gini coefficient is a measure of statistical dispersion most prominently used as a measure of inequality of income distribution or inequality of wealth distribution. It is defined as a ratio with values between 0 and 1: a low Gini coefficient indicates more equal income or wealth distribution, while a high Gini coefficient indicates more unequal distribution.

Conclusion
Creating peace cultures: the way forward

The Maldives has one of the lowest rates of domestic violence in Asia, and, in fact, in the world. The Maldives is certainly not free from violence; however, learning from a relatively non-violent society has profound implications for the direction of violence-prevention work. It shows us that violence against women is not inevitable, and helps us to envisage a future where families, communities and cultures are non-violent and gender equitable, and where relationships are respectful and non-discriminatory. Freeman (2001) argues that global processes are shaped, limited and redefined by local sites and actors. Similarly, I believe that global discourses and strategies on violence against women can be influenced by local experiences from a small island nation in South Asia.

Despite decades of work and millions of dollars spent trying to end violence against women, unfortunately there has been no aggregate decrease in the prevalence of domestic violence in Asia. In fact, I argue that the processes of globalization are contributing to an increase in intimate partner violence in the Maldives and possibly elsewhere. Until now there has been a necessary focus on highlighting violence against women as a serious human rights, development and public health issue with major consequences for individuals, communities and societies. This has been vital in bringing the issue to global attention, leading to much-needed legislative reform and improvements in health sector and criminal justice responses. However, while responding to the aftermath of violence remains essential, it alone will have only a limited impact on reducing violence itself. I believe that focusing primarily on the tragedy of the situation, only having a 'single story' (Adichie 2011), has limited our progress in ending violence against women. However, in the conclusion to this book I present the way forward for the field of violence against women, as I see it, based on the experiences from the Maldives.

Globalization from below: understanding domestic violence

Domestic violence is truly a global issue, and crosses borders both metaphorically and physically. It can no longer be understood outside the reality of globalization and social change. The example of the Maldives illustrates the double-edged nature of globalization. On the positive side, globalization and transnational feminist practice has promoted discourses on women's rights and brought the issue of violence against women into the spotlight (Grewal and Kaplan 1994; Kaplan 1994; Mohanty 2003). The Survey on Violence against Women in the Maldives was in and of itself a global process, using a global methodology that provides comparable data with countries as diverse as Peru, Tanzania, New Zealand and Japan (Garcia -Moreno et al. 2005). Globalization has contributed to economic growth and democratic reform. The Maldives had its first free and fair elections in 2008, and a new president was elected for the first time in 30 years, no doubt in part due to forces of globalization.

Despite the positive outcomes of globalization, this book has shown that the dramatic social changes that have accompanied the global flows of ideas, media, discourses and capital are in many ways eroding the very elements that have historically protected women in the Maldives from high rates of partner violence. With migration, urbanization and overcrowding, family homes have become structurally more closed and private, increasing the likelihood of violence taking place. The consumption of new ideals around love and romance through 'white weddings' and Bollywood love stories is challenging the once flexible and fluid practices of marriage and divorce. Divorce is becoming more difficult to access and more socially stigmatized, which puts women at increased risk of being trapped in violent relationships.

The global phenomenon of Islamism is being played out at multiple levels in the Maldives and is influencing gender relations and women's experiences of violence. I have suggested that there has been a backlash against attempts to promote gender equality in the Maldives with some groups reconstructing the idealized woman as a domesticated, dependent wife and mother. The erosion of the status of women is also reflected in the increasing prevalence of veiling and it is of concern that public debate around Islamism and patriarchy has been silenced. While the majority of Maldivians do not support fundamentalist ideologies, such views dominate public discourse while more moderate responses have been suppressed. Such changes have the very real potential to make women more vulnerable to experiences of violence by intimate partners.

Rapid social change has led to what many in the Maldives are calling a social crisis. The Maldives has witnessed mass internal migration that has led to increased urbanization, housing problems and high rates of youth unemployment. This has challenged the integrity of local communities and weakened the regulatory powers of social norms. Such a lack of social cohesion has the potential to increase violence, in part because it creates an experience of social isolation for women. Community fragmentation and increasing unemployment, among other things, have also led to a drug epidemic in the Maldives, which has serious implications for women's safety at home and on the streets. Crime is on the rise and the increasingly violent nature of society has the potential to create a situation where people learn that violence is an acceptable means of dealing with problems.

With globalization Maldivians are negotiating shifting meanings of femininity and masculinity. Young men in particular are experiencing a growing sense of powerlessness and are less able to fulfil hegemonic ideas of masculinity such as being the breadwinner of the family. Some men are therefore constructing alternative masculinities that promote dominance, power and control. It appears that this is already contributing to an increase in violence against women, with a rise in the number of rape cases in the Maldives. It is likely that this will also lead to an increase in violence in the home.

Concerns about women's economic marginalization, growing social isolation, increasing Islamism and men's feelings of powerlessness are shared by many other nations in Asia. While acknowledging the benefits that globalization has brought in terms of economic growth, the promotion of democratic principles and gender equality, we should be aware of the potentially detrimental impact globalization may have on women's experiences of violence in Asia. This requires progressive thinking and anticipation of the new challenges to gender equality. Globally, we must enhance feminist work that confronts pervasive conservative religious discourses around the world and the potentially negative impact they have on women's rights and position within society. We must work to address increasing levels of social disorganization and social isolation that reduce women's access to informal support networks such as friends and family. We must tackle the unequal benefits of economic development and the increasing social marginalization of women *and* men.

Holistic responses to domestic violence

Domestic violence cannot be understood as an isolated experience, or even from within a single country context. It must be examined within a larger human context. Work on violence against women has generally remained compartmentalized at the individual and family level. However, this book has shown that a complete understanding of gender violence requires looking at institutional, societal and even global patterns and practices. Violence does not have a single cause and is related to the convergence of specific factors within the broad context of power inequalities at the individual, community, national and global levels (Garcia-Moreno *et al.* 2005; Heise 1998; UN General Assembly 2006). Violence at the individual level is reproduced by the cultures of political, economic and social institutions and legitimized by ideologies that sanction hierarchies based not only on gender but other axes of inequality. This is particularly evident when we observe the linkages between economic marginalization, urbanization and social isolation or between global fundamentalism, education, divorce laws and local discourses on women's position within society.

Quantum physicist David Bohm's (1980) conception of order is useful in helping us understand such interconnectedness. From his perspective, all human beings are part of that unbroken whole that is continually unfolding. He articulates the fundamental idea that at a level we cannot see, there is an unbroken wholeness, or what he calls an 'implicate order' out of which seemingly discrete events arise (Bohm 1980). Therefore, seemingly separate events such as the industrialization of the fishing industry or the proliferation of Bollywood movies inevitably impact on the whole. From this perspective we can see that simplistic, piecemeal approaches to addressing violence against women that have dominated the field are inevitably unsuccessful because they fail to address the wholeness in which this phenomenon sits.

By taking a holistic approach we recognize that we need to work across multiple levels, in particular tackling the underlying causes of social violence including inequality, oppression, social isolation and marginalization, civil conflict and alcohol and drug abuse. For example, the dowry and bride price practices that are often associated with violence require attention (Rastogi and Therly 2006; Secretariat of the Pacific Community 2009; Umar 1998; Zaman 2005). Furthermore, transforming marriage practices that isolate a woman from her family of birth after marriage could be effective in reducing rates of violence. Promoting free and equal access to divorce rights and addressing any socio-cultural elements that stigmatize divorce or keep women trapped in abusive relationships is vital. The Maldives case study also highlights that prevention strategies must promote gender equality and empower women and girls. This may include promoting women's representation in the public sphere, including parliament, the judiciary and high-level managerial positions, and increasing women and girl's access to education.

The links between violence against children, male-on-male violence and violence against women indicates that prevention efforts need to address multiple forms of violence as interconnected. Prevention work should therefore include early childhood and family-based approaches, ending violence against children and corporal punishment, promoting positive parenting practices and integrating programmes on respectful relationships into the school curriculum. Flaherty (2010) suggests, and I agree, that we need education models that challenge authoritarian values and teach collaboration and respect and these models must dovetail with service provision. Such education and training ought to be about promoting creative and innovative citizens of humanity.

While violence prevention in the past has tended to focus on women's empowerment, this book indicates that work with boys and men needs to be prioritized alongside work with women and girls. Risk factor analysis in Chapter 2 clearly showed that male partner characteristics impact more significantly on women's risk of violence than women's own characteristics. The same has been found in other countries where similar research has been undertaken, such as in the Solomon Islands and Kiribati (Secretariat of the Pacific Community 2009, 2010). Many researchers agree that in order to address violence against women it is essential to challenge dominant models of masculinity (Eves 2007; Flood 2001; Michau 2005) and the Maldives example shows that notions of masculinity are not static or unchangeable. While the Maldives case study presents a trend towards more violent and dominant forms of masculinity, it also shows that change is possible. Further, it makes clear, as does recent research on alternative models of masculinity in Pakistan (Rozan 2012), that work on violence against women must connect the privilege associated with men's lives to men's own experiences of victimization and shifting power and authority.

Recent research on men's use of violence against women indicates that dominant notions of masculinity and violence practices are learnt early in life so prevention efforts must target young boys and men (Naved *et al.* 2011). Societies that have a hegemonic definition of masculinity connected to notions of aggression and violence should work on rescripting masculinities towards a culture of non-violence. This could include community mobilization programmes that encourage men, women and communities to examine their assumptions about gender norms and masculinity, understanding that changing social norms is a long-term process. Looking at the Maldives as a model in this regard could be useful in promoting notions of masculinity that stem from self-control, calmness and respect. Other promising practices include fatherhood programmes, sports and recreation programmes such as 'coaching boys into men', and school-based health relationship programmes with single-sex sessions.

However, broad sustainable change is only achieved when such activities are implemented in long-term and cumulative ways, mutually reinforced across various settings. One example of a systematic, sustained and cross-sectoral prevention policy is the Australian state government policy, *A Right to Respect: Victoria's Plan to Prevent Violence against Women 2010–2012* (State of Victoria 2009). While a change of government meant it was not implemented, it is still a useful example of a 'whole-of-government' approach that other countries could learn from. Significantly, the *Right to Respect* example and other studies have found that when it comes to ending violence, men, women and communities are more receptive to positive messages outlining what can be done rather than negative messages that promote fear or blame (Berkowitz 2004a, 2004b; Chattopadhay 2004; Kauffman 2001; McMahon and Dick 2011).

Creating peace cultures through positive approaches

A primary assumption of positive approaches is that in all human systems there are things that work well, or have in the past, and that these can be built on in envisioning and implementing system change (Liebler and

Sampson 2010). Positive approaches have a forward-looking orientation to producing change. Rather than focusing on analysing the ills of the past they place an emphasis on visioning and creating a positive image of a preferred future. Positive approaches should be culturally relevant and contextualized to each new situation. They value diversity as a source of creativity and innovation and offer tools for bringing people together to discover shared values and a common future (Sampson 2010: 5). This is what we need in violence prevention and the Maldives offers an example of a low-prevalence culture upon which we can build and envision social change.

In the Maldives, the relatively low prevalence of partner violence is associated with gender equitable attitudes and an open and peaceable culture. Based on this case study, I propose that we need a fundamental paradigm shift in the way we understand and respond to violence against women. I believe that to help end violence against women we need to work towards creating cultures of peace, not simply 'non-violence'. Flaherty (2010) similarly argues that to create a world beyond intimate partner abuse requires an active, constructive focus on skills for 'living peace' and truly healthy living.

Making a shift in the discourse from stopping violence to creating peace helps us to see the bigger picture. While work on violence against women tends to be compartmentalized at the individual or family level, peace building is seen as a lifelong process; a continuum from the family to global institutions (Boulding and Ikeda 2010). This change in discourse also helps us to move from a deficit, problem-focused model of violence prevention to a creative, positive model, and positive approaches have much greater potential to tap into the potential power of human beings to create meaningful social change.

The distinction in language that I am talking about, and the power it has to change practice, is perhaps well represented by the Hiroshima Peace Park in Japan that stands in stark contrast to other war memorials. The Peace Park's purpose is to advocate for peace, rather than simply memorialize victims of war. Peace declarations are made every year and the mayor of Hiroshima pledges that the city will do everything in its power to abolish nuclear weapons and build lasting world peace.

It may seem like an impossible task to create peaceful societies in the midst of such violence, oppression and inequality that the world faces. However, peace activist and teacher, Elise Boulding (in Boulding and Ikeda 2010: 92), referencing the Dutch sociologist Fred Polak, shows that 'societies that believe in their own future repeatedly demonstrated the dynamic power to overcome hardships creatively. But societies that were apathetic and fearful could not generate the energy needed for positive change'. So while positive violence prevention approaches require the focus of another book entirely, it is useful to share some positive examples to start the discussion on a paradigm shift in the field of violence prevention.

Safer cities projects that aim to challenge planning's gendered nature towards securitizing urban spaces and present alternative approaches to making safer places have had some success. The Making Safer Places project, run by Women's Design Service from 2003 to 2005, had the purpose of empowering local women in Bristol, London and Manchester to improve the design, access and facilities in their neighbourhoods (Beebeejaun 2009). Comité d'action femmes et sécurité urbaine (CAFSU) in Montreal is challenging paternalistic ways of thinking about tackling violence against women (Beebeejaun 2009). We can also look at the Gandhigram (Gandhi Villages) in India where they aim to create a classless society based on Gandhi's teachings of non-violence.

The power of creativity to prevent violence is reflected in the Big hART social change arts organization. It worked in a notorious central Sydney housing estate nicknamed 'Suicide Towers', enabling it to become the first public housing estate to achieve WHO designation as a Safe Community. Big hART produced various art pieces and films and ultimately saw safety to be about social connectedness and relationships, agency, well-being, functional physical environment and a positive image within the broader community (Coggan *et al.* 2008). The project showed that art can enable people to become more employable, more involved, more confident and more active in contributing to the development of their local communities.

Another example that takes a positive, peace-promoting approach is Youth Empowerment Solutions for Peaceful Communities (YES): community-level youth violence prevention programme engaging youth to carry out community change projects designed by youth. The long-term goals of the programme are to change structural and environmental factors contributing to youth violence. This also involves creative processes such as Photovoice: a participatory research method based on health promotion principles, involving participants in taking pictures, writing narratives and influencing policy (Zimmerman *et al.* 2011).

Elise Boulding's workshops on 'Imaging a Nonviolent World' are based on the recognition that positive images of the future have empowered creative action for social change in societies of the past (Boulding 2010). In Guinea, 'proventive peacebuilding' has been successfully applied – which identifies, affirms, celebrates and strengthens the values, instruments and processes that nurture and sustain peace in a society (Doe 2010: 147).

John Pail Lederach (2010) suggests that a more holistic and creative view of peace building motivates action not directly on the problem but rather in the relational spaces that surround the problem. At this stage I would like to return to Bohm's (1980: 48) theory of implicate order in which he uses the analogy of a flowing stream:

> On this stream, one may see an ever-changing pattern of vortices, ripples, waves and splashes, etc., which evidently have no independent existence as such. Rather, they are abstracted from the flowing movement, arising

132   Conclusion

and vanishing in the total process of the flow. Such transitory subsistence as may be possessed by these abstracted forms implies only a relative independence or autonomy of behaviour, rather than absolutely independent existence as ultimate substances.

If we focus positive and creative efforts on changing the 'ripples' – the people, relationships, institutions and environments – this process will ultimately change the problem itself. This collective effort will create a world where diversity is celebrated, all people are valued and respected equally, and have the freedom to fulfil their possibilities.

Appendices

Appendix 1: operational definitions of partner violence used in the Maldives Survey on Violence against Women (replicating WHO Multi-Country Study)

Emotional abuse by an intimate partner
- Was insulted or made to feel bad about herself
- Was belittled or humiliated in front of other people
- Perpetrator had done things to scare or intimidate her on purpose (e.g. by yelling or smashing things)
- Perpetrator had threatened to hurt her or someone she cared about

Physical violence by an intimate partner
- Was slapped or had something thrown at her that could hurt her
- Was pushed or shoved or had her hair pulled
- Was hit with fist or something else that could hurt
- Was choked or burnt on purpose
- Perpetrator threatened to use or actually used a weapon against her

Sexual violence by an intimate partner
- Was physically forced to have sexual intercourse when she did not want to
- Had sexual intercourse when she did not want to because she was afraid of what partner might do
- Was forced to do something sexual that she found degrading or humiliating

Physical violence in pregnancy
- Was slapped, hit or beaten while pregnant
- Was punched or kicked in the abdomen while pregnant

Appendix 2: Statistical tables of results from the Maldives Survey on Violence against Women

Table A1 Prevalence of physical and/or sexual violence by an intimate partner among ever-partnered women, according to when the violence took place (n = 1,731)

	Physical partner violence by period		Sexual partner violence by period		Sexual and/or physical partner violence by period	
	No.	%	No.	%	No.	%
Current (last 12 months)	99	5.7	35	2.0	110	6.4
Lifetime	212	17.9	81	6.7	227	19.5
Total	1,731	100.0	1,731	100.0	1,731	100.0

Table A2 Severity of physical partner violence reported by ever-partnered women (n = 1,731)

	No.	%
No violence	1,420	82.1
Moderate violence only	122	7.0
Severe violence	189	10.9

Table A3a Frequency of intimate partner violence, by type

	Physical partner violence		Sexual partner violence		Emotional partner violence	
	No.	%	No.	%	No.	%
Never	1,419	84.1	1,616	94.1	1,224	64.4
Once	83	4.9	20	1.2	74	4.5
A few times	122	7.2	51	3.0	200	12.1
Many times	64	3.8	30	1.7	154	9.3

Table A3b Association between frequency and severity of physical partner violence, among ever-partnered women aged 15–49

	Moderate physical violence only		Severe physical violence	
	No.	%	No.	%
Once	56	47.1	25	17.0
A few times	50	42.0	71	48.3
Many times	13	10.9	51	34.7
Total	119	100.0	147	100.0

Table A4a Percentage of ever-partnered women reporting various controlling behaviours by their intimate partners (n = 1,731)

Type of controlling behaviour	No.	%
Keeps her from seeing friends	121	7.0
Restricts her contact with family	65	3.8
Wants to know where she is at all times	532	30.7
Ignores her, treats her indifferently	136	7.9
Gets angry if she speaks with other men	344	19.9
Often suspicious that she is unfaithful	163	9.4
Controls her access to health care	328	19.0
At least one act of controlling behaviours	798	46.4

Table A4b Percentage of ever-partnered women reporting controlling behaviour by partner according to their experience of physical and/or sexual partner violence

		Never experienced controlling behaviour by partner		Experienced controlling behaviour by partner	
		No.	%	No.	%
Ever experienced sexual or physical violence by partner	No (n = 1,394)	829	59.5	556	39.9
	Yes (n = 337)	94	27.9	242	71.8

Table A4c Mean number of acts of controlling behaviour reported by ever-partnered women according to their experiences of intimate partner violence

Ever experienced sexual or physical violence by partner	Mean	No.
No	0.7	1,394
Yes	2.2	337
Total	1.0	1,731

Table A5a Percentage of women who experienced controlling behaviour, by severity of physical partner violence

	Experienced controlling behaviour	
	No.	%
No physical partner violence	574	40.7
Moderate physical violence only	72	59.5
Severe physical violence	151	80.7
Total	797	46.4

Table A5b Percentage of women who experienced controlling behaviour, by frequency of partner violence

Frequency of intimate partner violence	Experienced controlling behaviour	
	No.	%
No partner violence	574	40.7
Once	45	54.2
A few times	89	73.6
Many times	51	79.7
Total	759	45.2

136 Appendices

Table A5c Logistic regression model for association between controlling behaviour and experiences of physical partner violence

	COR	95% CI	P value
'Moderate' physical violence	2.1	1.5–3.0	p < 0.001
'Severe' physical violence	3.0	1.9–4.9	p < 0.001
Experienced physical violence once	1.7	1.1–2.7	p = 0.016
Experienced physical violence 'a few times'	4.1	2.7–6.2	p < 0.001
Experienced physical violence 'many times'	5.7	3.1–10.6	p < 0.001

Key: COR: crude odds ratio; CI: confidence interval.

Table A6a Percentage of women aged 15–49 who have ever experienced financially controlling behaviour from their current husband, by women's experiences of IPV[a]

	Ever-partnered women (n = 1,330)		Never experienced partner violence (n = 1,065)		Experienced partner violence (n = 265)		P value[c]
	No.	%	No.	%	No.	%	
Given up/refused job because of partner	195	14.7	132	12.4	63	23.7	p < 0.001
Partner taken earnings/savings against her will[b]	37	2.8	22	2.1	15	5.7	p = 0.001
Partner refuses to give money for household expenses	63	4.8	27	2.5	36	13.6	p < 0.001

Notes
[a] Among women who are currently married.
[b] Among women who are currently married and earning their own income.
[c] P value is for 2×2 chi-square test of the difference between never experienced partner violence and experienced partner violence.

Table A6b Logistic regression models for association between financially controlling behaviour and experiences of intimate partner violence

	COR	95% CI	AOR	95% CI
Given up/refused job because of partner	2.2	1.6–3.1	2.2	1.6–3.1
Partner taken earnings/savings against her will	2.9	1.5–5.6	2.9	1.5–5.8
Partner refuses to give money for household expenses	6.1	3.6–10.2	6.2	3.6–10.5

Key: COR: crude odds ratio; AOR: adjusted odds ratio (adjusted for site, age group, marital status and educational level); CI: confidence interval.

Table A7a Percentage of women, who have ever been in a relationship, reporting selected symptoms of ill health, according to their experience of physical and/or sexual partner violence

	Never experienced partner violence (n = 1,394) No.	Never experienced partner violence (n = 1,394) %	Experienced physical and/or sexual partner violence (n = 337) No.	Experienced physical and/or sexual partner violence (n = 337) %	P value (significance levels), Pearson chi-square test
Poor/very poor general health	104	7.5	45	13.4	p = 0.003
Problems walking	167	12.0	55	16.3	p = 0.106
Difficulties with activities	165	11.8	72	21.4	p < 0.001
Recent pain	436	31.3	167	49.6	p < 0.001
Problems with memory	138	9.9	63	18.8	p < 0.001
Recent dizziness	368	26.4	123	36.5	p = 0.001
Vaginal discharge	167	12.0	53	15.7	p = 0.100

Table A7b Logistic regression models for the associations between selected health conditions and experiences of intimate partner violence among ever-partnered women

Health condition	COR	95% CI	AOR	95% CI
Poor/very poor health	1.8	1.2–2.7	1.7	1.1–2.5
Problems walking	1.3	0.9–1.9	1.2	0.9–1.7
Difficulties with activities	2.0	1.4–2.7	1.8	1.3–2.5
Recent pain	2.1	1.7–2.7	2.1	1.6–2.7
Problems with memory	2.0	1.5–2.8	2.0	1.4–2.8
Recent dizziness	1.6	1.2–2.0	1.5	1.2–2.0
Vaginal discharge	1.3	0.5–1.9	1.4	1.0–2.0

Key: COR: crude odds ratio; AOR: adjusted odds ratio (adjusted for site, age group, marital status and educational level); CI: confidence interval.

Table A8a Percentage of ever-pregnant women reporting having had a miscarriage, abortion, stillbirth or child who died, according to their experience of partner violence

	Ever experienced sexual or physical violence by partner				Beaten while pregnant			
	No		Yes		No		Yes	
	No.	%	No.	%	No.	%	No.	%
Respondent ever pregnant[a]	1,020	73.2	296	87.8	1,224	100.0	82	100.0
Ever-partnered women	**1,394**	**100.0**	**337**	**100.0**	**1,224**	**100.0**	**82**	**100.0**

138   *Appendices*

Table A8a cont.

| | Ever experienced sexual or physical violence by partner |||| Beaten while pregnant ||||
| | No || Yes || No || Yes ||
	No.	%	No.	%	No.	%	No.	%
Ever had a miscarriage[b]	213	20.9	88	29.7	268	21.9	30	36.6
Ever had a stillbirth[b]	56	5.5	28	9.5	74	6.0	10	12.2
Ever had an abortion[b]	18	1.8	13	4.4	28	2.3	2	2.4
Ever had a child who died[b]	179	17.5	73	24.7	234	19.1	18	22.0
Ever-pregnant women	**1,020**	**100.0**	**296**	**100.0**	**1,224**	**100.0**	**82**	**100.0**

Notes
[a] Among ever-partnered women.
[b] Among ever-pregnant women.

Table A8b Logistic regression models for the association between selected reproductive health outcomes and experiences of intimate partner violence, among ever-pregnant women

	COR	95% CI	AOR	95% CI	P value
Ever had a miscarriage	1.6	1.2–2.1	1.6	1.2–2.2	p = 0.003
Ever had a stillbirth	1.8	1.1–2.9	1.8	1.1–2.9	p = 0.020
Ever had an abortion	2.6	1.2–5.3	2.9	1.3–6.1	p = 0.011
Ever had a child who died	1.5	1.1–2.1	1.5	1.0–2.1	p = 0.009

Key: COR: crude odds ratio; AOR: adjusted odds ratio (adjusted for site, age group, marital status and educational level); CI: confidence interval.

Table A9a Physical and/or sexual partner abuse and circumstances of last pregnancy, among women who gave birth in last five years

| | | Ever experienced sexual or physical violence by partner ||||
| | | No || Yes ||
		No.	%	No.	%
Respondent wanted last pregnancy?	Wanted to become pregnant then	308	64.3	59	41.5
	Wanted to wait until later/did not want (more) children	99	20.7	53	37.4
	Did not mind either way	72	15.0	30	21.1
Total		479	100.0	142	100.0

		\multicolumn{4}{c}{Ever experienced sexual or physical violence by partner}
		\multicolumn{2}{c}{No}	\multicolumn{2}{c}{Yes}
		No.	%	No.	%
Partner wanted last pregnancy?	Wanted to become pregnant then	322	67.2	69	48.9
	Wanted to wait until later/did not want (more) children	88	18.4	37	26.1
	Did not mind either way	66	13.8	34	23.9
	Don't know	3	0.6	2	1.1
Total		479	100.0	142	100.0

Table A9b Logistic regression models for the association between unplanned pregnancies and experiences of intimate partner violence, among ever-pregnant women

	COR	95% CI	AOR	95% CI	P-value
Woman did not want last pregnancy	2.3	1.5–3.5	1.8	1.2–2.8	p < 0.001
Partner did not want last pregnancy	1.6	1.0–2.5	1.2	0.8–2.0	p = 0.040

Key: COR: crude odds ratio; AOR: adjusted odds ratio (adjusted for site, age group, marital status and educational level); CI: confidence interval.

Table A10a Comparison of suicidal ideation and behaviour for ever-partnered women according to their experiences of physical partner violence

		\multicolumn{2}{c}{Never experienced physical partner violence}	\multicolumn{2}{c}{Experienced physical partner violence}
		No.	%	No.	%
Ever thought about ending life	Yes	105	7.4	57	18.3
	No	1,312	92.6	254	81.7
Total women		1,420	100	311	100
Ever tried taking life*	Yes	9	8.6	8	14.0
	No	96	91.4	49	85.9
Total women		105	100	57	100

Note

* Among women who reported suicidal thoughts.

Table A10b Logistic regression models for associations between suicidal thoughts and experiences of intimate partner violence

	COR	95% CI	AOR	95% CI	P-value (significance levels), Pearson chi-square test
Ever thought about ending life	3.1	2.2–4.3	4.0	2.8–5.8	$p < 0.001$
Ever tried taking life	2.0	0.7–5.5	1.9	0.6–6.2	$p = 0.19$

Key: COR: crude odds ratio; AOR: adjusted odds ratio (adjusted for site, age group, marital status and educational level); CI: confidence interval.

Table A11a Percentage of ever-partnered women aged 15–49 who experienced partner violence in past 12 months, by background characteristics

Characteristics		Women who have experienced IPV in past 12 months (current)	
		No.	%
Age	15–19	11	6.8 (ns)
	20–34	61	8.0
	35–49	34	6.8
Education	None	12	9.7 (ns)
	Primary	57	7.6
	Secondary	35	6.8
	Higher	2	5.6
Marital status	Currently married	83	7.4 (ns)
	Current partner, living apart	15	6.1
	Divorced, separated	8	15.4
	Widowed	0	0.0
Respondent chose partner herself	Chose partner herself	61	6.5***
	Did not chose partner herself	35	14.0
Can count on family for help	Yes	94	6.8***
	No	11	24.4
Polygamy	Husband has only one wife	93	8.0 (ns)
	Husband has more than one wife	3	13.0
Children from more than one relationship	Never married	10	4.3
	No children	22	5.8***
	Children from one relationship only	56	6.2
	Children from more than one relationship	28	19.4

Characteristics		Women who have experienced IPV in past 12 months (current)	
		No.	%
Employment	Not earning an income	55	6.6 (ns)
	Earning an income	31	8.0
Father beat mother	Yes	21	13.2**
	No	85	6.7
Experienced non-partner physical abuse > 15 yrs	Yes	20	17.5***
	No	86	6.5
Experienced non-partner sexual violence > 15 yrs	Yes	19	26.8***
	No	87	6.4
Experienced childhood sexual abuse	Yes	30	18.4***
	No	76	6.0
Attitudes to IPV	Agrees with at least one reason for a husband hitting his wife	99	7.7 (ns)
	Agrees with no reasons for husband hitting his wife	6	4.2
Attitudes about sexual autonomy within marriage	Agrees with at least one reason for a wife refusing sex with her husband	101	7.4 (ns)
	Agrees with no reason for a wife refusing sex with her husband	5	7.8

Notes

Asterisk denotes bivariate associations that are statistically significant based on the chi-square test; one test per variable (p < 0.05); ***: p < 0.001, **: p < 0.01, p < 0.05, ns = not significant.

Table A11b Percentage of ever-partnered women aged 15–49 who experienced partner violence in past 12 months, by husband's characteristics

Characteristics		Women who have experienced IPV in the past 12 months (current)	
		No.	%
Age	15–19	1	1.7**
	20–34	60	9.7
	35–49	31	5.1
	50+	14	9.9

Table A11b cont.

Characteristics		Women who have experienced IPV in the past 12 months (current)	
		No.	%
Education	None	15	9.4 (ns)
	Primary	37	6.8
	Secondary	33	7.5
	Higher	1	2.4
Employment status	Not unemployed (working, retired, student)	100	7.2 (ns)
	Unemployed	5	12.5
Alcohol/drug use	Never used intoxicating substances	91	6.5***
	Uses intoxicating substances	15	44.1
Father beat mother	Yes	7	15.9*
	No	99	7.3
Frequently beaten as a child	Yes	6	16.7*
	No	100	7.4
Violent with other men	Yes	11	40.7***
	No	95	6.8
Had a relationship concurrently	Yes	40	25.6***
	No	66	5.2
Exhibits controlling behaviour	Yes	88	14.4***
	No	18	2.2

Note

Asterisk denotes bivariate associations that are statistically significant based on the chi-square test; one test per variable (p < 0.05); ***: p < 0.001, **: p < 0.01, p < 0.05, ns = not significant.

Table A11c Correlates of ever-partnered woman's likelihood of having ever experienced partner violence in the past 12 months: adjusted odds ratios estimated using multivariate logistic regression

Characteristic	AOR (adjusted for all other risk factors)	95% CI for OR		P value
		Lower	Upper	
Children (r: no children)				
Children by one partner	0.84	0.37	1.87	0.66
Children by more than one partner	3.14	1.25	7.89	0.015
Arranged marriage (r: respondent chose partner herself)				

Characteristic	AOR (adjusted for all other risk factors)	95% CI for OR Lower	Upper	P value
Respondent did not choose partner herself	2.66	1.54	4.60	0.000
Family support (r: can count on family for support)				
Cannot count on family for support	4.22	1.73	10.30	0.002
Partner's intoxicating substance use (r: never uses intoxicating substances)				
Partner uses intoxicating substances	10.57	3.83	29.12	0.000
Controlling behaviour (r: none)				
Partner has exhibited controlling behaviour	6.21	3.26	11.85	0.000
Affair (r: none)				
Partner has had an affair	4.09	2.33	7.19	0.000
Partner violent with other men (r: never)				
Partner has been violent with other men	7.67	2.03	29.04	0.003
Non-partner physical abuse > 15 yrs (r: never)				
Woman experienced non-partner physical violence	1.26	0.55	2.87	0.59
Non-partner sexual abuse > 15 yrs (r: never)				
Woman experienced non-partner sexual violence	1.83	0.73	4.60	0.20
CSA (r: none)				
Woman experienced childhood sexual abuse	2.78	1.40	5.52	0.003
Partner frequently beaten as a child (r: no)				
Partner frequently beaten as a child	0.45	0.10	2.08	0.31
Woman's father beat mother (r: no)				
Woman's father beat mother	1.66	0.79	3.48	0.18
Partner's father beat mother (r: no)				
Partner's father beat mother	1.50	0.45	4.99	0.51
Constant	0.054			

144 Appendices

Table A11c cont.

Characteristic	AOR (adjusted for all other risk factors)	95% CI for OR		
		Lower	Upper	P value
Number of women	1,142			

Notes

Shading represents bivariate relationships that are found to be statistically significant (p < 0.05)
r = Reference (omitted) category
Appendix Table A11c presents multivariate logistic regression analysis to determine the factors significantly associated with intimate partner violence. Factors considered include all the characteristics discussed in the bivariate analysis (Tables A11a and A11b) that were found to have a statistically significant association with partner violence. The dependent variable analysed is whether a woman experienced physical and/or sexual partner violence in the last 12 months, where a respondent is coded '1' if she has experienced violence and '0' otherwise.

Glossary of foreign terms

Buruga	headscarf
Dhivehi	Maldivian language
Dhivehi Rajje	The Maldives
Dhivehin	Maldivian people
Fanditha	magic
Faskh (divorce)	court-ordered dissolution of marriage based on woman-initiated petition
Gifili	outdoor toilet
Haram	prohibited in Islam
Hijab	headscarf
Ishq	romantic love (Arabic)
Izzat	family honour (Arabic)
Khul (divorce)	type of divorce where the woman offers compensation
Loabi	love/cute
Majlis	Maldivian Parliament
Raaveri	toddy collectors
Raivaru	traditional Maldivian poetry/song
Ramazan	fasting month
Rihaakuru	fish paste
Rufiyaa	Maldivian currency
Ruju (divorce)	a type of divorce where the man pronounces 'I divorce thee' three times
Shahada	Muslim testimony of belief
Shari'a	Islamic law
Talaq	'I divorce thee' pronouncement
Undholi	large wooden swing
Zina	crime of sexual misconduct

Bibliography

Abaza, M. (2001) 'Shopping malls, consumer culture and the reshaping of public space in Egypt', *Theory, Culture & Society*, 19(5): 97–122.
Abraham, M. (2000) *Speaking the unspeakable: Marital violence in South Asian immigrant communities in the United States*, New Brunswick, NJ: Rutgers University Press.
Abramsky, T., Watts, C., Garcia-Moreno, C., Devries, K., Kiss, L., Ellsberg, M., Jansen, A.F.M. and Heise, L. (2011) 'What factors are associated with recent intimate partner violence? Findings from the WHO Multi-Country Study on Women's Health and Domestic Violence', *BMC Public Health*, 11: 109.
Abu-Lughod, L. (1991) 'Writing against culture', in Fox, R.G. (ed.) *Reprinting anthropology*, Santa Fe, NM: School of American Research Press.
Adamson, C. (2007) 'Gendered anxieties: Islam, women's rights and moral hierarchy in Java', *Anthropological Quarterly*, 80(1): 5–37.
Adduvas (2006) 'What the MPs said against allocating seats to women', *Adduvas*, Malé, p. 10–2.
Adhikari, R. and Tamang, J. (2010) 'Sexual coercion of married women in Nepal', *BMC Women's Health*, 10: 31–9.
Adichie, C. (2011) 'The danger of a single story', TED Lecture Series. Online. Available HTTP: www.ted.com/talks/chimamanda_adichie_the_danger_of_a_single_story.html (accessed 20 July 2011).
Ahmed, A.S. (2004) *Postmodernism and Islam, predicament and promise*, London and New York: Routledge.
Ahmed, F. (2007) 'DRP and MDP back appointment of women judges', *Haveeru*, 26 May, Malé, pp. 3, 34.
Ahmed, L. (2011) *A quiet revolution: The veil's resurgence, from the Middle East to America*, New Haven, CT: Yale University Press.
Akpinar, A. (2003) 'The honour/shame complex revisited: Violence against women in the migration context', *Women's Studies International Forum*, 26(5): 425–42.
Al-Hibri, A. (2003) 'An Islamic perspective on domestic violence', *Fordham International Law Journal*, 27: 195–200.
Ali, S. (2006) 'Sex, drugs and kids', *Adduvas Weekly*, 13 July, Malé, p. 12.
Aljazeera (2 March 2012) 'Coup in the coral islands?', in *101 East*, Aljazeera.
Amnesty International (2003) *Republic of Maldives: Repression of peaceful political opposition*, Malé: Amnesty International.
Andaya, B.M. (1998) 'From temporary wife to prostitute: Sexuality and economic change in early modern Southeast Asia', *Journal of Women's History*, 9(4): 11–34.

Bibliography 147

Andersson, N., Cockcroft, A., Anasari, N., Omer, K., Chaudhry, U.U., Khan, A. and Pearson, L. (2009) 'Collecting reliable information about violence against women safely in household interviews: Experience from a large-scale national survey in South Asia', *Violence Against Women*, 15(4): 482–96.

Aniya, A. (2010) 'Comment: An evening with Mrs Naik', *Minivan News*, 29 May, Malé, p. 19.

Aniya, A. (2007) 'Are women the germs that spread social ills?', *Minivan News*, 20 March, Malé, p. 19.

Appadurai, A. (1991) 'Global ethnoscapes: Notes and queries for a transnational anthropology', in Fox, R.G. (ed.) *Recapturing anthropology: Working in the present*, Santa Fe, NM: School of American Research Press.

Arias, I. (1998) 'Complexities of family violence and the need for belongingness', in Klein, R.C.A. (ed.) *Multidisciplinary perspectives on family violence*, London and New York: Routledge.

Ayubi, N. (1993) *Political Islam: Religion and politics in the Arab world*, London and New York: Routledge.

Ayyub, R. (2007) 'The many faces of domestic violence in the South Asian American Muslim community', in Dasgupta, S.D. (ed.) *Body evidence: Intimate violence against South Asian women in America*, New Brunswick, NJ and London: Rutgers University Press.

Aziz, Z.A. (2010) 'Malaysia: Trajectory towards secularism or Islamism?', in Derichs, C. and Fleschenberg, A. (eds) *Religious fundamentalisms and their gendered impacts in Asia*, Berlin: Friedrich-Ebert-Stiftung.

Babu, B.V. and Kar, S.K. (2010) 'Domestic violence in Eastern India: Factors associated with victimization and perpetration', *Public Health*, 124(3): 136–48.

Bahramitash, R. (2005) *Liberation from liberalization: Gender and globalization in Southeast Asia*, London: Zed Books.

Bajaj, V. (2012) 'Behind Maldives' glamor, a struggling democracy', *New York Times*, 12 February. Online. Available HTTP: www.nytimes.com/2012/02/13/world/asia/behind-maldives-glamor-a-struggling-democracy.html?pagewanted=all&_r=0 (accessed 20 February 2012).

Barker, D.K. (1998) 'Dualisms, discourse and development', *Hypatia: Feminist Journal of Philosophy*, 13(3): 83–94.

Barker, G., Contreras, M., Heilman, B., Singh, A., Verma, R. and Nascimento, M. (2011) *Evolving men: Initial results from the International Men and Gender Equality Survey*, Washington, DC: International Center for Research on Women.

Bates, L.M., Schular, S.R., Islam, F. and Islam, K. (2004) 'Socioeconomic factors and processes associated with domestic violence in rural Bangladesh', *International Family Planning Perspectives*, 30(4): 190–9.

Battuta, I. (1929) *Travels in Asia and Africa, 1325–1354*, trans. H.A.R. Gibb. New York: Routledge.

Beasley, C. (2008) 'Rethinking hegemonic masculinity', *Men and Masculinities*, 11(1): 86–103.

Beebeejaun, Y. (2009) 'Making safer places: Gender and the right to the city', *Security Journal*, 22: 219–29.

Bell, H.C.P. (1940) *The Maldive Islands: Monograph on the history, archaeology, and epigraphy*, Colombo: Ceylon Government Press.

Bell, K.M. and Naugle, A.E. (2008) 'Intimate partner violence theoretical considerations: Moving towards a contextual framework', *Clinical Psychology Review*, 28: 1096–107.

Bibliography

Bennett, L.R. and Manderson, L. (2003) 'Introduction: Gender inequality and technologies of violence', in Manderson, L. and Bennett, L.R. (eds) *Violence against women in Asian societies*, London and New York: Routledge Curzon.

Berkowitz, A.D. (2004a) *Working with men to prevent violence against women: An overview (part I)*, Applied Research Forum: National Electronic Network on Violence against Women.

Berkowitz, A.D. (2004b) *Working with men to prevent violence against women: Program modalities and formats (part II)*, Applied Research Forum: National Electronic Network on Violence against Women.

Bhattacharjee, A. (1992) 'The habit of ex-nomination: Nation, women and the Indian immigrant bourgeoisie', *Public Culture*, 5: 19–43.

Bhattacharya, S. (2011) 'Fundamentalist backlash (Terror Watch)', *Calcutta Tube*. Online: Available HTTP: http:calcuttatube.com/fundamentalist-backlash/149752 (accessed 25 June 2011).

Blackwood, E. (1995) 'Senior women, model mothers, and dutiful wives: Managing gender contradictions in a Minangkabau village', in Ong, A. and Peletz, M.G. (eds) *Bewitching women, pious men, gender and body politics in Southeast Asia*, Berkeley, CA: Berkeley University Press.

Blau, J.R. and Blau, P.M. (1982) 'The cost of inequality: Metropolitan structure and violent crime', *American Sociological Review*, 47: 114–28.

Bohm, D. (1980) *Wholeness and the implicate order*, London and Boston: Routledge & Kegan Paul.

Boston.com (2011) 'Thousands demonstrate in Maldives over Islamic law', *Boston.com*, 23 December. Online. Available HTTP: www.boston.com/news/world/asia/articles/2011/12/23/thousands_demonstrate_in_maldives_over_islamic_law (accessed 24 March 2012).

Boulding, E. (2010) 'Peace cultures for today and tomorrow', in Sampson, C., Abu-Nimer, M., Liebler, C. and Whitney, D. (eds) *Positive approaches to peacebuilding: A resource for innovators*, Chargrin Falls, OH: Taos Institute Publications.

Boulding, E. and Ikeda, D. (2010) *Into full flower: Making peace cultures happen*, Cambridge, MA: Dialogue Path Press.

Brah, A. (2002) 'Global mobilities, local predicaments: Globalization and the critical imagination', *Feminist Review*, 70: 30–45.

Brecklin, L.R. (2002) 'The role of perpetrator alcohol use in the injury outcomes of intimate assaults', *Journal of Family Violence*, 17(3): 185–97.

Brewster, M.P. (2003) 'Power and control dynamics in prestalking and stalking situations', *Journal of Family Violence*, 18: 207–17.

Brown, J.K. (1992) 'Introduction: Definitions, assumptions, themes and issues', in Counts, D.A., Brown, J.K. and Campbell, J.C. (eds) *Sanctions and sanctuary: Cultural perspectives on the beating of wives*, Oxford: Westview Press.

Browning, C.R. (2002) 'The span of collective efficacy: Extending social disorganization theory to partner violence', *Journal of Marriage and Family*, 64(4): 833–50.

Burke, L.K. and Follingstad, D.R. (1999) 'Violence in lesbian and gay relationships: Theory, prevalence, and correlational factors', *Clinical Psychology Review*, 19(5): 487–512.

Castles, S. (2001) 'Studying social transformation', *International Political Science Review*, 22(1): 13–32.

CEDAW (2007) *Concluding comments of the Committee on the Elimination of Discrimination against Women: Maldives*, New York: United Nations.

Chakravarti, U. (2005) 'From fathers to husbands: Love, death and marriage in North India', in Welchman, L. and Hossain, S. (eds) *'Honour': Crimes, paradigms and violence against women*, Victoria: Spinifex Press.

Charrad, M.M. (2001) *States and women's rights: The making of postcolonial Tunisia, Algeria, and Morocco*, Berkeley, CA: University of California Press.

Chattopadhay, T. (2004) *Advocacy brief: Role of men and boys in promoting gender equality*, Bangkok: UNESCO Bangkok.

Coan, J., McFarlane, J., Parker, B., Soeken, K., Silva, C. and Reel, S. (1998) 'Violent pornography and abuse of women: Theory to practice', *Aggressive Behaviour*, 23: 375–88.

Cocker, A.L., Smith, P.H., McKeown, R.E. and King, M.J. (2000) 'Frequency and correlates of intimate partner violence by type: Physical, sexual and psychological battering', *American Journal of Public Health*, 90: 553–9.

Coggan, C., Saunders, C. and Grenot, D. (2008) 'Art and safe communities: The role of Big hART in the regeneration of an inner city housing estate', *Health Promotion Journal of Australia*, 19: 4–9.

Coid, J., Petruckevich, A., Feder, G., Chung, W.S., Richardson, J. and Moorey, S. (2001) 'Relation between childhood sexual and physical abuse and risk re-victimization in women: A cross-sectional survey', *The Lancet*, 358: 450–4.

Connell, J. (2003) 'Island dreaming: The contemplation of Polynesian paradise', *Journal of Historical Geography*, 29(4): 554–81.

Connell, R.W. (1995) *Masculinities*, Berkeley, CA: University of California Press.

Coomaraswamy, R. (2005) 'Preface: Violence against women and "crimes of honour"', in Welchman, L. and Hossain, S. (eds) *'Honour': Crimes, paradigms and violence against women*, Victoria: Spinifex Press.

Counts, D.A. (1999) '"All men do it": Wife beating in Kaliai, Papua New Guinea', in Counts, D.A., Brown, J.K. and Campbell, J.C. (eds) *To have and to hit: Cultural perspectives on wife beating*, Urbana, IL: University of Illinois Press.

Counts, D.A., Brown, J.K. and Campbell, J.C. (eds) (1992) *Sanctions and sanctuary: Cultural perspectives on the beating of wives*, Oxford: Westview Press.

Crowell, N.A. and Burgess, A.W. (eds) (1996) *Understanding violence against women*, Washington, DC: National Academy Press.

Das, A. and Kemp, S. (1997) 'Between two worlds: Counseling South Asian Americans', *Journal of Multicultural Counseling and Development*, 25: 23–33.

Dasgupta, S.D. (2000a) 'Broken promises: Domestic violence murders and attempted murders in the US and Canadian South Asian communities', in Nankani, S. (ed.) *Breaking the silence: Domestic violence in the South Asian-American community*, Philadelphia: Xlibris Corporation.

Dasgupta, S.D. (2000b) 'Charting the course: An overview of domestic violence in the South Asian community in the United States', *Journal of Social Distress and the Homeless*, 9: 173–85.

Davis, M. (2012) *Mutiny in the Maldives*, television documentary, *SBS Australia*. Online. Available HTTP: www.sbs.com.au/dateline/story/about/id/601405/n/Mutiny-in-the-Maldives (accessed 1 March 2012).

Davis, R.E. (2002) '"The strongest women": Explorations of the inner resources of abused women', *Qualitative Health Research*, 12(9): 1248–63.

De Munck, V.C. (1996) 'Love and marriage in a Sri Lankan Muslim community: Toward a reevaluation of Dravidian marriage practices', *American Ethnologist*, 23(4): 698–716.

150 Bibliography

DeLillo, D., Giuffre, D., Tremblay, G. and Peterson, L. (2001) 'A closer look at the nature of intimate partner violence reported by women with history of child sexual abuse', *Journal of Interpersonal Violence*, 16: 116–32.

Derichs, C. and Fleschenberg, A. (2010) 'Religious fundamentalism and their gendered impacts in Asia', in Derichs, C. and Fleschenberg, A. (eds) *Religious fundamentalism and their gendered impacts in Asia*, Berlin: Friedrich-Ebert-Stiftung.

Derné, S. (2008) 'Globalizing gender culture: Transnational cultural flows and the intensification of male dominance in India', in Ferguson, K.E. and Mironesco, M. (eds) *Gender and globalization in Asia and the Pacific*, Honolulu, HI: University of Hawaii Press.

Didi, Z.H. (2006) 'The great divider', *Evening Weekly*, Malé, p. 19.

Diwan, P. (1990) *Dowry and protection to married women*, New Delhi: Deep and Deep Publication.

Dobash, R. (1996) *Re-education programmes for violence men: An evaluation*, London: Home Office Research and Statistics Directorate.

Dobash, R.E. and Dobash, R. (1980) *Violence against wives: A case against the patriarchy*, London: Open Books.

Doe, S.G. (2010) 'Proventive peacebuilding in the Republic of Guinea: Building peace by cultivating the positives', in Sampson, C., Abu-Nimer, M., Liebler, C. and Whitney, D. (eds) *Positive approaches to peacebuilding: A resource for innovators*, Chargrin Falls, OH: Taos Institute Publications.

Doherty, B. (2012) 'Female flogging on rise in Maldives', *Sydney Morning Herald*, 25 January. Online. Available HTTP: www.smh.com.au/world/female-flogging-on-rise-in-maldives-20120124-1qfmd.html (accessed 3 February 2012).

Donnan, S. (2006) 'Aceh enforces Sharia law with the lash of a cane', *Financial Times*, 6 October.

Doyal, L. (2002) 'Putting gender into health and globalization debates: New perspectives and old challenges', *Third World Quarterly*, 23: 233–50.

Dunkle, K., Jewkes, R., Brown, H., Gray, G., McIntyre, J. and Harlow, S. (2004) 'Gender-based violence, relationship power, and risk of HIV infection in women attending antenatal clinics in South Africa', *The Lancet*, 363(9419): 1415–21.

Duvvury, N. (2000) 'Violence against women in the marital home: Results of a household survey in India', in Consultation on Sexual Violence against Women, 18–20 May, Melbourne.

Dwyer, R. (2006) 'Kiss or tell? Declaring love in Hindi films', in Orsini, F. (ed.) *Love in South Asia: A cultural history*, Cambridge: Cambridge University Press.

Eisikovits, Z. and Buchbinder, E. (2000) *Locked in a violent embrace: Understanding and intervening in domestic violence*, Thousand Oaks, CA: Sage Publications.

Elliot, P. (1996) 'Shattering illusions: Same-sex domestic violence', *Journal of Gay & Lesbian Social Services*, 4(1): 1–8.

Ellis, R. (1998) *A man for all islands: A biography of Maumoon Abdul Gayoom*, Singapore: Times Editions Publishers.

Ellsberg, M. (2000) 'Candies in hell: Women's experiences of violence in Nicaragua', *Social Science and Medicine*, 51: 1595–610.

Ellsberg, M.C., Pena, R., Herrera, A., Liljestand, J. and Winkvist, A. (1999) 'Wife abuse among women of child-bearing age in Nicaragua', *American Journal of Public Health*, 89: 241–4.

Euben, R.L. (1999) *Enemy in the mirror: Islamic fundamentalism and the limits of modern rationalism*, Princeton, NJ: Princeton University Press.

Evans, J. (2008) 'Opposition calls for urgent drug reform as methadone programme launched', *Minivan News*, 26 October, Malé, p. 5.

Eves, R. (2007) *Exploring the role of men and masculinities in Papua New Guinea in the 21st century: How to address violence in ways that generate empowerment for both men and women*, Alexandria, NSW: Caritas Australia.

Evins, G. and Chescheir, N. (1996) 'Prevalence of domestic violence among women seeking abortion services', *Women's Health Issues*, 6: 204–10.

Fantuzzo, J. and Linquist, C. (1989) 'The effects of observing conjugal violence on children: A review and analysis of research methodology', *Journal of Family Violence*, 4(1): 77–94.

Fantuzzo, J., Depaola, L., Lambert, L., Martino, T., Anderson, G. and Sutton, S. (1991) 'Effect of interparental violence on the psychological adjustment and competence of young children', *Journal of Clinical and Consulting Psychology*, 14: 144–61.

Fealy, G. (2005) 'Islamization and politics in Southeast Asia', in Lahoud, N. and Johns, A.H. (eds) *Islam in world politics*, London and New York: Routledge.

Featherstone, M. (1998) 'The flaneur, the city and the virtual public life', *Urban Studies*, 35(5–6): 909–25.

Fehringer, J.A. and Hindin, M.J. (2009) 'Like parent, like child: Intergenerational transmission of partner violence in Cebu, the Philippines', *Journal of Adolescent Health*, 44(4): 363–71.

Ferguson, K.E., Merry, S.E. and Mironesco, M. (2008) 'Introduction', in Ferguson, K.E. and Mironesco, M. (eds) *Gender and globalization in Asia and the Pacific: Method, practice and theory*, Honolulu, HI: University of Hawaii Press.

Fergusson, D.M., Horwood, J.L. and Ridder, E.M. (2005) 'Partner violence and mental health outcomes in a New Zealand birth cohort', *Journal of Marriage and Family*, 67(5): 1103–19.

Finkelhor, D., Gelles, R.J., Hotaling, G.T. and Straus, M.A. (1983) *The dark side of families: Current family violence research*, Newbury Park, CA: Sage.

Flaherty, M.P. (2010) 'Constructing a world beyond intimate partner abuse', *Affilia*, 25: 224–35.

Flood, M. (2001) 'Men's collective anti-violence activism and the struggle for gender justice', *Development*, 44(3): 42–7.

Ford, M. and Lyons, L. (eds) (2012) *Men and masculinities in Southeast Asia*, London: Routledge.

Frankenberg, R. (1997) 'Introduction: Local whiteness, localizing whiteness', in Frankenberg, R. (ed.) *Displacing whiteness: Essays in social and cultural criticism*, Durham, NC and London: Duke University Press.

Freeman, C. (2001) 'Is local: global as feminine: Masculine? Rethinking the gender of globalization', *Signs: Journal of Women in Culture and Society*, 26(4): 1007–37.

Frisk, S. (2009) *Submitting to God: Women and Islam in urban Malaysia*, Copenhagen: NIAS Press.

Frye, V., Galea, S., Tracey, M., Bucciarelli, A., Putnam, S. and Wilt, S. (2008) 'The role of neighborhood environment and risk of intimate partner femicide in a large urban area', *American Journal of Public Health*, 98(8): 1473–9.

Fulu, E. (2004) *Gender-based violence in the Maldives: Report of the findings of qualitative research*, Malé: Ministry of Gender, Family Development and Social Security.

Fulu, E. (2007a) 'Domestic violence and women's health in the Maldives', *Regional Health Forum*, 11(2): 25–32.

Bibliography

Fulu, E. (2007b) 'Gender, vulnerability, and the experts: Responding to the Maldives tsunami', *Development and Change*, 38(5): 843–67.

Fulu, E. (2007c) *The Maldives study on women's health and violence against women: Initial results on prevalence, health outcomes and women's responses to violence*, Malé: Ministry of Gender and Family.

Garbarino, J. and Crouter, A. (1978) 'Defining the community context for parent–child relations: The correlates of child maltreatment', *Child Development*, 4: 604–16.

Garcia-Moreno, C., Jansen, H.A.F.M., Ellsberg, M., Heise, L. and Watts, C. (2005) *WHO multi-country study on women's health and domestic violence against women: Initial results on prevalence, health outcomes and women's responses*, Geneva: World Health Organization.

Geffner, R., Igleman, R.M. and Zellner, J. (2003) *The effects of intimate partner violence on children*, New York: Haworth Press.

Gelles, R.J. and Straus, M.A. (1979) 'Determinants of violence in the family: Toward a theoretical integration', in Burr, W.R., Hill, R., Nye, F.I. and Reiss, I.T. (eds) *Contemporary theories about the family: Research-based theories, vol. I*, New York: Free Press.

Gender and Development Cambodia (2010) *A preliminary analysis report: Deoum Troung Pram Hath in Modern Cambodia – A qualitative exploration of gender norms, masculinity and domestic violence*, Phnom Penh: GADC.

Gerami, S. (2005) 'Islamist masculinity and Muslim masculinities', in Kimmel, M.S., Hearn, J. and Connell, R.W. (eds) *Handbook of studies on men and masculinities*, Thousand Oaks, CA, London and New Delhi: Sage Publications.

Giddens, A. (1990) *The consequences of modernity*, Stanford, CA: Stanford University Press.

Giddens, A. (2003) *Runaway world: How globalization is reshaping our lives*, New York: Routledge.

Göle, N. (2002) 'Islam in public: New visibilities and new imaginaries', *Public Culture*, 14(1): 173–90.

Gondolf, E.W. (1988) 'Who are those guys? Toward a behavioural typology of batterers', *Violence and Victims*, 3: 187–203.

Government of Viet Nam (2010) *'Keeping silent is dying': Results from the National Study on Domestic Violence against Women in Viet Nam*, Hanoi: United Nations Viet Nam.

Graham-Bermann, S.A. (1998) 'The impact of woman abuse on children's social development: Research and theoretical perspectives', in Holden, G.W., Geffner, R. and Jouriles, E.N. (eds) *Children exposed to marital violence: Theory, research and applied issues*, Washington, DC: American Psychological Association.

Grewal, I. and Kaplan, C. (1994) *Scattered hegemonies: Postmodernity and transnational feminist practices*, London: University of Minnesota Press.

Hajjar, L. (2004) 'Religion, state power, and domestic violence in Muslim societies: A framework for comparative analysis', *Law and Social Inquiry*, 29(1): 1–38.

Haleem, A. (2006) 'President urges public to involve more women in all development efforts', *Haveeru*, Malé, 6 December, pp. 4, 55.

Hama Jamiyya (2006) *NGO shadow report on CEDAW, Maldives: Reviewing the government's implementation of CEDAW*, Malé: Hama Jamiyya.

Hameed, I. (2006a) 'Poor and vulnerable: Why is the average Maldivian finding life so hard in the Maldives?', *The Evening Weekly*, Malé.

Hameed, I. (2006b) 'Religious freedom?', *The Evening Weekly*, Malé, p. 17.
Hammel, J. (2009) 'Toward a gender-inclusive conception of intimate partner violence research and theory: Part 2 – New directions', *International Journal of Men's Health*, 8(1): 41–59.
Haneez (2007) 'Letter to the editor on Aniya's article, translated from Dhivehi to English by Shaarif Ali', *Minivan News*, 21 March, Malé, p. 20.
Hanmer, J. (2000) 'Domestic violence and gender relations: Contexts and connections', in Quaid, S. and Wigglesworth, D. (eds) *Home truths about domestic violence: Feminist influences on policy and practice – A reader*, London and New York: Routledge.
Hassan, Y. (1995) 'The haven becomes hell: A study of domestic violence in Pakistan', in Cantt, L. (ed.) *Pakistan: Women living under Muslim laws*, Paris: Women Living under Muslim Laws (WLUML) Publications.
Haveeru News Service (2006) 'Recovering drug addicts need compassion and support: UNICEF', *Haveeru*, 28 June, Malé, p. 5.
Haveeru News Service (2007a) 'Reader's feedback for "Judicial Service Commission considers appointing two women judges, one woman magistrate", translated from Dhivehi to English by Shaarif Ali', *Haveeru*, Malé, p. 9.
Haveeru News Service (2007b) 'Uniform with headscarf introduced for Immigration staff', *Haveeru News*, Malé, p. 3.
Hefner, R.W. (1997) 'Islamization and democratization in Indonesia', in Hefner, R.W. and Horvatich, P. (eds) *Islam in an era of nation-states*, Honolulu, HI: University of Hawai'i Press.
Heise, L. (1998) 'Violence against women: An integrated, ecological framework', *Violence Against Women*, 4: 262–90.
Heise, L. (2011) *What works to prevent partner violence? An evidence overview*, working paper, London: Department for International Development.
Heise, L. (2012) *Determinants of partner violence in low and middle-income countries: Exploring variation in individual and population-level risk*, PhD thesis, London School of Hygiene and Tropical Medicine.
Heise, L. and Garcia-Moreno, C. (2002) 'Violence by intimate partners', in Krug, E.G. (ed.) *World report on violence and health*, Geneva: World Health Organization.
Heise, L., Ellsberg, M. and Gottemoeller, M. (1999) *Ending violence against women: Population reports*, Baltimore, MD: Johns Hopkins University School of Public Health, Population Information Program.
Heise, L., Pitanguy, J. and Germaine, A. (1994) *Violence against women: The hidden health burden*, World Bank Discussion Paper 225, Washington, DC: World Bank.
Helie-Lucas, M.-A. (1987) 'Bound and gagged by the family code', in Davis, M. (ed.) *Third world – Second sex: Women's struggles and national liberation*, London: Zed Books.
Heyat, F. (2006) 'Globalization and changing gender norms in Azerbaijan', *International Feminist Journal of Politics*, 8(3): 394–412.
Heyerdahl, T. (1986) *The Maldives mystery*, London: George Allen & Unwin.
Hien, P.T.T. (2008) 'Sexual coercion within marriage in Quang Tri, Vietnam', *Culture, Health and Sexuality*, 10(S1): S177–S87.
Hilsdon, A.-M. (2003) 'Violence against Maranao Muslim women in the Philippines', in Manderson, L. and Bennett, L.R. (eds) *Violence against women in Asian societies*, London and New York: Routledge Curzon.

Hirsch, J.S. (2007) '"Love makes a family": Globalization, companionate marriage, and the modernization of gender inequality', in Padilla, M.B., Hirsch, J.S., Munoz-Laboy, M., Sember, R.E. and Parker, R.G. (eds) *Love and globalization: Transformations of intimacy in the contemporary world*, Nashville, TN: Vanderbilt University Press.

Hoelter, L., Axinn, W. and Ghimire, D. (2004) 'Social change, premarital nonfamily experiences and marital dynamics', *Journal of Marriage and Family*, 66(5): 1131–51.

Hoffman, K.L., Demo, D.H. and Edwards, J.N. (1994) 'Physical wife abuse in a non-western society: An integrated approach', *Journal of Marriage and the Family*, 56: 131–46.

Holtzworth-Munroe, A. (2000) 'A typology of men who are violent towards their female partners: Making sense of the heterogeneity in husband violence', *Current Directions in Psychological Science*, 9(4): 140–3.

Hosking, P. (2006) *The 'rights' side of life: A baseline human rights survey – Survey report*, Malé: Human Rights Commission and UNDP.

Hotaling, G.T. and Sugarman, D.B. (1986) 'An analysis of risk markers in husband to wife violence: The current state of knowledge', *Violence and Victims*, 1: 101–24.

Hottocks, R. (1994) *Masculinity in crisis*, New York: St Martin's.

Howell, S. and Willis, R. (1989) *Societies at peace: Anthropological perspectives*, London and New York: Routledge.

Human Rights Council (2007) *Report of the Special Rapporteur on freedom of religion or belief, Asma Jahangir*, Geneva: Human Rights Council.

Hunjan, S. and Towson, S. (2007) '"Virginity is everything": Sexuality in the context of intimate partner violence in the South Asian Community', in Dasgupta, S.D. (ed.) *Body evidence: Intimate violence against South Asian women in America*, New Brunswick, NJ: Rutgers University Press.

Hursheed, M. (2006) 'The fights between rival street gangs and the security forces seem to be escalating', *The Evening Weekly*, 27 June, Malé, p. 4.

Hynes, M., Ward, J., Robertson, K. and Crouse, C. (2003) 'A determination of the prevalence of gender based violence among conflict-affected populations in East Timor', *Disasters*, 28(3): 294–321.

Ibrahim, M. (1991) *National machinery for the advancement of women in the Maldives: Evaluation and suggestions*, Malé: Department of Women's Affairs.

ICRW (2002) *Men, masculinity and domestic violence in India: Summary report of four studies*, Washington, DC: International Center for Research on Women.

Idrus, N.I. and Bennett, L.R. (2003) 'Presumed consent: marital violence in Bugis society', in Manderson, L. and Bennett, L.R. (eds) *Violence against women in Asian societies*, London and New York: Routledge Curzon.

Imam, U. and Akhtar, P. (2005) 'Researching Asian children's experiences of domestic violence: The significance of cultural competence and shared ethnicities of participants in research process', in Skinner, T., Hester, M. and Malos, E. (eds) *Researching gender violence: Feminist methodology in action*, Cullompton: Willan Publishing.

Inhorn, M.C. (2007) 'Loving your infertile Muslim spouse: Notes on the globalization of IVF and its romantic commitments in Sunni Egypt and Shia Lebanon', in Padilla, M.B., Hirsch, J.S., Munoz-Laboy, M., Sember, R.E. and Parker, R.G. (eds) *Love and globalization: Transformations of intimacy in the contemporary world*, Nashville, TN: Vanderbilt University Press.

Island, D. and Letellier, P. (1991) *Men who beat men who love them: Battered gay men and domestic violence*, New York: Harrington Park Press.
Jaffe, P., Wolfe, D.A. and Wison, S.K. (1990) *Children of battered women*, New York: Sage.
Jahangir, A. (2006) 'Press conference statement by the Special Rapporteur on Freedom of Religion and Belief', *Minivan News*, 9 August, Malé, p. 3.
Jankowiak, W.R. and Fischer, E.F. (1992) 'A cross-cultural perspective on romantic love', *Ethnology*, 31(2): 149–55.
Jayasinghe, A. (2012) 'Trouble in paradise: Maldives and Islamic extremism', *AFP*. Malé. Online. Available HTTP: www.google.com/hostednews/afp/article/ALeqM5gpQRnwpootZot3dABRpSl68QzLbg (accessed 12 February 2012).
Jehu, P. (1988) *Beyond sexual abuse: Therapy with women who were victims in childhood*, Chichester: Wiley & Sons.
Jejeebhoy, S.J. (1998) 'Wife-beating in rural India: A husband's right?', *Economic and Political Weekly*, 23(15): 588–862.
Jewkes, R. and Abrahams, N. (2002) 'The epidemiology of rape and sexual coercion in South Africa: An overview', *Social Science & Medicine*, 55: 1231–44.
Jewkes, R., Levin, J. and Penn-Kekana, L. (2002) 'Risk factors for domestic violence: Findings from a South African cross-sectional study', *Social Science & Medicine*, 55: 1603–17.
Jimenez, A.C. (2005) 'Changing scales and the scales of change', *Critique of Anthropology*, 25(2): 157–76.
Johnson, H. (1996) *Dangerous domains: Violence against women in Canada*, Toronto: International Thomson Publishing.
Jolly, M. (1997) 'From Point Venus to Bali Ha'i: Eroticism and exoticism in representations of the Pacific', in Jolly, M. and Manderson, L. (eds) *Sites of desire, economies of pleasure: Sexualities in Asia and the Pacific*, Chicago, IL: University of Chicago Press.
Jones, A.S., Gielen, A.C., Campbell, J.C., Schollenberger, J., Dienemann, J.A., Kub, J., O'Campo, P.J. and Wynne, E.C. (1999) 'Annual and lifetime prevalence of partner abuse in a sample of female HMO enrollees', *American Journal of Obstetrics and Gynecology*, 9(6): 295–305.
Jordan, W. (2007) 'Aniya arrested over article "against Islam"', *Minivan News*, 3 May, Malé, p. 1.
Jory [Pseudonym], S. (2005) *Muslim by law: A right or a violation of rights? A study about the Maldives*, unpublished thesis.
Joseph, S. (1988) 'Feminization, feminism, self and politics', in Altorki, S. and El-Solh, C.F. (eds) *Arab women in the field: Studying your own society*, New York: Syracuse University Press.
Josephides, L. (1994) 'Gendered violence in a changing society: The case of urban Papua New Guinea', *Journal de la Societe des Oceanistes*, 99: 187–96.
Kabeer, N. (1994) *Reversed realities: Gender hierarchies in development thought*, London: Verso.
Kallivayalil, D. (2007) 'Mental and emotional wounds of domestic violence in South Asian women', in Dasgupta, S.D. (ed.) *Body evidence: Intimate violence against South Asian women in America*, New Brunswick, NJ: Rutgers University Press.
Kandiyoti, D. (1991) *Women, Islam and the state*, London: Macmillan.
Kandiyoti, D. (2007) 'Between the hammer and the anvil: Post-conflict reconstruction, Islam and women's rights', *Third World Quarterly*, 23(3): 503–17.

Kaplan, C. (1994) 'The politics of location as transnational feminist practice', in Grewal, I. and Kaplan, C. (eds) *Scattered Hegemonies: Postmodernity and Transnational Feminist Practices*, Minneapolis and London: University of Minnesota Press.

Kassam, Z. (ed.) (2010) *Women and Islam*, Santa Barbara, CA: ABC-CLIO.

Katz, J. and Chambliss, W.J. (1991) 'Biology and crime', in Sheley, J.F. (ed.) *Criminology: A contemporary handbook*, Belmont, CA: Wadsworth.

Kauffman, M. (2001) 'Building a movement of men working to end violence against women', *Development*, 44(3): 9–14.

Keck, M. (2012) 'Women lead defense of Maldivian democracy', *Huffington Post*, 19 March. Online. Available at HTTP: www.huffingtonpost.com/mary-keck/women-maldives_b_1336729.html (accessed 20 March 2012).

Kendall, L. (1996) *Getting married in Korea: Of gender, morality, and modernity*, Berkeley, CA: University of California Press.

Khan, A. and Hussain, R. (2008) 'Violence against women in Pakistan: Perceptions and experiences of domestic violence', *Asian Studies Review*, 32(2): 239–53.

Kimmel, M. (2007) 'Contextualizing men's violence: The personal meets the political', in O'Toole, L., Schiffman, J.R. and Edwards, M.L.K. (eds) *Gender violence: Interdisciplinary perspectives*, New York: New York University Press.

Kingdom of Cambodia (2009) *Violence against women 2009 follow-up survey: Final study report*, Phnom Penh: Ministry of Women's Affairs.

Kirkwood, C. (1993) *Leaving abusive partners: From the scars of survival to the wisdom for change*, London: Sage.

Kishor, S. and Johnson, K. (2004a) *Domestic violence in nine developing countries: A comparative study*, Calverton, MD: ORC MACRO International.

Kishor, S. and Johnson, K. (2004b) *Profiling domestic violence: A multi-country study*, Calverton, MD: ORC MARCO International.

Kocacik, F., Kutlar, A. and Erselcan, F. (2007) 'Domestic violence against women: A field study in Turkey', *Social Science Journal*, 44: 698–720.

Koenig, M.A., Ahmed, S., Hossain, M.B. and Mozumder, A.B.M.K.A. (2003) 'Women's status and domestic violence in rural Bangladesh: Individual- and community-level effects', *Demography*, 40(2): 269–88.

Krug, E.G., Dahlber, L.L., Mercy, J.A., Zwi, A.B. and Lozano, R. (2002) *World report on violence and health*, Geneva: World Health Organization.

Kulsum, M. (2006) 'Bill to allocate seats to women fails to pass in Majlis, translated from Dhivehi to English by Shaarif Ali', *Minivan News*, Malé, p. 6.

Kyriacou, D.N., Anglin, D., Taliaferro, E., Stone, S., Tubb, T., Linden, J.A., Muelleman, R., Barton, E. and Kraus, J.F. (1999) 'Risk factors for injury to women from domestic violence', *New England Journal of Medicine*, 341(25): 1892–8.

Lahoud, N. and Johns, A.H. (2005) 'Introduction', in Lahoud, N. and Johns, A.H. (eds) *Islam in world politics*, London and New York: Routledge.

Landenburger, K. (1989) 'A process of entrapment and recovery from an abusive relationship', *Issues in Mental Health Nursing*, 10: 209–27.

Larkin, B. (1997) 'Indian films and Nigerian lovers: Media and the creation of parallel modernities', *Africa Today*, 67(3): 406–39.

Latheef, H. (2006) 'The Adhaalath Party and religion: Elephants in our rooms', *Minivan News*, Malé, p. 19.

Latheef, M. (2007) 'Freedom of expression without boundaries, translated from Dhivehi to English by Shaarif Ali', *Haveeru*, Malé, pp. 8, 35.

Lederach, J.P. (2010) 'The "wow factor" and a non-theory of change', in Sampson, C., Abu-Nimer, M., Liebler, C. and Whitney, D. (eds) *Positive approaches to peacebuilding: A resource for innovators*, Chagrin Falls, OH: Taos Institute Publication.

Lee, E. (2007) 'Domestic violence and risk factors among Korean immigrant women in the United States', *Journal of Family Violence*, 22: 141–9.

Letellier, P. (1994) 'Gay and bisexual male domestic violence victimization: Challenges to feminist theory and responses to violence', *Violence and Victims*, 9(2): 95–106.

Levinson, D. (1989) *Family violence in cross-cultural perspective*, Newbury Park, CA: Sage Publications.

Liebler, C. and Sampson, C. (2010) 'Appreciative inquiry in peacebuilding: Imagining the possible', in Sampson, C., Abu-Nimer, M., Liebler, C. and Whitney, D. (eds) *Positive approaches to peacebuilding: A resource for innovators*, Chargrin Falls, OH: Taos Institute Publications.

Lilja, M. (2010) *Gender mapping of Cambodia: Gender helpdesk*, Stockholm: Stockholm University.

Lindberg, A. (2009) 'Islamization, modernization or globalization? Changed gender relations among South Indian Muslims', *South Asia: Journal of South Asian Studies*, 32(1): 86–109.

Loue, S. (2001) *Intimate partner violence: Societal, medical, legal and individual response*, New York: Kluwer Academic/Plenum Publishers.

Lu, L. and Chen, C. (1996) 'Correlates of coping behaviors: Internal and external resources', *Counselling Psychology Quarterly*, 9(3): 297–308.

Lubna, H. (2012) 'Security forces use water cannon on MDP women's sit-down protest', *Minivan News*, 6 March. Online. Available HTTP: http://minivannews.com/politics/security-forces-use-water-cannon-on-mdp-womens-sit-down-protest-32897 (accessed 10 March 2012).

Machrusah, S. (2010) 'Islam and women's political participation in Indonesia: discourses and practices', in Derichs, C. and Fleschenberg, A. (eds) *Religious fundamentalism and their gendered impacts in Asia*, Berlin: Friedrich-Ebert-Stiftung.

McMahon, S. and Dick, A. (2011) '"Being in a room with like-minded men": An exploratory study of men's participation in a bystander intervention program to prevent intimate partner violence', *Journal of Men's Studies*, 19(1): 3–18.

Mahajan, A. (1995) *Family violence and abuse in India*, New Delhi: Deep and Deep Publications.

Mahmood, S. (2005) *The politics of piety: The Islamic revival of the feminist subject*, Princeton, NJ: Princeton University Press.

Mak, W.W.S., Chong, E.S.K. and Kwong, M.M.F. (2010) 'Prevalence of same-sex intimate partner violence in Hong Kong', *Public Health*, 124(3): 149–52.

Makan, A. (2007) 'Day of turmoil for female dissidents', *Minivan News*, 24 April, Malé, p. 5.

Maldives Dissent (2009) 'The religious right calls for violence against women and children to continue', *Maldives Dissent Blogspot*. Online. Available HTTP: http://maldivesdissent.blogspot.co.uk/search?updated-min=2009-01-01T00:00:00-08:00&updated-max=2010-01-01T00:00:00-08:00&max-results=26 (accessed 24 July 2009).

Maloney, C. (1976) 'The Maldives: New stresses in an old nation', *Asian Survey*, 16(7): 654–71.

Maloney, C. (1980) *People of the Maldives Islands*, New Delhi: Orient Longman.
Mandaville, P. (2007) 'Globalization and the politics of religious knowledge: Pluralizing authority in the Muslim world', *Theory, Culture & Society*, 24(2): 101–15.
Marchand, M.H. and Runyan, A.S. (2000) 'Introduction: Feminist sightings of global restructuring – Conceptualizations and reconceptualizations', in Marchand, M.H. and Runyan, A.S. (eds) *Gender and global restructuring: Sightings, sites and resistances*, New York: Routledge.
Marcotte, R.D. (2005) 'Identity, power, and the Islamist discourse on women: an exploration of Islamism and gender issues in Egypt', in Lahoud, N. and Johns, A.H. (eds) *Islam in world politics*, London and New York: Routledge.
Marsden, M. (2007) 'Love and elopement in northern Pakistan', *Journal of the Royal Anthropological Institute*, 13: 91–108.
Martin, S., Moracco, K., Garro, J., Tsui, A.O., Kupper, L.L. and Chase, J.L. (2002) 'Domestic violence across generations: Findings from northern India', *American Journal of Epidemiology*, 31: 560–72.
Masamura, W.T. (1979) 'Wife abuse and other forms of aggression', *Victimology International Journal*, 4(1): 46–59.
Mazumdar, R. (1998) 'Marital rape: Some ethical and cultural considerations', in Dasgupta, S.D. (eds) *A patchwork shawl: Chronicles of South Asian women in America*, New Brunswick, NJ: Rutgers University Press.
Mendieta, D. (2007) *Global fragments: Latinamericanisms, globalizations, and critical theory*, New York: State University of New York Press.
Merry, S.E. (2001) 'Rights, religion and community: Approaches to violence against women in the context of globalization', *Law and Society Review*, 35(1): 39–88.
Michalski, J. (2004) 'Making sociological sense out of trends in intimate partner violence', *Violence against Women*, 10(6): 652–75.
Michau, L. (2005) 'Good practice in designing a community-based approach to prevent domestic violence', in *Expert Group Meeting Workshop Violence against women: Good practices in combating and eliminating violence against women*. Vienna: UN Division for the Advancement of Women in collaboration with UN Office on Drugs and Crime.
Miller, S.L. (1994) 'Expanding the boundaries: Toward a more inclusive and integrated study of intimate violence', *Violence and Victims*, 9: 183–99.
Ministry of Gender Family Development and Social Security (2004) *Untold stories: Violence against women in the Maldives*, Malé: Club Hulhevi.
Ministry of Justice (2006) *Malé and Island Court sentences for zineh, 2003–2005*, Malé: Ministry of Justice.
Minivan News (2005) 'The Paateys: Heroin addiction in the Maldives', *Minivan News*, 13 January, Malé, p. 2.
Minivan News (2006a) 'An island divided', *Minivan News*, Malé, p. 19.
Minivan News (2006b) 'Justice Minister slams UN Special Rapporteur', *Minivan News*, Malé, p. 1.
Minivan News (2006c) 'MDP politician seconded supreme council clause', *Minivan News*, Malé, p. 1.
Minivan News (2006d) 'Rogue Islamic scholar sentenced', *Minivan News*, Malé, p. 19.
Minivan News (2007) 'Sheikh Fareed arrested', *Minivan News*, 24 January, Malé, p. 1.
Mir-Hosseini, Z. (1992) 'Women and politics in post-Khomeini Iran: Divorce, veiling and emerging feminist voices', in Afshar, H. (ed.) *Women and politics in the Third World*, London: Routledge.

Misra, A. (2004) 'Theorising "small" and "micro" state behaviour using the Maldives, Bhutan and Nepal', *Contemporary South Asia*, 13(2): 133–48.
Mitchell, W.E. (1992) 'Why Nape men don't beat their wives: Constraint towards domestic tranquility in a New Guinea society', in Counts, D.A., Brown, J.K. and Campbell, J.C. (eds) *Sanctions and sanctuary: Cultural perspectives on the beating of wives*, Oxford: Westview Press.
Mittra, S. and Kumar, B. (2004) *Encyclopedia of women in South Asia: Maldives*, Delhi: Kalpaz Publications.
Moghadam, V.M. (2001) 'Feminism and Islamic fundamentalism: A secularist interpretation', *Journal of Women's History*, 13(1): 42–5.
Moghadam, V.M. (2003) *Modernizing women: Gender and social change in the Middle East*, Boulder, CO: Lynne Rienner.
Moghissi, H. (1999) *Feminism and Islamic fundamentalism: The limits of postmodern analysis*, London and New York: Zed Books.
Mohamed, A. (2007) 'Women protest against drugs', *Minivan News*, 24 April, Malé, p. 3.
Mohanty, C.T. (1991) 'Under Western eyes: Feminist scholarship and colonial discourses', in C.T. Mohanty, A. Russo, and L. Torres (eds) *Third World women and the politics of feminism*. Bloomington, IN: Indiana University Press.
Mohanty, C.T. (2003) *Feminism without borders: Decolonizing theory, practicing solidarity*, London: Duke University Press.
Moosa, H.F. and Shareef, A. (2007) 'Islam doesn't ask us to wear black: President Gayoom', *Minivan News*, Malé, p. 5.
Moraes, C.L. and Reichenheim, M.E. (2002) 'Domestic violence during pregnancy in Rio de Janeiro, Brazil', *International Journal of Gynecology and Obstetrics*, 79: 269–77.
Mouzos, J. and Makkai, T. (2004) *Women's experiences of male violence: Findings from the Australian component of the International Violence against Women Survey (IVAWS)*, Canberra: Australian Government; Australian Institute of Criminology.
Musthaq, F. (2006) 'That sinking feeling', *The Evening Weekly*, Malé, 31 October, p. 5.
Naik, Z. (2008a) 'Dr Zakir Naik and the controversy', TwoCircles.net. Online. AvailableHTTP:http://twocircles.net/2008nov12/dr_zakir_naik_and_controversy.html (accessed 2 April 2011).
Naik, Z. (2008b) 'Dr. Zakir Naik: Airhostess – a decent job?', YouTube. Online. Available HTTP: www.youtube.com/watch?v=nT_7m_XjnB4 (accessed 2 April 2011).
Naik, Z. (2009) 'Is dating forbidden (haram) in Islam?'. Online. Available HTTP: http://ourislamicweb.blogspot.co.uk/2011/01/is-dating-forbidden-haram-in-islam-dr.html (accessed 2 April 2011).
Naish, A. (2009) 'Contentious article of Child Abuse Act to be reassessed', *Minivan News*, 23 November, Malé, p. 2.
Narayan, K. (1993) 'How native is a "native anthropologist"?', *American Anthropologist*, 95: 671–85.
Narayan, U. (1997) *Dislocating cultures/identities, traditions, and Third-World feminism*, New York and London: Routledge.
Naseem, A. (2010) 'Domestic violence accepted and justified in the Maldives, says report', *Minivan News*, 20 October. Online. Available HTTP: http://minivannews.com/politics/domestic-violence-accepted-and-justified-in-the-maldives-says-report-12500 (accessed 24 March 2012).

Nash, J. (1992) 'Factors relating to infrequent domestic violence among the Nagovisi', in Counts, D.A., Brown, J.K. and Campbell, J.C. (eds) *Sanctions and sanctuary: Cultural perspectives on the beating of wives*, Oxford: Westview Press.
Nasheed, M. (2012) 'The dregs of dictatorship', *New York Times*, 8 February. Online. Available HTTP: www.nytimes.com/2012/02/08/opinion/in-the-maldives-strangled-democracy.html (accessed 9 February 2012).
Naved, R.T., Huque, H., Farah, S. and Shuvra, M.M.R. (2011) *Men's attitudes and practices regarding gender and violence against women in Bangladesh: Preliminary findings*, Dhaka: icddr,b; UNFPA and Partners for Prevention.
Nazeer, A. (2010) 'Islamic Ministry expresses concern over isolated congregations', *Minivan News*, 14 April, Malé, p. 5.
Nelson, E. and Zimmerman, C. (1996) *Household survey on domestic violence in Cambodia*, Phnom Penh: Ministry of Women's Affairs and the Project against Domestic Violence.
Newcomb, R. (2006) 'Gendering the city, gendering the nation: Contesting urban space in Fes, Morocco', *City & Society*, 18(2): 288–311.
Nielsen, J.M., Endo, R.K. and Ellington, B.L. (1992) 'Social isolation and wife abuse: A research report', in Viano, E.C. (ed.) *Intimate violence: Interdisciplinary perspectives*, Washington, DC: Hemisphere Publishing Corp.
NNCB (2003) *Rapid situation assessment of drug abuse in Maldives*, Malé: Narcotics Control Board.
Nurmila, N. (2009) *Women, Islam and everyday life: Renegotiating polygamy in Indonesia*, London and New York: Routledge.
O'Campo, P., Gielen, A., Faden, R., Xue, X., Kass, N. and Mei-Cheng, W. (1995) 'Violence by male partners against women during the childbearing years: A contextual analysis', *American Journal of Public Health*, 85: 1092–7.
Omidi, M. (2009) 'Amnesty calls for moratorium on flogging', *Minivan News*, 9 July. Online. Available HTTP: http://minivannews.com/society/amnesty-calls-for-moratorium-on-flogging-1371 (accessed 24 July 2009).
Orsini, F. (2006) 'Introduction', in Orsini, F. (ed.) *Love in South Asia: A cultural history*, Cambridge: Cambridge University Press.
Ortega, L.R. (2010) 'Discrepancies in rape statistics highlighted in NGOs report', *Minivan News*, 22 March. Online. Available HTTP: http://minivannews.com/society/ngo-press-release-4731 (accessed 4 February 2012).
Osella, C. and Osella, F. (2000) 'Friendship and flirting: Micro-politics in Kerela, South India', *Journal of the Royal Anthropological Institute*, 4: 189–206.
O'Shea, M. (2004) *Dhon Hiyala and Ali Fulhu: Background and origins*, Malé: Novelty Press.
O'Toole, L., Schiffman, J.R. and Edwards, M.L.K. (2007) 'Preface: Conceptualizing gender violence', in O'Toole, L., Schiffman, J.R. and Edwards, M.L.K. (eds) *Gender violence: Interdisciplinary perspectives*, New York and London: New York University Press.
Padilla, M.B., Hirsch, J.S., Munoz-Laboy, M., Sember, R.E. and Parker, R.G. (2007) 'Introduction: Cross-cultural reflections on an intimate intersection', in Padilla, M.B., Hirsch, J.S., Munoz-Laboy, M., Sember, R.E. and Parker, R.G. (eds) *Love and globalization: Transformations of intimacy in the contemporary world*, Nashville, TN: Vanderbilt University Press.
Pateman, C. (2008) 'Democracy, human rights and a basic income in a global era', 12th BIEN Congress: Inequality and Development in a Globalized Economy, Dublin.

Peletz, M.G. (2009) *Gender pluralism: Southeast Asia since early modern times*, New York: Taylor & Francis.
Pence, E. and Paymar, M. (1993) *Education groups for men who batter: The Duluth model*, New York: Springer.
Pinnewala, P. (2009) 'Good women, martyrs, and survivors: A theoretical framework for South Asian women's responses to partner violence', *Violence against Women*, 15(1): 81–105.
Plitcha, S. (1992) 'The effects of female abuse on health care utilization and health status: A literature review', *Women's Health*, 2: 154–61.
Pottenger, J.R. (2005) 'Islam and ideology in Central Asia', in Lahoud, N. and Johns, A.H. (eds) *Islam in world politics*, London and New York: Routledge.
Pyrard, F. (1619) *The voyage of Francois Pyrard of Laval to the East Indies, The Maldives, The Moluccas and Brazil*, New York: Burt Franklin.
Radford, L. and Tsutsumi, K. (2004) 'Globalization and violence against women: Inequalities in risks, responsibilities and blame in the UK and Japan', *Women's Studies International Forum*, 27: 1–12.
Rani, M. and Bonu, S. (2009) 'Attitudes towards wife beating: A cross-country study in Asia', *Journal of Interpersonal Violence*, 24(8): 1371–97.
Rao, S. (2007) 'The globalization of Bollywood: An ethnography of nonelite audiences in India', *Communication Review*, 10: 57–76.
Rao, V. (1997) 'Wife-beating in rural South India: A qualitative and economic analysis', *Social Science & Medicine*, 44: 1169–80.
Rasheed, A. (2006a) 'Islam, Maldives and the reform movement', *Minivan News*, 7 October, Malé, p. 19.
Rasheed, A. (2006b) 'Unwrapping violence', *Adduvas*, Malé, pp. 27–9.
Rasheed, A. (2006c) 'Who's responsible for the increasing number of street fights?', *The Evening Weekly*, 22 August, Malé.
Rasheed, A. (2007a) 'Delay: The key word', *Minivan News*, Malé, p. 23.
Rasheed, A. (2007b) 'Letter to the editor', *Minivan News*, Malé, p. 15.
Rasheed, H. (2007) 'Attacks against expatriates almost a daily occurrence', *Haveeru News Service*, 27 August, Malé, p. 2.
Rasheed, Z. (2008) '"It's in my heart": A remote island struggles for change', *Minivan News*, 26 October, Malé, p. 19.
Rastogi, M. and Therly, P. (2006) 'Dowry and its link to violence against women in India', *Trauma, Violence and Abuse*, 7(1): 66–77.
Razee, H. (2000) *Gender and development in the Maldives: A review of twenty years 1979–1999*, Malé: UN Theme Group on Gender with the support of the Ministry of Women's Affairs and Social Security.
Razee, H. (2006) *'Being a good woman': Suffering and distress through the voices of women in the Maldives*, unpublished thesis, University of New South Wales.
Rege, S. (2003) 'More than just tacking women on to the "macropicture": Feminist contributions to globalization discourses', *Economic and Political Weekly*, 38(43): 4555–63.
Renzetti, C.M. and Miley, C.H. (eds) (1996) *Violence in gay and lesbian domestic partnerships*, New York: The Haworth Press.
Republic of Maldives (1998) *Republic of Maldives vulnerability and poverty assessment 1*, Malé: Ministry of Planning and National Development and United Nations Development Programme.
Republic of Maldives (2005a) *Millennium development goals: Maldives country report 2005*, Malé: Ministry of Planning and National Development.

Republic of Maldives (2005b) *National recovery and reconstruction plan: Programmes and plans*, Malé: Ministry of Planning and National Development.
Republic of Maldives (2005c) *Statistical yearbook of Maldives 2005*, Malé: Ministry of Planning and National Development.
Republic of Maldives (2006a) *Republic of Maldives vulnerability and poverty assessment 2*, Malé: Ministry of Planning and National Development and United Nations Development Programme.
Republic of Maldives (2006b) *The national gender policy of the Government of the Republic of the Maldives*, Malé: Republic of Maldives.
Republic of Maldives (2008a) *Analytical report: Population and housing census 2006*, Malé: Ministry of Planning and National Development.
Republic of Maldives (2008b) *Constitution of the Maldives, 2008*, Malé: Ministry of Legal Reform, Information and Arts.
Republic of Maldives (2008c) *Statistical yearbook of Maldives, 2008*, Malé: Ministry of Planning and National Development.
Republic of Maldives (2011a) *Millennium Development Goals: Maldives country report 2011* Malé: Department of National Planning.
Republic of Maldives (2011b) *Statistical yearbook 2011*, Malé: Department of National Planning.
Republic of Sri Lanka (2004) *Campaign to end domestic violence against women launched*, Colombo: Republic of Sri Lanka.
Rinaldo, R. (2008) 'Muslim women, middle class habitus, and modernity in Indonesia', *Contemporary Islam*, 2(1): 23–39.
Rishana, H. (2006) 'Sex and adolescents', *The Evening Weekly*, Malé, p. 5.
Robertson, N. and Busch, R. (1994) ' Not in front of the children: Spousal violence and its effects on children', *Butterworths Family Law Journal*, 6: 107–15.
Robertson, R. (1990) *Globalization, social theory and global culture*, London: Sage.
Robertson, R. and Khondker, H.H. (1998) 'Discourses of globalization: preliminary considerations', *International Sociology*, 13(1): 25–40.
Robinson, J. (2010a) 'Apostate publicly represents and rejoins Islam, after counselling', *Minivan News*, 1 June. Online. Available HTTP: http://minivannews.com/politics/apostate-publicly-repents-and-rejoins-islam-after-counselling-7704 (accessed 1 June 2010).
Robinson, J. (2010b) 'Islamic Ministry completes religious unity regulations', *Minivan News*, 6 May, Malé, p. 1.
Robinson, J. (2012) 'Amnesty condemns violent MNDF attack on a group of "peaceful women protesters" in Addu', *Minivan News*, 1 March. Online. Available HTTP: http://minivannews.com/politics/amnesty-condemns-violent-mndf-attacks-on-peaceful-women-protesters-in-addu-32709 (accessed 10 March 2012).
Robinson, K.M. (2009) *Gender, Islam and democracy in Indonesia*, Abingdon and New York: Routledge.
Rocca, C.H., Rathod, S., Falle, T., Pande, R.P. and Krishnan, S. (2009) 'Challenging assumptions about women's empowerment: Social and economic resources and domestic violence among young married women in urban South India', *International Journal of Epidemiology*, 38: 577–85.
Roces, M. and Edwards, L. (2000) 'Contesting gender narratives, 1970–2000', in Edwards, L. and Roces, M. (eds) *Women in Asia: Tradition, modernity and globalization*, St Leonards: Allen & Unwin.
Romero-Frias, X. (2003) *The Maldives Islanders: A study of the popular culture of an ancient Ocean Kingdom*, 3rd rev. edn, Barcelona: Nova Ethnographia Indica.

Rony, F.T. (1996) *The third eye: Race, cinema and ethnographic spectacle*, Durham, NC and London: Duke University Press.
Rosenberg, M. (2008) 'A Maldivian island into itself', *Sunday Canberra Times*, Canberra, 10 February, p. 26.
Roy, A. (2002) *The algebra of infinite justice*, London: Flamingo.
Rozan (2012) *Will the real men please stand up? Stories of five men and their affirmative action against sexual violence*, Islamabad: Rozan.
Sadiq, A. (1976) *Dhon Hiyala and Ali Fulhu*, Malé: Novelty Press.
Saeed, A. (2006) *Islamic thought: An introduction*, London and New York: Routledge.
Saeed, S., Naseem, I., Moosa, D. and Afaal, A. (2003) *Reproductive and sexual health of adolescents in the Maldives*, Malé: UNRC.
Sahgal, G. and Yuval-Davis, N. (1991) 'Refusing Holy Orders', *Women Living under Muslim Laws Dossier*, 9(10): 23–6.
Salim, A. (2007) 'Dynamic legal pluralism in modern Indonesia: The state and the sharia (court) in the changing constellations of Aceh', First International Conference on Aceh and Indian Ocean Studies, Banda Aceh, 24–26 February 2007.
Saman, M. (2007) 'MDP activist defends the veil, translated from Dhivehi to English by Shaarif Ali', *Minivan News*, 25 March, Malé, p. 6.
Sampson, C. (2010) 'Introduction', in Sampson, C., Abu-Nimer, M., Liebler, C. and Whitney, D. (eds) *Positive approaches to peacebuilding: A resource for innovators*, Chargrin Falls, OH: Taos Institute Publications.
Sampson, C., Abu-Nimer, M., Liebler, C. and Whitney, D. (2010) *Positive approaches to peacebuilding: A resource for innovators*, Chargrin Falls, OH: Taos Institute Publications.
Sandbrook, R. and Romano, D. (2004) 'Globalization, extremism and violence in poor countries', *Third World Quarterly*, 25: 1007–30.
Saunders, D.G. (1992) 'A typology of men who batter: Three types derived from cluster analysis', *American Journal of Orthopsychiatry*, 62: 264–75.
Schafer, J., Caetano, R. and Cunradi, C.B. (2004) 'A path model of risk factors for intimate partner violence among couples in the United States', *Journal or Interpersonal Violence*, 19(2): 127–42.
Schuler, S.R., Hashemi, S.M., Riley, A.P. and Akhter, S. (1996) 'Credit programs, patriarchy and men's violence against women in rural Bangladesh', *Social Science and Medicine*, 43(12): 1729–42.
Scott, K., Schafer, J. and Greenfield, T.K. (1999) 'The role of alcohol in physical assault perpetration and victimization', *Journal of Studies of Alcohol*, 60: 528–36.
Secretariat of the Pacific Community (2009) *Solomon Islands Family Health and Safety Study Report*, New Caledonia: Ministry of Women, Youth and Children Affairs and Secretariat of the Pacific Community.
Secretariat of the Pacific Community (2010) *Kiribati Family Health and Support Study Report*, New Caledonia: Ministry of Internal and Social Affairs and Secretariat of the Pacific Community.
Seedat, M., Niekerk, A.V., Jewkes, R., Suffla, S. and Ratele, K. (2009) 'Violence and injuries in South Africa: Prioritising an agenda for prevention', *The Lancet*, 374(9694): 1101–22.
Sen, P. (2005) '"Crimes of honour", value and meaning', in Welchman, L. and Hossain, S. (eds) *'Honour': Crimes, paradigms and violence against women*, Victoria: Spinifex Press.
Sev'er, A. (2002) *Fleeing the house of horrors: Women who have left abusive partners*, Toronto: University of Toronto Press.

Bibliography

Shaikh, S.D. (2007) 'A Tafsir of praxis: Gender, marital violence, and resistance in a South African Muslim community', in Maguire, D.C. and Shaikh, S. (eds) *Violence against women in contemporary world religions: Roots and cures*, Cleveland, OH: Pilgrim Press.

Shareef, I.A. (2006) 'An equation for rebellion', *Evening Weekly*, Malé.

Sharify-Funk, M. (2008) *Encountering the transnational: Women, Islam and the politics of interpretation*, Aldershot and Burlington, VT: Ashgate Publishing.

Shauna, A. (2008) 'Politicians must face the real religious crisis', *Minivan News*, Malé, p. 19.

Shepard, M.F. and Pence, E.L. (eds) (1999) *Coordinating community responses to domestic violence: Lessons from the Duluth model and beyond*, Thousand Oaks, CA: Sage.

Siedler, H. (1980) *Report on the survey of island women*, Malé: National Planning Agency, Government of Maldives in collaboration with the Overseas Education Fund.

Silberschmidt, M. (2001) 'Disempowerment of men in rural and urban East Africa: Implications for male identity and sexual behaviour', *World Development*, 29(4): 657–71.

Smith, M. (1990) 'Patriarchal ideology and wife beating: A test of a feminist hypothesis', *Violence and Victims*, 5: 257–73.

Spark, C. (2011) 'Gender trouble in town: Educated women eluding male domination, gender violence and marriage in PNG', *Asia Pacific Journal of Anthropology*, 12(2): 164–79.

Sparr, P. (1994) *Mortgaging women's lives: Feminist critiques of structural adjustment*, London and Atlantic Highlands, NJ: Zed Books.

Stark, E. (2007) *Coercive control: The entrapment of women in personal life*, Oxford: Oxford University Press.

State of Victoria (2009) *A right to respect: Victoria's plan to prevent violence against women 2010–2020*, Melbourne: Office of Women's Policy.

Stivens, M. (1998) 'Modernizing the Malay mother', in Ram, K. and Jolly, M. (eds) *Maternities and modernities: Colonial and postcolonial experiences in Asia and the Pacific*, Cambridge: Cambridge University Press.

Stivens, M. (2006) '"Family values" and Islamic revival: Gender, rights and state moral projects in Malaysia', *Women's Studies International Forum*, 29(4): 354–67.

Strauchler, O., McCloskey, K., Malloy, K., Sitaker, M., Grigsby, N. and Gillig, P. (2004) 'Humiliation, manipulation, and control: Evidence of centrality in domestic violence against an adult partner', *Journal of Family Violence*, 19(6): 339–54.

Straus, M.A. (1994) 'State-to-state differences in social inequality and social binds in relation to assaults on wives in the United States', *Journal of Comparative Family Studies*, 25: 7–24.

Straus, M.A., Gelles, R.J. and Smith, C. (eds) (1990) *Physical violence in American families: Risk factors and adaptations to violence in 8,145 families*, Brunswick, NJ: Transaction.

Swiss, S. and Giller, J. (1993) 'Rape as a crime of war: A medical perspective', *Journal of the American Medical Association*, 270: 612–5.

Tewari, N., Inman, A. and Sandhu, D. (2003) 'South Asian Americans: Culture, concerns and therapeutic strategies', in Mio, J. and Iwamasa, G. (eds) *Culturally diverse mental health: The changes of research and resistance*, New York: Brunner-Routledge.

The Hindu Online (2004) 'Maldives ready for change, says Gayoom: Excerpts from an interview with V.S. Sambandan', *The Hindu* Online, New Delhi, 5 September. Online. Available HTTP: http://www.hindu.com/2004/09/05/stories/2004090501771400.htm (accessed 17 October 2010).

The Jakarta Post (2006) 'Unease in Aceh as morality police crack down', *The Jakarta Post*, p. 3.

Tjaden, P. and Thoennes, N. (2000) *Extent, nature and consequences of intimate partner violence: Findings from the national violence against women survey*, Washington, DC: National Institute of Justice, Centers for Disease Control and Prevention.

Torres, S. and Han, H.R. (2003) 'Women's perceptions of their male batterers' characteristics and level of violence', *Issues in Mental Health Nursing*, 24: 667–79.

Trawick, M. (1990) *Notes on love in a Tamil family*, Berkeley, CA: University of California Press.

Ulrich, Y. (1998) 'What helped most in leaving spousal abuse', in Campbell, J. (ed.) *Empowering survivors of abuse*, Thousand Oaks, CA: Sage.

Umar, M. (1998) *Bride burning in India*, New Delhi: A.P.H. Publishing Corporation.

UNDP (2007) *Human development report 2007/2008: Fighting climate change – Human solidarity in a divided world*, New York: Palgrave Macmillan.

UNDP (2008) *Human development report 2007/2008*, New York: United Nations Development Programme.

UNDP (2010) *Human development report 2009*, New York: United Nations Development Programme.

UNDP Maldives (2010) *Summary report on women in public life in the Maldives: Situational analysis*, Malé: United Nations Development Programme.

UN General Assembly (2006) *In-depth study on all forms of violence against women: Report of the Secretary General*, Geneva: United Nations.

UNHCR (1995) *Sexual violence against refugees: Guidelines on prevention and response*, Geneva: United Nations High Commission for Refugees.

UNIFEM (2010) *Investing in gender equality: Ending violence against women*, New York: UNIFEM

US Department of State (2010a) *2009 Country Report on Human Rights Practices: Maldives*. Online. Available HTTP: www.state.gov/j/drl/rls/hrrpt/2009/sca/136090.htm (accessed 8 February 2012).

US Department of State (2010b) *International religious freedom report: Maldives*, Washington, DC: Bureau of Democracy, Human Rights, and Labor.

Velezinee, A. (2004) *Embedded gender contracts: The Family Law and lived realities in Malé, Maldives*, unpublished thesis, Institute of Social Studies, Graduate School of Development Studies.

Velzeboer, M., Ellsberg, M., Arcas, C.C. and Garcia-Moreno, C. (2003) *Violence against women: The health sector responds*, Washington, DC: Pan American Health Organization (PAHO).

Venkataramani-Kothari, A. (2007) 'Understanding South Asian immigrant women's experiences of violence', in Dasgupta, S.D. (ed.) *Body evidence: Intimate violence against South Asian women in America*, New Brunswick, NJ and London: Rutgers University Press.

Walby, S. and Allen, J. (2004) *Domestic violence, sexual assault and stalking: Findings from the British Crime Survey*, London: Home Office Research, Development and Statistics Directorate.

Walker, L.E. (1999) 'Psychology and domestic violence around the world', *American Psychologist*, 54: 21–9.
Warrington, M. (2001) '"I must get out": the geographies of domestic violence', *Royal Geographical Society*, 26: 365–82.
Watts, C., Heise, L., Ellsberg, M., Williams, L. and Garcia-Moreno, C. (1998a) *WHO multi-country study of women's health and domestic violence, core protocol*, Geneva: World Health Organization.
Watts, C., Keogh, E., Ndlovu, M. and Kwaramba, R. (1998b) 'Withholding of sex and forced sex: Dimensions of violence against Zimbabwean women', *Reproductive Health Matters*, 6(12): 57–65.
Webb, P.A. (1988) *Maldives: People and environment*, Bangkok: Media Transasia Limited.
Wekerle, C. and Wolfe, D.A. (1999) 'Dating violence in mid adolescence: Theory, significance, and emerging prevention initiatives', *Clinical Psychology Review*, 19: 435–56.
Welchman, L. and Hossain, S. (2005) 'Introduction: "Honour", rights and wrongs', in Welchman, L. and Hossain, S. (eds) *'Honour': Crimes, paradigms and violence against women*, Victoria: Spinifex Press.
Werbner, P. (2005) 'Honour, shame and the politics of sexual embodiment among South Asian Muslims in Britain and beyond: An analysis of debates in the public sphere', *International Social Science Review*, 6(1): 25–47.
Wesely, J.K., Allison, M.T. and Schneider, I.E. (2000) 'The lived body experience of domestic violence survivors: An interrogation of female identity', *Women's Studies International Forum*, 23(2): 211–22.
White, H.R. and Chen, P.H. (2002) 'Problem drinking and intimate partner violence', *Journal of Studies of Alcohol*, 63: 205–14.
Whitfield, C.L., Anda, R.F. and Felitti, V.J. (2003) 'Violence childhood experiences and the risk of intimate partner violence in adults: Assessment in a large health maintenance organization', *Journal of Interpersonal Violence*, 18(2): 166–85.
Whitney, D., Liebler, C. and Cooperrider, D. (2010) 'Appreciative inquiry in organizations and international development: An invitation to share and learn across fields', in Sampson, C., Abu-Nimer, M., Liebler, C. and Whitney, D. (eds) *Positive approaches to peacebuilding: A resource for innovators*, Chargrin Falls, OH: Taos Institute Publications.
WHO (2002) *World report on violence and health*, Geneva: World Health Organization.
Widom, C. (1989) 'The cycle of violence', *Science*, 244: 160–6.
Wieringa, S.E. (2005) 'Islamization in Indonesia: Women activists' discourses', *Signs: Journal of Women in Culture and Society*, 32(1): 1–8.
Wilcox, P. (2006) *Surviving domestic violence: Gender, poverty and agency*, Houndmills: Palgrave Macmillan.
Williams, C. (2004) 'Islamic extremism and Wahhabism', in Jones, D.M. (eds) *Globalization and the new terror: The Asia Pacific dimension*, Northampton, MA: Edward Elgar.
Williams, K.R. (1984) 'Economic sources of homicide: Reestimating the effects of poverty and inequality', *American Sociological Review*, 49: 283–9.
Williamson, L. (2006) 'Aceh wary over new Sharia police', *BBC News Online*, 8 December. Online. Available HTTP: http://news.bbc.co.uk/1/hi/world/asia-pacific/6220256.stm.

Wilt, S. and Olson, S. (1996) 'Prevalence of domestic violence in the United States', *Journal of the American Medical Women's Association*, 51(3): 77–82.

World Bank, Asian Development Bank and United Nations System (2005) *Maldives Tsunami: Impact and recovery, joint needs assessment*, Malé: World Bank–ADB–UN System.

Yllo, K. (1993) 'Through a feminist lens: Gender, power, and violence', in Gelles, R.J. and Loseke, D.R. (eds) *Current controversies on family violence*, Newbury Park, CA: Sage.

Yllo, K. (2005) 'Through a feminist lens: Gender, diversity and violence – Extending the feminist framework', in Loseke, D.R., Gelles, R.J. and Cavanaugh, M.M. (eds) *Current controversies on family violence*, Thousand Oaks, CA: Sage Publication.

Zaman, H. (2005) 'Domestic violence: South Asia', in Joseph, S., Najmabadi, A., Peteet, J., Shami, S., Siapno, J. and Smith, J.I. (eds) *Encyclopedia of women and Islamic cultures, vol. II: Family, law and politics*, Leiden and Boston: Brill.

Zimmerman, C.A., Stewart, S.E., Morrel-Samuels, S., Franzen, S. and Reischl, T.M. (2011) 'Youth empowerment solutions for peaceful communities: Combining theory and practice in a community level violence prevention curriculum', *Health Promotion Practice*, 12(3): 425–39.

Index

Note: n after a page number denotes that the topic referred to appears in a numbered note at the end of the chapter.

abuse *see* domestic violence
Adhaalath Party 1, 8, 9, 81–3, 85, 98
Adichie, Chimamanda Ngozie 3, 125
anger in Maldivian society 57
Aniya, Aishath, Secretary-General of the MDP 105–7
arranged marriages 28, 41, 44, 47, 68
Azerbaijan, influences of globalization 70, 88, 108

Bangladesh: crime of marital rape 22; dowry 50; prevalence of partner violence 10; women's rights 109
Bohm, David, theory of implicate order 128, 131
Bollywood *see* marriage, Maldivian
Buddhism 1, 4–5
buruga see headscarf

Cambodia: masculinity 63
childhood sexual abuse 40, 44
Child Sex Abuse Act (2009) 85
Committee on the Elimination of Discrimination against Women (CEDAW) 85
community support networks: as protection against partner violence 50
conservatism, Islamic *see* fundamentalism
Constitution of the Republic of Maldives: defines president as 'Protector of Islam' 72, 105; denies non-Muslims Maldivian citizenship 72, 104; Islam official state religion 72; women's eligibility for presidency 53, 95

contraception 22
controlling behaviours 26–7, 30, 43, 44, 86
crime in the Maldives: *see* social changes in the Maldives
cultural crisis: and development of Islamism 81
culture, Maldivian: and anger 57; effects on lower rate of partner violence 58; harmonious, non-violent 57; ideals of masculinity 61–3; modesty 25; no longer preserved 115; peaceful 58; romantic love 45; traditional components of family life 52; unifying 57; unity at risk from global influences 73

degradation as abusive control 22, 25, 29
democratization: impacts of 4, 78, 115; and the Indian Ocean tsunami 80–1
Dhivehi language 5, 45, 46
Dhivehi Rayyithunge Party (Maldivian People's Party) *see* DRP
Didi, Aishath Mohamed, 2006–8 Maldivian Minister of Gender and Family 49, 58, 60, 77, 79, 80, 86, 102, 103
divorce practices in the Maldives: as escape from partner violence 51–2; flexibility and acceptability 51; giving protection against partner violence 44; and Islamic law 51; under the Maldivian Family Law Act (2001) 75–8; new definition as a social problem 75; women's vulnerability to violence post-Family Law Act 76–8

divorce types under the Maldivian Family Law Act: *ruju, khul, faskh* 75–8; and *talaq* pronouncements 75–7
domestic violence: changes in women's experiences of 15; continuum of experiences 21; definitions 12, 36n3, 133; denial 9–10; emotional abuse 22, 24, 25, 26; factors increasing women's vulnerability to 108–9; and globalization 13–14, 17, 127; hidden 10; increases reported after 2008 124; as indicator of status of women 2; limitations to strategies for ending 125; linkages between causes 127–8; Maldives Domestic Violence Act 53; Maldivians historically non-violent 58–9; multiple technologies 21, 35; not culturally justified in the Maldives 60; physical forms 20–1; related to social change in the Maldives 3, 116–17; retaliation by women 25–6; sexual abuse 21–2; and women's disobedience 59; *see also* intimate partner violence (IPV)
dowry 46–7, 50, 52, 128
DRP (Dhivehi Rayyithunge Party; Maldivian People's Party) 8, 94, 98, 116
drug use *see* social changes

economic control of women 22, 24, 26, 36, 52
economic development: and globalization 15, 126–7; house structures 66; and marginalization of women 91–4, 97, 108, 127; and social changes in the Maldives 4–6, 112–14, 118; tourism 5, 73, 91
education levels: in the Maldives 6; as risk factor for partner violence 13, 39, 40
emotional abuse *see* domestic violence

family law *see* Maldivian Family Law (2001)
family support: loss of in restructured homes 67–8; as protective factor against partner violence 44, 49, 119
faskh see divorce types under the Maldivian Family Law Act
femininity 25, 63, 120, 127
financial abuse as controlling behaviour 27–8, 29

flexible marriage practices in the Maldives 44–50, 51; erosion by conservative Islamism 84–5; residence after marriage 49, 128; *see also* divorce practices in the Maldives
flogging, public, as punishment 53, 72; debate in the Maldives 99–100
focus group discussions: on community beliefs about violence against women 4; conservatism of young men 83–4; with health-care professionals 31, 34; of husband's sexual needs 23; marital rape 23; methodology in Maldives Survey 17n1; on the obedience of wives 65; on social isolation as abusive control 28
Freedom in the World Index 7
fundamentalism: arising from Maldivian youths studying abroad 79–80; disproportionate effect on women 89; Himandhoo Island conflict 78–9; as response by conservative Islamists to western influences 88–9; as vehicle of protest against liberal Islamism 79; *see also* Islamism

Gayoom, Maumoon Abdul (Maldivian President 1978–2008) 7; and Islamic revival 72–5, 78–9, 80–1, 94, 101–2, 104
Gender Advocacy Working Group 2
gender empowerment measure (GEM): decrease in the Maldives 94
gender equality: conflicts between women's public roles and conservatism 95–6; education 55; and lower prevalence of partner violence 52, 56; low Gender Inequality Index (GII) 55; majority belief in 55; objections to appointment of female judges 98–9; promoted during Gayoom's presidency 94; proposed legal reforms 95; women's historical role in Maldivian politics and society 54, 61
gender inequality: and codes of masculinity 63; controlled by regulations under Ministry of Islamic Affairs 87; defeat of proposed female quota in parliament 90, 96; increases likelihood of abuse in relationships 93; increasing under democratization 89; and response to the tsunami 92; sites in the Maldives 52–3

gender roles: in Maldivian marriage 69; promotion of women's rights opposed by conservative Islamists 95–7; public roles of women, impact of globalization on 90–1; in response to the tsunami 92–3; traditional household roles in the Maldives 48–9, 83–4
globalization: cultural complexities 15–16, 81; definition 15; effects on women's lives in the Maldives and Asia 88–9; further studies needed 17; and gender 16; gendered separation of public/private spheres 108; and Indian films 70–1; negative impacts 127; positive outcomes 126; promotion of democracy by international agencies 8, 80–1; and social disorganization 17, 112; and women's public roles 17
Globalized Ecological Model (*Fig.I.1* 14): five levels of factors as framework for the study of partner violence in the Maldives 13–16, 39; individual 39–44; community 52–6; family 44–52; society 56–60; global 63, 65–88 passim
'god-given right': justification of violence against women 94

headscarf (*buruga*): absence blamed for society's ills 97; and conservative Islamist views 87–8; as hair covering for modesty 24–5; increased use under Adhaalath Party influence 82; and the Indian Ocean tsunami 80; lack of choice 102–3; not formerly worn in the Maldives 71, 101; *see also* veiling
Himandhoo Island conflict 78–9
home: changes to family support structures 67–8; open structure in the Maldives 66; and privacy 66; as private space 14, 65–6; recent family restructuring to exclude outsiders 66–8; seclusion facilitates domestic violence 67–8
honour/shame complex 17; as a culturally specific means of patriarchal control in South Asia 55; not a gendered control in the Maldives 56
Human Development Index 5

humiliation, as abusive control 22, 25, 29, 36
husbands: control over wife's sexuality 22; sexual drive 22–3

income distribution in the Maldives *see* economic development
India: alcohol consumption as risk factor 43; availability of abortion 32; Bollywood influences 68, 70–1, 126, 128; dowry 50; education as risk factor 40; Gandhigram (Gandhi Villages) 131; masculinity 63, 123
Indian Ocean tsunami *see* tsunami, Indian Ocean
Indira Gandhi Memorial Hospital (IGMH): health care staff's recognition of partner violence 31, 34
Indonesia: defining the Islamic community 109–10; globalization and young Muslims' Islamic faith 15; Islamic revival movement 72; polygamy in 86; public democratization 89; roles of women under Islam 97; veiling and religious rules 102
intimate partner violence (IPV): definition of intimate partner 36n2; definitions of violence 12, 36n3, 133; effects of patriarchal values in South Asian culture 54; impacts on victims' children 35; impacts on women's health 29–31; initiated by women 12; lower prevalence rate in the Maldives 3, 9, 17; Maldives Survey 4; a multi-disciplinary problem 13; not result of Maldivian women's disobedience 20, 50; patterns of, in the Maldives 20–2; perceived prevalence in the Maldives 10; prevalence rates in countries other than the Maldives 3, 10–11; recognition by health care providers 30–1, 33–4; socio-cultural elements providing protection against 11; used to exert coercive control 35; use of health facilities by victims 34; women's vulnerability increased by Maldives 'social crisis' 122, 124; *see also* domestic violence
intimidation as abusive control 22, 24, 26
Islam: conservatism and Maldivian women's public roles 99; interpretation regarding sexual

obligations 22; as part of Maldivian daily life 72; public discussion 104–6; representative voice in the Maldives 103–5
Islamic Democratic Party 8
Islamic extremism: blamed for 2007 Malé bombing 116; controlled by Ministry of Islamic Affairs regulations 86–7; Nasheed on abuse of freedom of speech laws by 81; reaction to a non-Muslim in the Maldives 88; and resignation of President Nasheed 1
Islamic feminists: interpretation of the Qur'an on violence against women 84
Islamic revival: Arab/Islam religious schools 73–4; and change of Maldivian Constitution 72; as a global movement 72; and non-Islamic religions 73; and perceived need for strengthening families by legislation 75; and protection of Islamic religious unity 73–4; shift to a fundamentalist movement 78–80; *see also* Gayoom, Maumoon Abdul (Maldivian President 1978–2008)
Islamism: causes of change in domestic violence in the Maldives and Asia 3, 4, 15, 88–9, 126; in discourses about gender 4, 108; enabled by political uncertainties 116; in patriarchal family ideology 78, 83–4; as resistance to western influences 73, 78, 81
isolation of women by male partner: after marriage 49, 128; as means of abusive control 22, 25, 26, 28, 30, 36; social isolation as risk factor for violence 29, 42, 49, 67, 118–19; and stronger religious practices 89
izzat (Arabic) *see* honour/shame complex

judges, female 98–9

khul see divorce types under the Maldivian Family Law Act
Kiribati: acceptance of partner violence 59; prevalence of partner violence 11, 129

Malaysia: globalization and young Muslim's Islamic faith 15; Muslim women's legislated rights reduced 89, 109; state as interpreter of Islam 110
Maldives, Republic of: Constitution 53, 72, 95, 104, 105; economy 5; education 5–6; geography 4, 5; health 5–6; Human Development Index 5; language 5; Millennium Development Goals 5; politics 7–8; population density 6; religion 4–5, 74; services 6; tourism 5, 73
Maldives Democratic Party *see* MDP
Maldives Domestic Violence Act (2012) 53
Maldives Domestic Violence Bill 100
Maldives Survey (*Maldives Survey on Violence against Women*) 4, 9, 11; case studies 19, 20, 23–4, 26, 28, 30; feminist epistemology 13; restrictions on discussion of family problems 67
Maldivian culture *see* culture, Maldivian
Maldivian Family Law (2001) 75–8
Maldivian historical ruling queen 54–5
Maldivian law: discriminatory against women 53; Maldives Domestic Violence Act 53; and *zina* 53
Maldivian People's Party *see* DRP
Malé (capital of Maldives): evidence of 'social crisis' 112–14; housing 7; political demonstrations 8; problems of mass internal migration 6, 66, 113, 126; rate of growth 6–7
Maloney, Clarence (anthropologist) 4, 56, 57, 69, 71
marriage, arranged *see* arranged marriages
marriage, flexible *see* flexible marriage practices
marriage, Maldivian: changing expectations 68–9, 71; global influences 70–2; influence of Bollywood 68, 70–1, 126, 128; outside legal systems 84–5; and polygamy 84–5; and romantic love 45, 68; a traditional Maldivian *raivaru* 46–8; views on roles within 83–4; white weddings 69–70; *see also* divorce practices in the Maldives
masculinity, Maldivian: changes under Islamization 88–9; contrasted with ideals of, in other countries 61–3; and low prevalence of partner violence 63; marginalization of young men

111, 121–2, 127; preference by some for non-violence 121–2; recent changes towards violence 120–1; violence prevention 129
massage parlours, legitimate salons for women, closure under Adhaalath Party influence 82
MDP (Maldives Democratic Party): calling for new elections in 2012 1; concessions to Islamist parties to achieve power 82; discredited by President Gayoom 73; endorsement of female judges 98; establishment in exile in Sri Lanka 8; and political divisions 115–16; return to Maldives from exile 81; *see also* Aniya, Aishath, Secretary-General of the MDP
mental health consequences of violence: depression, anxiety and suicidal thoughts 33–4; emotional distress 32–3; help-seeking behaviour 34–5
Millennium Development Goals (MDG) 5
Ministry of Gender and Family 92; *see also* Didi, Aishath Mohamed 2006–8 Maldivian Minister of Gender and Family
Ministry of Islamic Affairs 82; regulations governing religion 86–7; and religious conflict 116; 2008 replaced Supreme Council of Islamic Affairs 87
modesty 25; *see also* reputation
multi-party democracy *see* political reform process

Nasheed, Mohamed: election to Presidency 8; forced resignation 1, 9, 115; on Islamic extremists 81
Nasir, Ibrahim, first president of the Republic of Maldives 7
National Gender Policy: recognition of gender equality by Islam 94–5
National Museum, Malé, destruction of artefacts 1
National Recovery and Reconstruction Programme (NRRP) *see* tsunami, Indian Ocean
National Women's Development Policy (NWDP) (Bangladesh): opposed by fundamentalists 109
Nepal: crime of marital rape 22; dowry 50; education as risk factor 40; family honour 55; partner's alcohol consumption 43; patriarchal control 43; prevalence of partner violence 10

obedience: and the influence of Islamism 83; a requirement of wives 20, 59
obligations, sexual 22

Pakistan: arranged marriages 41; crime of marital rape 22; dowry 50; education as risk factor 40
Papua New Guinea: acceptance of partner violence 59; non-violent masculinity 63; partner violence and failed masculinity 123; vulnerability of educated women 123
partner violence *see* intimate partner violence
patriarchal family ideology 78, 83–4
peace cultures, creation of 129–32
physical abuse *see* domestic violence
political parties *see* Adhaalath Party, DRP, Islamic Democratic Party, MDP
political reform process under international pressure 81
political tensions 7–8
polygamy 44, 51, 53, 84–5, 107–8
pregnancy: and abortion 32; unintended 32; violence during 28, 31, 32, 40
Protection of Religious Unity Act (1994) 74, 79; 2010 amended extensively by Ministry of Islamic Affairs 82–3
protective factors against partner violence in the Maldives: family support 42, 49; flexibility of marriage and divorce practices 17, 44, 51
protests, political 8, 115

Qur'an: on commands for self-reasoning 105; compulsory in Maldivian schools 73; on constraints to women's rights 96; as justification for gender inequality 83–4; and NWDP 109; on the obedience of women 83–4; recited at Maldivian wedding 69; reinterpretation by progressive Muslims 123; silent on women veiling 102

raivaru 45–8
Ramazan 72, 78
rape, marital 22, 23; Maldivian interpretation 24
Razee, H. (Maldivian ethnographer): on Maldivians' view of their country as peaceful 57; on women's household responsibilities 54
religion *see* Islamic revival
religious fundamentalism *see* fundamentalism
religious unity 73–4, 78–9
Religious Unity Act (1994) *see* Protection of Religious Unity Act (1994)
reproductive heath consequences of violence 31–2
reputation: as social control in the Maldives 56; *see also* honour/shame complex; modesty
risk factors for partner violence in the Maldives: affairs by partner 43; arranged marriages 48; childhood sexual abuse 40, 44; generality of partner violence 42–3; for individuals 39–44; lower incidence in the Maldives 44; modified by family support 42, 49; partner's use of alcohol or drugs 43–4; post-marriage residence decisions 49; social isolation 42
roles *see* gender roles
ruju see divorce types under the Maldivian Family Law Act

safer cities projects 131
sexual abuse *see* domestic violence
Shari'a: application of civil law based on, by Maldivian courts 72; discriminatory punishment 53; and female judges 99; implementation promoted by Adhaalath Party 81; and marriage 69
social changes in the Maldives 2–4; community fragmentation 116–17; drug use 116–17, 119–20; effects on prevalence of domestic violence 3; increase in crime 111, 117–18, 120, 122, 124, 126; linked with violence against women 117–18; political divisions 115–16; symptoms and causes of contemporary 'social crisis,' 111, 126

social media: Maldivians' use of in discussions of Islam 107; use of in demonstrations 2
Sri Lanka: crime of marital rape 22; establishment of MDP in exile 8; prevalence of partner violence 10
suicide, Maldivian societal attitudes to 33
Supreme Council of Islamic Affairs 74; replaced by Ministry of Islamic Affairs 87

talaq see divorce types under the Maldivian Family Law Act
tourism 5; and employment of women 91; separation from local Maldivian life 73
tsunami, Indian Ocean: international pressure on local politics 8, 80–1; international response and the economic marginalization of women 92–3; linked to women's immorality in South Asia 80; National Recovery and Reconstruction Programme (NRRP) 92–3; perceived as result of Allah's wrath 80; physical effects 8; Tsunami Impact Assessment of women's livelihoods 92–3

UNIFEM (United Nations Development Fund for Women) 52
United Nations Development Programme (UNDP): and women's lost livelihoods from the tsunami 92
UN Special Rapporteur on Freedom of Religion: controversy over visit to the Maldives 2006 104
urbanization: and domestic violence 6; reconfiguration of domestic housing 66

veiling 47–8; indicator of public/private separations 101, 109; rapid rise in use of 107; and rise in religious conservatism 100–3; *see also* headscarf (*buruga*)
violence, partner: operational definitions used in the Maldives Survey 36n3, 133; *see also* domestic violence, intimate partner violence
violence prevention 128–9; positive approaches 129–30; *see also* peace cultures, creation of

Waheed, Mohamed: supported by Adhaalath Party 83; sworn in as President 8

Wahhabi movement, funding from Middle East 80

wealth, personal *see* economic development

western culture and influences: imposed by globalization 15; Islamism as resistance to 73, 79; on marriage 68, 71; threat to Islam 106

white weddings *see* marriage, Maldivian

WHO Multi-Country Study on Women's Health and Domestic Violence survey methodology 9, 40

women: appointed as judges 98–9; as distracting sexual objects for men 98; economic marginalization of 91–2, 127; labour force participation rate in the Maldives 91; loss of financial independence through globalization 91, 94; protest demonstrations in the Maldives 2; 'should be kept hidden in Islam' 98–9

World Health Organization (WHO) 9

Yoosuf, Rashidha (former Minister of Women's Affairs and Social Security, Republic of Maldives) 9–10, 96

youth unemployment *see* economic development